CONCISE ENGLISH-TAGALOG DICTIONARY

CONCISE
ENGLISH-TAGALOG
DICTIONARY

by Jose Villa Panganiban
[A.B., Ph.B., B.S.E., M.A., Ph.D.]

CHARLES E. TUTTLE COMPANY: PUBLISHERS
Rutland, Vermont & Tokyo, Japan

Published by the Charles E. Tuttle Company, Inc.
of Rutland, Vermont & Tokyo, Japan
with editorial offices at
2-6 Suido, 1-chome, Bunkyo-ku, Tokyo 112

© *1969 by Charles E. Tuttle Publishing Co., Inc.*

LCC Card No. 69-13501
ISBN 0-8048-1962-9

First Tuttle edition, 1969
First Tuttle paperback edition, 1994
Sixth printing, 1998

Printed in Singapore

To My Children
Jose Maria
Rosamyrna
Juan Virgilio
Consuelina Lourdes

Table of Contents

vii

Table of Contents

Publisher's Foreword

There is a definite need for this book by schools, teachers, students, translators, and anyone intent upon studying Tagalog.

The main objectives of this dictionary are simplicity, facility of reference, and accuracy. The Tagalog equivalents in the dictionary have been selected for their accuracy of meaning, but in some cases, because of translation difficulties, it has been necessary to sacrifice accuracy in favor of closeness or nearness in meaning. However, the orthography of the Tagalog meanings conforms with the rules of the official grammar published by the Institute of National Language.

Pronunciation and Accentuation

TO understand quickly the accentuation system used in this book, which is the same as that prescribed by the *Balarilà* of the Institute of National Language, consider two important things: STRESS and GLOTTAL STOP.

STRESS means syllabic emphasis. It is marked by the acute accent (á) on the vowel of the syllable, on whichever syllable the stress falls, except on the penultimate which does not need to be marked because majority of Tagalog words are penultimate. (It is important to note that when a word has no accent mark at all in its last two syllables, it is penultimate in stress).

1. Acute stress (i. e. on the last syllable) :—*Buháy, talagá, hambóg, maliít.*

2. Penultimate stress (i. e. on the syllable before the last),—no accent mark: — *buhay, aral, pato. sabɩ, laganap, dalaga.*

3. Stress on a syllable before the penultimate (i. e. on the third, fourth, etc.. syllable before the last) :—(a) in combination with the penultimate: *táhanan, símulain, nárarapat, mákita;*—(b) in combination with the acute stress: *káwanihán, kágawarán, náririyán, náririto.*

NOTE WELL: The acute accent marks ONLY the syllabic stress.

GLOTTAL STOP refers to the end-vowel of a word that is pronounced with an arrested sound at the epiglottis. The accent mark used is the grave accent (à). This particular accent is found in words with the glottal end-vowel but penultimate in stress:—*Batà, binatà, luhà, labì, turò, paglalaho.*

But, (and this is important) if a word of acute stress happens to end also in a glottal vowel, we get, first: the acute accent (á) for the stress, and second: the grave (à) for the glottal end-vowel, which results into a combination which we call the circumflex accent because of its similarity to the accent of the same name in international phonetics: (â).—*dagt*â, *sir*â, *bint*î, *panibugh*ô, *busl*ô.

* * *

The importance of understanding the system of accentuation as guide to correct pronunciation cannot be minimized. It would solve many problems, among them the following:

1. We would not have to grope for the correct pronunciation of a word.

2. Non-Tagalog Filipinos and foreigners trying to learn the language would have a clear guide to correct pronunciation.

3. Uniformity of pronunciation throughout the nation would result, as there are many localisms and regional idiosyncracies which education should remove in favor of a national standard.

We should bear in mind that there are a great number of Tagalog words that change in meaning by a change in accent. Take this sentence which Prof. Lope K. Santos, Director of the Institute of National Language, habitually presents to his students:

Lalaki ang aso. The dog is male.—Without accent marks on *lalaki* and *aso* they are to be pronounced as penultimate words. *Lalaki* means "male" or "masculine". *Aso* means "dog."—If we should use stress accents on *lalaki* to make it *lálakí,* the word becomes the future tense form of the infinitive *lumakí,* to grow big. Thus, *Lálakí ang aso* would mean "The dog will grow big."—Let us also put an acute stress on *aso,* to become *asó,* smoke. *Lálakí ang asó* means "The smoke will grow big." Of course, it would be ridiculous to write: *Lalaki ang asó* because no smoke is ever masculine in the Tagalog language, although we say *"el humo"* in Spanish.

Observe the differences in meaning in the following groups of words:

1. *kaibigan,* friend
   kaibigán, desire, inclination, preference
   káibigán, mutual consent
   kaíbigan, sweetheart, boy-friend or girl-friend
2. *baga,* glowing ember
   bagá, (an interrogative particle)
   bagà, lungs
   bagâ, tumor in the breast
3. *buhay,* life
   buháy, alive
4. *kita,* earnings; seen, obvious, conspicuous
   kitá, (pronoun with a compound meaning, I to you)
5. *bata,* Spanish word used in Tagalog meaning "robe", especially "bathrobe", or other robes used while at home
   batà, child
   batá, root-word for a verb, as *magbatá,* to suffer.

The mastery of Tagalog is mastery of stresses and glottal vowels, aside from understanding of sentence structures. But any one trained in some language, as English or Spanish, at school or elsewhere, and having a sense of expression, would be able to construct sentences. It is not everyone that can pronounce correctly according to standard pronunciation,—even in languages other than Tagalog,—until he has become familiar with what is standard. For the sake of uniformity, the initiative of the Institute of National Language should be considered authoritative, as it certainly is by law. The INL we understand bases the standard pronunciation upon the preferences of literate Manila, which is the metropolitan in which all Tagalogs of differing accents meet and in which certain mannerisms gain a more or less permanent foothold. We must have a standard,—and Manila being the sea where all rivers meet, let us take the resulting taste and consistency of the sea.

* * *

Tagalog Word Forms

Much of the vocabulary of the student of Tagalog could be built quicker and easier if the student should try to master the different word structures. The following is intended to show briefly how words are formed in Tagalog.

First, we consider the particles (*katagâ*) which are mostly monosyllabic words that have no meaning in themselves when alone but become definite parts of speech when combined with other words. Among such words are: *din* (*rin*), *man* (*namán*), *pa*, *na*, *ngâ;* the postpositive pronouns *ka, ko, mo, niyá*, etc.

Second, the root-words, mostly disyllabic but some have more than three syllables and only a few monosyllabic. All these root-words are used to form reduplicated, affixed, and compound words, but the majority of them can stand as single parts of speech.—*bahay, lupà, lasa, sugat, bulaklák, lagarì*, etc.

Third, the reduplicated words, in which a syllable, two syllables, or the whole word is repeated—*Lálakí, magandágandá, mabuting-mabutì.*

Fourth, the affixed word formed by either a prefix, infix, or suffix added to a root-word, or by any two or all of the affixes with the root. Prefixed: *ma*buhay, *pa*gawâ, *mang*gamót. Infixed: ki*n*atawán, bi*n*alimbíng, t*um*ayô. Suffixed: ubu*hín*, lutu*in*, tawa*nan*, tamá*an*. Prefixed and infixed: *kINa*kasama, *ipINa*gágawâ. Prefixed and suffixed: *mag*sálita*an*, *pag*tawan*án*, *pa*bil*hín*, *ka*tulung*in*. All affixes: *pagpUM*ilit*an*, *pINa*kiking*gán*, *kINa*tátayu*án*.

Fifth, the compound word, in which two different words or roots are combined (a) in literal sense, without losing the original meanings of the combined words: *buhay-*

Maynilà, dalagang-bukid, bahay-parì; (b) in the figurative sense, i. e., losing the original meaning of the combined words in favor of a third: *hampaslupà, Bagumbayan, dalagambukid.*

As in the changes in accentuation, changes in word structure also produce many shades of meaning.

bahay, house
bahay-bahay, every house
magbahay, to own or build a house
pagbahayan, to build a house (on a certain place)
kabahay, fellow living in the same house
kabahayan, the central portion of a house
mamahay, to reside in
pamamahay, household
bahay-parì, convent, monastery
bahay-batà, uterus
bahay-langgám, ant-hill
bahay-harì, royal palace
bahay-bayan, public house
bahay-sanglaan, pawnshop
bahay-kalakal, business house
maybahay, housekeeper, wife
etc., etc.

The foregoing list gives only a few that can be formed out of the root-word *bahay.* Majority of Tagalog roots can be transformed agglutinatively into scores of other words with different meanings, with the root as the central relation.

How to Use this Book

Facility of reference and real utility can be obtained from any vocabulary or dictionary if the user is familiar with its organization and structure. This vocabulary, being a bilingual presentation, and having been prepared with a certain point of view, has its own characteristic organization of materials somewhat different from other books of the same kind. The user, therefore, is advised to study the following explanations of organization and structure.

1. The English entries are immediately followed by their respective parts of speech.

> CORNER, n. *sulok.*
> DISOBEY, v. *sumuwáy, suwayin.*

See the list of abbreviations for these parts of speech.

2. After the part of speech, the Tagalog equivalent or equivalents follow, but if the original entry has no exact correspondence in Tagalog, or can be interpreted in some other meanings, secondary English key-words are provided. In this way, accuracy is achieved.

> CRUSH, v. to break into pieces or
> flatten by pressure, *pisaín;*
> grind to powder, *ligisín;* squeeze
> with the fingers or the hand,
> *pisilín;* pulverize, *durugin.*

3. If the English entry belongs to two or more parts of speech, a dash (—) separates the second or third part of speech from the first. Often, an idiomatic combination or common expression using the entry is given. In this case, the entry is printed with its initial letter alone, to save space.

> CROSS, n. *kurús, krus,* Sp.—v.
> To mark with a c., *kurusán.*—
> to move to the opposite side, *tu-*
> *mawíd; tawirín.*—To make the
> sign of the c., *mag-antandâ.*—
> adj. ill-tempered, *mainit ang ulo.*

4. If a "Tagalog" equivalent is not really Tagalog but derived from a foreign language, the abbreviation of the language of derivation follows the word.

> DEAN, n. *dekano*, Sp.
> GERM, n. seed, *binhî*; sprout,
> *paltók*, (of mongos, *toge, tawge,*
> Ch.); microbe, *mikrobyo*, Sp.;
> origin, *pinagmuián.*

Some of the words in our national language are derived from the Latin (Lat.), French (Fr.), Chinese (Ch.), Arabic (Ar.), Hebrew (Heb.). Words from the Malay are not marked. The reason is that we have no authoritative reference at present to allow us to make such indications. Old Tagalog words being revived or resuscitated are marked "O.T." Tagalog terms not in common use but deemed needed are indicated by "nc." Coined words which the author considered as possibly useful are followed by "cw."

5. Technical terms belonging to a particular branch of science or art are introduced by the name of the branch of science or art in parentheses, as (Gram.) Grammar, (Bot.) Botany, etc.

> GENDER (Gram.) *kasarian.—*
> Feminine g., *kasariang pamba-*
> *bae. —* Masculine g., *kasariang*
> *panlalaki.*

6. Often, to save space and too much repetition, or to indicate slight differences under the same meaning, secondary key-words in English are presented in parentheses:

> ACQUIRE, v. (by self-exertion)
> *mátamó, makuha;* (by purchase)
> *mábili;* (by inheritance) *má-*
> *mana.*
> CAPE, n. wrap, *abrigo*, Sp.; head-
> land (narrow), *lungos;* (short)
> *imus;* (high) *tangos;* (wide and
> long) *tangwáy.*

xviii

Abbreviations Used in this Dictionary

Abbr., *abbreviation*
adj., *adjective*
adv. *adverb*
Anat., *anatomical term*
Ar., *derived from the Arabian*
art., *article*

Biol., *biological term*
Bis., *derived from the Bisayan*
Bot., *botanical term*

Ch., *derived from the Chinese*
Colloq., *colloquialism*
Com., *commercial term*
conj., *conjunction*
Cub., *derived from the Cuban*
cw., *a coined word*

Eccl., *an ecclesiastical term*
Elec., *an electrical term*
Eng.. *derived from English*

fem., *feminine gender*
fig., *of figurative usage*
Fr., *derived from the French*

Geom., *geometrical term*
Gram., *grammatical term*

Haw., *derived from the Hawaiian*
Hnd., *derived from the Hindu*

Ilok., *derived from the Ilokano*
inter., *interjection*

Lat., *derived from the Latin*

masc., *masculine gender*
Math.. *mathematical term*
Med., *medical term*
Mex., *derived from the Mexican*

n., *noun*
nc., *term not commonly used*

Ornith., *ornithological term*
O. T., *old Tagalog term*

Pam., *derived from the Pampango*
pl., *plural number*
prep., *preposition*
pron., *pronoun*

sing., *singular number*
Sl., *slangy expression*
Sp., *derived from the Spanish*

v., *verb*
vul., *vulgar*

Zool., *Zoological term*

References

1. *New English-Spanish and Spanish-English Dictionary* by Antonio Cuyás. Revised and enlarged by Antonio Llano. New York, 1930. D. Appleton and Company.
2. *Webster's Elementary Dictionary.* New York, 1935. American Book Company.
3. *The Winston Dictionary*, Encyclopedic edition. Philadelphia, 1945. The John C. Winston Company.
4. *The Secretary's Desk Book* by William J. Pelo. Philadelphia, 1945. The John C. Winston Company.
5. *The Tagalog Language* by Constantino Lendoyro, second edition, Manila, 1909. Juan Fajardo.
6. *Diccionario Hispano-Tagalog* por Pedro Serrano Laktaw, Primera Parte. Manila, 1889. Estab. tipográfico "La Opinión" á cargo de G. Bautista.
7. *Diccionario Tagalog-Hispano* por Pedro Serrano Laktaw, Segunda Parte. Manila, 1914. Imp. y Lit. de Santos y Bernal.
8. *Ang Wika at Baybaying Tagalog* ni G. E. Tolentino. Maynila, 1937.
9. *Gramática na Isinauicang Tagalog nang sa Castilà* ni Don Asisclo F. Vallin at Bustillo at ni Don Z. Villamarin. Maynila, 1886. Establecimiento Tipográfico "La Industrial".
10. *Estudios Gramaticales sobre la Lengua 'Iagalog* por Pedro Serrano Laktaw (Obra Póstuma). Manila, 1929. Imprenta de Juan Fajardo.
11. *A Manual of the Philippine National Language* by Cecilio Lopez, third edition. Manila, 1941. Bureau of Printing.
12. *Arte de la Lengua Tagala y Manual Tagalog* por Fray Sebastian de Totanes. Binondo, 1865. Imprenta de Miguel Sanchez y Cia.
13. *Gramatikang Inggles-Tagalog* ni Ramona Desiderio Marquez at Sofronio G. Calderón. Maynila, 1919. Palimbagan ni P. Sayo Balo ni Soriano.
14. *Lecciones de Gramática Hispano-Tagala* por D. Fr. José Hevia Campomanes, duodecima primera edición. Manila, 1930. Tip. de la Univ. de Sto. Tomás.
15. *Elements of Tagalog Grammar* by Henry Demond, S. V. D. Manila, 1929. Catholic Trade School.
16. *Fundamental Tagalog* by J. Villa Panganiban, second edition, second printing. Manila, 1940. Philippine Education Co.
17. *Preliminary Studies on the Lexicography of the Philippine Languages.* Publications of the Institute of National Language, Vol. I, Nos. 1-9. Manila, 1937.

18. *A Preliminary Study of the Affixes in Tagalog* by Cecilio Lopez. Publications of the Institute of National Language, Vol. II. Manila, 1937.

19. *An Outline Syntax of Buddhistic Sanskrit* by Sukumar Sen. Journal of the Department of Letters, Vol. XVII, 1928. Calcutta University Press.

20. *A Study of Tagalog Grammar and What Elements of It Should Be Taught* by J. Villa Panganiban, doctoral thesis. Manila, 1941. University of Santo Tomas.

21. *Vocabulario de la Lengua Tagala* por el P. Juan de Noceda y el P. Pedro de Sanlucar. Reimpreso en Manila, 1860. Imprenta Ramirez y Giraudier.

22. *Pangasinan: Gramática tan Diccionario* by Ernest A. Rayner. Manila, 1923. Methodist Publishing House.

23. *Vocabulario Iloco-Español* por M.R.P. Fr. Andres Carro, 2.a edición. Manila, 1888. Establecimiento Tipo-litográfico de M. Perez, hijo.

24. *Munting Diccionario na Inglés-Tagalog* ni Sofronio G. Calderon. Manila, 1916. Imprenta y Libreria de P. Sayo Vda. de Soriano.

25. *Balarilà ng Wikang Pambansá.* Surián ng Wikang Pambansá, Maynila, 1940. Bureau of Printing.

26. *A Tagalog-English Vocabulary*, first edition. Institute of National Language, Manila, 1940. Bureau of Printing.

27. *Balarilang Pilipino* ni I. Evangelista. Tondo, 1923. Bulalakao's Printing Press.

28. *Diccionario Manual de Términos Comunes Español-Tagalo* por Don Rosalio Serrano. Manila, 1913. Libreria y Papeleria de J. Martinez.

29. *Vocabulario de la Lengua Pampanga* por M.P.R. Lector Fr. Diego Bergano. Reimpreso, Manila, 1860. Imprenta de Ramirez y Giraudier.

30. *Ortografía y Reglas de la Lengua Tagalog* por Don Pedro Andres de Castro. Madrid, 1930. Libreria General de Victoriano Suárez.

Acknowledgments

THE original and main part of this vocabulary was prepared in several periods. At the start, in 1941, the suggestions and aid of Dr. Eufronio M. Alip proved useful. The interest displayed and the critical suggestions of Rev. Fr. Evergisto Bazaco, O.P., in the preparation of the letter "A" helped the author to a great extent in finding a "foothold" so-to-speak.

When Japan bombed Pearl Harbor on December 8, 1941, the manuscript, completed until letter "C", evacuated with the author to the Barrio of Bungkalot, Tanauan, Batangas. The author's advisers became the old people of the barrio and transient evacuees. From March, 1942, Mrs. Fidela C. de Panganiban, the author's mother; Mrs. Consuelo T. Panganiban, the author's better-half; and Mrs. Leonila L. Torres, acted as advisers and consultants, although very little work was done.

In 1943, back in the city, the author availed himself of the many suggestions and advices of Maj. Jose M. Hernandez, P.A., Mr. Antonio Zacarias, and Dr. Eufronio M. Alip. In 1944, after an interview with Director Lope K. Santos of the Institute of National Language, the manuscript (though at this time had reached until letter "M") was revised with a new organization of material. Director Santos and Mr. Julian Cruz Balmaseda provided the author with valuable suggestions at this time.

After the first bombing of the Port of Manila by the Americans in September, 1944, the author and his family evacuated to Tanauan, Batangas. Work on the manuscript became more intensive. The late Dr. Brigido Carandang, believed to have been killed by the Japanese early in 1945, made it a habit to look in at the author at work, to read the manuscript and ridicule some entries. The good doctor's ridicule helped the author a great deal in improving the work.

When, after Christmas of 1944, the Japanese airfield at Lipa and the railroad station at Tanauan became the object of daily air-raids by the Americans, the author and his family evacuated with the manuscript to Barrio Wawang Balili, near Lake Taal, within sight of Taal Volcano and Tagaytay City on the famous ridge of Cavite. Once again, the author had a chance to consult natural "Tagalists", among them the barrio headman Mang Atong Salisi; Mr. Dionisio Atienza, an ex-teacher; and various other persons, natives and evacuees.

The manuscript was on letter "S" when the 11th Airborne Division of the U.S. Army landed paratroops on Tagaytay and the author was called upon by local guerrillas to act as Liaison Officer in meeting the paratroopers. In February, 1945, the massacre of the towns of Santo Tomas, Tanauan, and Lipa, by the Japanese occurred. With thousands of other evacuees, the author, with his manuscript carefully packed under one arm and food for a few days under another, fled across hills and forests to Cabuyao, Laguna, guarded by a guerrilla band captained by the gallant Remigio Maiquis who had the presence of mind to hide under some bushes the Royal typewriter (specially equipped with Tagalog accents) on which the author wrote the manuscript. When the Japanese burned and razed the barrio of Wawang Balili to the ground, among the few things saved from the barrio was the said typewriter.

Back in Manila by March, 1945, work on the manuscript was resumed with the constructive suggestions of Mr. Vicente Sabalvaro and Atty. Teodoro L. Valencia, while the author worked for PCAU 20, and later, for the Military Censorship Detachment, USAFFE. The manuscript was completed by June, 1945.

At this time, Mr. Arsenio R. Afan saw the manuscript which had reached over 1,400 pages. Mr. Afan was instrumental in interesting Dr. Jose M. Aruego of the University Publishing Company who asked for an abridgment of the work in order to produce a low-priced vocabulary.

The manuscript had to be rewritten, therefore, to meet the requirement of the publishers, and in this preparation the help of Mrs. Antonia H. Villanueva proved very valuable. When, finally, the manuscript went to press, the proofs were gone over by Director Lope K. Santos, Mr. Marcelo P. Garcia, Mr. Leonardo Dianzon, and Mr. Leonardo C. Paner. Mrs. Paulina Flores Hidalgo and Miss Aurea Mercado went over the final printed sheets for errata which are corrected in this second printing.

As may be seen, hundreds of people had a hand in the preparation of this small vocabulary. To all these people, the author hereby expresses his thanks and acknowledges sincerely their aid, without which this book could not have found itself published in the way it is.

* * *

Legally Speaking . . . .

1. "The National Assembly shall take steps toward the development and adoption of a common national language based on one of the existing native languages."—*Constitution of the Philippines, Art. XIV, Sec. 3.*

2. The Institute of National Language is created to choose the native tongue which is to be used as the basis for the evolution and adoption of the Philippine National Language.— *Commonwealth Act No. 184,* Oct. 28, 1946. (The Institute of National Language was organized by Executive Order, Jan. 12, 1937.)

3. Adoption of Tagalog as the basis for the National Language of the Philippines, by recommendation of the Institute of National Language, to take effect Dec. 30, 1939.—*Executive Order No. 134* by President Manuel L. Quezon, Dec. 30, 1937.

4. An appropriation of ₱100,000 was approved for the National Language Institute—*Commonwealth Act 333,* June 18, 1938. (This appropriation, however, was made available only until 1940. After that... the Budget for 1941 was ₱35,268.)

5. The Filipino National Language is declared as one of the official languages of the Philippines, effective July 4, 1946. —*Commonwealth Act No. 570,* June 7, 1940.

6. Statement by President Sergio Osmeña, April 2, 1946: "No backward step will be taken by the administration in connection with the National Language."

[Note: *During the Japanese Occupation, the National Language was given emphasis in the schools, in society, and over the radio. There was a Military Administration Decree on the National Language and there were several Executive Orders and Ministry of Education Circulars.*]

A

A, art. isá (one) usually with -ng: isáng. A man, isáng tao.

ABANDON, v. to leave, iwan: forsake, pabayaan.

ABIDE, v. to wait for, maghintáy; dwell, reside, tumirá.

ABILITY, n. kakayahán.

ABLE, adj. maykaya.

ABODE, n. home, táhanan; residence, tírahan.

ABOLISH, v. to take away, alisín, kaltasin.

ABOUT, adv. nearly, halos; more or less, humigit-kumulang.— prep. concerning, hinggíl sa, tungkól sa.

ABOVE, adv. sa itaás; on top, sa ibabaw—prep. on top of, sa ibabaw ng—Above all, higít sa lahát.

ABRIDGE, v. paikliin.

ABROAD, adv. in other countries, sa ibáng bansá; out-of-doors, sa labás.

ABSENT, adj. walâ. He is absent, Walâ siyá.

ABSOLUTE, adj. positive, complete, lubós, ganáp.

ABUNDANT, adj. saganà, masaganà.

ABUSE, v. to treat badly or cruelly, magmalupit; pagmamalupit; pagmalupitán; take undue advantage, magmalabis.

ACCENT, n. (Gram.) tuldík. Acute a., tuldík na pahilís; grave a., tuldík na paiwà; circumflex a., tuldík na pakupyâ.

ACCEPT, v. tumanggáp; tanggapín.

ACCIDENT, n. sakunâ.

ACCOMPANY, v. to go with, sumama; samahan; (in music) sumaliw, saliwan.

ACCOMPLISH, v. to fulfill, tuparín; complete, ganapín.

ACCORDING TO, prep. ayon sa.

ACCORDINGLY, adv. kayá; kayâ ngâ.

ACCOUNT, v. to take into account, ipagpalagáy; answer for, managót; give an explanation for, magpaliwanag; ipaliwanag. —n. debt, utang, pagkakautang; record, talâ; report, ulat; explanatory statement, salaysáy, paliwanag, palinaw.

ACCUSE, v. (in a law court) magsakdál; isakdál; (to a superior) magsumbóng; isumbóng, (falsely) magbintáng; pagbintangán.

ACCUSTOM, v. (oneself) magbihasá, magsanay; to become accustomed, mabihasa, masanay, mahirati.

ACHE, v. sumakít.—n. sakít.

ACKNOWLEDGE, v. to recognize (as authority) kilalanin; (as true) pananggapán.

ACQUAINT, v. to inform, ipatalós, ipabatíd.

ACQUAINTANCE, n. (a person one knows slightly) kakilala; knowledge, kaalamán, kabatirán.

ACQUIRE, v. (by self-exertion) mátamó, makuha; (by purchase) mábili; (by inheritance) mámana.

ACROSS, adv. patawíd, pakabilâ. —prep. sa kabilá ng, sa ibayo ng.

ACT, n. deed, *gawâ* (in a stage play) *yugtô;* (of law) *batás;* motion, *galáw, kilos.*—v. to perform, *gumanáp;* do, make, *gumawâ;* move, *gumaláw, kumilos.*

ACTION, see Act, n.

ACTIVE, adj. quick, *maliksí;* alive, *buháy;* lively, *masiglá.* —a. voice (Gram.) *tinig táhasan.*

ACTOR, n. (in general) *artista,* Sp.

ACTUAL, adj. *tunay;* present, *kasalukuyan.*

ACUTE, adj. *malubhâ; talamák.*

ADAPT, v. *iagpáng, ibagay.*

ADD, v. *magdagdág, idagdág;* (together) *pagsamahin.*

ADDITION, n. *pagdaragdág; pagsasama.*

ADDRESS, n. *direksiyón,* Sp.; residence, *tinitirahán.*— v. to talk, *kausapin;* deliver a speech, *magtalumpatì.*

ADMIRATION, n. *paghangà.*

ADMIRE, v. *humangà; hangaan.*

ADMIT, v. to allow to enter, *papasukin;* acknowledge, *pananggapán.*

ADOPT, v. (a child) *ampunín.*

ADORE, v. *sumambá; sambahín.*

ADULT, adj.-n. *matandâ; maygulang.*

ADVANCE, n. progress, *pagsulong, pag-unlád.*—v. to go forward ahead of others, *magpáuná, umuna.*

ADVANCED, adj., progressive, *masulong;* made or given ahead of others or time, *páuná.*

ADVANTAGE, n. *bentaha,* Sp.; (superiority) *kahigtán.*

ADVENTURE, n. experience, *karanasan.*

ADVERTISE, v. *mag-anúnsiyo,* Sp.

ADVERTISEMENT, n. *anúnsiyo,* Sp.

ADVICE, n. counsel, *payo;* notification, *pahiwatig.*

ADVISE, v. counsel, *magpayo, pagpayuhan.*

ADVISER, n. *tagapayo.*

AFFAIR, n. a matter, *bagay;* a concern, *pákialamín.* — Private a., *sariling kapakanán;* public a., *kapakanáng-bayan;* love a., *palásintahan.*

AFFECT, v. (well) *makabuti;* (badly) *makasamâ;* to cause anger, *makagalit;* cause pleasure, *makalugód.*

AFFECTION, n. a feeling of love, *pag-ibig;* a great fondness, *paggiliw.*

AFFIDAVIT, n. sworn statement, *apidabit,* Lat.; *panunumpâ; alusithâ,* O.T.

AFFORD, v. to have money enough to buy, *makabili;* *makakayang bumili.*—Can't afford, *di-kaya.*

AFRAID, adj. *takót, natátakot.*

AFTER, prep. (used with a person or thing) *pagkatapos ng;* (with the name of a person) *pagkatapos ni;* (with time) *pagkaraan ng.*

AFTERNOON, n. *hapon.*

AGAIN, adv. *ulî, mulî.*

AGAINST, prep. *laban sa.*

AGE, n. length of time lived, *gulang;* *edád,* Sp.; period of time, *panahón.*—Of legal a., *may karampatang gulang;* of minor a., *batà pa; walâ pa sa edád.*

AGENT, n. *ahente,* Sp.

AGITATE, v. to shake, *kalugín;* excite, *manulsól, sulsulán.*

AGITATOR, n. *mánunulsól.*

AGONY, n. last sufferings of a dying person or animal, *paghihingalô;* extreme suffering, *paghihirap.*

AGREE, v. to assent, *umayon;* consent, *pumayag.*

AGREEABLE, adj. pleasing, *nakalúlugód.*

AGREEMENT, n. *kásunduan.*

AGRICULTURE, n. *agrikultura,* Sp.; *pagsasaka.*

AHEAD, adv. in front, *nasa-unahán;* leading, *nangúnguna.*—Go ahead (go on), *Sige na,* Sl., Sp.; *magpatuloy ka.*

AID, n. *tulong;* succor, *saklolo;* contribution, *ambág; abuloy.*

AIM, n. purpose, *hangád, hángarin;* object, *layon, pakay;* act of pointing a firearm, *pagtudlâ, pagtutok.*—v. a. a firearm at, *itudlâ, ıtutok.*

AIR, n. wind, *hangin;* tune, *himig.* A. mail, *palipád-sulat.*—v. expose to the a., *pahanginan.*

AISLE, n. space between, *pagitan.*

ALARM, n. fear, *takot, pangambá;* warning of danger, *hudyát ng panganib.*

ALIEN, n. & adj. *dayuhan; tagaibáng-bansá, banyagà.*

ALIKE, adj. *magkatulad.*

ALIVE, adj. *buháy; maybuhay.*

ALL, pron. *lahát.*

ALLEGIANCE, n. *pagkatig.*

ALLOW, v. to permit, *itulot;* grant, *igawad.*

ALMIGHTY, adj. *makapangyarihan.*—God Almighty, *Diyós na Makapangyarihan.*

ALMOST, adv. *halos.*

ALONE, adj. *nag-íisá;* only, *lamang, lang.*

ALOUD, adv. loudly, *malakás;* out loud (in voice) *pasigáw.*

ALPHABET, n. *abakada, katitikan; alpabeto,* Sp.

ALREADY, adj. *na.*

ALSO, adv. *din, rin, man, namán;* including, *patí.*

ALTAR, n. *dambanà; altár,* Sp.

ALTHOUGH, conj. *bagamá't (bagamán at); kahit, káhit na.*

ALTOGETHER, adv. wholly, *lubós, ganáp.*

ALWAYS, adv. *lagì, lagì na; palagì, palagì na; parati, paráti na.*

AM, see BE, v.

AMAZE, v. to astonish greatly, *papagtakahín.*

AMBASSADOR, n. *sugò;* representative, deputy, *kinatawán.*

AMBIGUOUS, adj. *di-malinaw; taluhimig.*

AMBITION, n. *ambisyón,* Sp.; eager desire to improve one-self, *paghahangád, hángarin;* aim or object for which one strives, *láyunin, pita.*

AMBITIOUS, adj. *mapaghangád, mapaglayon, mapagpita.*

AMBULANCE, n. *ambulansiyá,* Sp.

AMEND, v. *susugan,* to alter, *baguhin.*

AMENDMENT, n. *susog, pagbabago.*

AMERICA, n. *Amériká,* Sp.-Eng.

AMERICAN, adj. & n., *Amerikano,* Sp.

AMONG, prep. in the midst of, *sa gitnâ ng mga;* in company with, *kasama ng mga.*

AMOUNT, n. a sum, *halagá;* totality, *kabuuán.*

AMPLE, adj. large, *malaki;* plenty, *marami;* extensive, *malawak.*

AMUSE, v. (self) *mag-aliw, maglibáng;* (others) *aliwín, libangín.*

AMUSEMENT, n. *áliwan, libangan.*

ANCESTOR, n. *ninunò.*

ANCHOR, n. *pasangit; sinipete.*— v. *dumaóng.*

ANCIENT, adj. *sinauna; sáunahín.*

AND, conj. *at; at sakû.*

ANGEL, n. *anghél,* Sp.

ANGER, n. *galit.*

ANGLE, n. *panulukan;* corner, *sulok.*

ANGRY, adj. *galit.*

ANIMAL, n. *hayop.*

ANKLE, n. *buól; bukong-bukong.*

ANNOUNCE, v. to make known publicly, *ihayág.*

ANNOY, v. to disturb by bothering, *abalahin;* vex, *yamutin;* pester, *buwisitin.*

ANNUAL, adj. *táunan;* a year at a time, *santáunan.*

ANOTHER, pron. *ibá;* one more, *isá pa.*

ANSWER, n. *sagót;* reply, *tugón.*—v. *sumagót, sagutín;* reply, *tumugón, tugunín.*

ANT, n. *langgám; guyam.*

ANXIOUS, adj. deeply concerned, *balisá.*

ANY, pron.-adj. *alinmán; anumán.*

ANYBODY, pron. *sínumán.*

ANYHOW, adv. *papaánumán.*

ANYWHERE, adv. *saanmán; kahit saán.*

APART, adv. *bukód; hiwaláy.*

APARTMENT, n. *aksesorya,* Sp.

APIECE, adv. for each one, *sa bawa't isá.*

APPARATUS, n. *aparato,* Sp.; tool, *kasangkapan;* equipment, *kagamitán.*

APPARENT, adj. *sa malas, sa wari.*

APPEAL, v. to make a plea, *mamanhík;* (Law) *umapelá,* Sp.

APPEAR, v. to become visible, *lumitáw;* come out, *lumabás.*

APPEARANCE, n. act of becoming visible, *paglitáw;* act of coming out, *paglabás;* the look of a person or thing, *anyô; itsura,* Sp.

APPETITE, n. *gana,* Sp.

APPLE, n. *mansanas,* Sp.

APPLICANT, n. *ang may kahílingan.*

APPLICATION, n. petition, *hiling, kahilingan.*

APPLY, v. to ask for, *humiling, hilingín;* put to practical use, *ilapat; isagawâ, gawín.*

APPOINT, v. *hirangin;* be appointed, *máhirang.*

APPOINTMENT, n. act of appointing, *paghirang;* of having been appointed, *pagkáhirang;* (the a. itself) *nombramyento,* Sp.

APPRECIATE, v. to value at true worth, *magpahalagá, pahalagahán;* enjoy intelligently, *kalugdán.*

APPROACH, v. to draw near, *lumapit.*

APPROVE, v. to have a favorable opinion, *mabutihin, magalingín;* (legislative) *pagtibayin.*

APRON, n. *apron,* Eng.; *dilantál,* Sp.; *tapî.*

ARCHITECT, n. *arkitekto,* Sp.

AREA, n. *lawak, lakí, sukat ng lupang may sandaáng metrong parisukat.*

ARGUE, v. *mangatwiran;* to debate with, *makipagtalo.*

ARGUMENT, n. *katwiran;* discussion, debate, *pagtatalo.*

ARISE, v. *bumangon;* to spring up, *sum ból.*

ARITHMETIC, n. *aritmétiká,* Sp.; *palátuusan,* nc.

ARM, n. *bisig; braso,* Sp.

ARMOR, n. *baluti; kutamaya*, Sp.

ARMY, n. *hukbó.*

AROUND, adv. & prep. *sa palibot, sa paligid.*

ARRANGE, v. *ayusin, iayos.*

ARRANGEMENT, n. *ayos.*

ARREST, v. *dumakip, dakpín;* to catch, *humuli, hulihin.*

ARRIVAL, n. *pagdating.*

ARRIVE, v. *dumating.*

ARROW, n. *panà, tunod.*

ART, n. *sining; arte*, Sp.

ARTICLE, n. thing, *bagay;* section, *pangkát;* (for newspaper or magazine) *lathálain;* (Gram.) *pantukoy.*

ARTIST, n. *artista*, Sp.

AS, adv. to the same amount (given as prefix) *kasing-, kasim-, kasin-.*—conj. because, *sapagká't;* since, *yayamang.*—prep. like, *tulad sa, gaya ng.*

ASCEND, v. to climb, *umakyát.*

ASH, ASHES, n. *abó.*

ASHAMED, adj. *nahihiyâ, nápapahiyâ.*

ASHORE, adv. *sa kati; sa pampáng.*

ASIDE, adv. apart, *bukód, hiwaláy.*—prep. a. from, *bukód sa.*

ASLEEP, adj. *natútulog.*

ASSEMBLE, v. *magtipun-tipon.*

ASSEMBLY, n. *pagtitipon;* (legislative) *kapulungan.*

ASSIGN, v. to give as task to be done, *ipagawà, ipatupád;* set apart, *iukol;* (Law) transfer. *ilipat;* grant, *igawad.*

ASSIST, v. to help, *tumulong, tulungan;* attend, be present, *dumaló.*

ASSISTANCE, n. help, *tulong;* presence, *pagdaló.*

ASSOCIATE, n. companion, *kasama;* partner (in business) *kabakas;* helper, assistant, *katulong.*—adj. as n.—v. *sumama, makisama;* join things together, *pagsamá-samahin.*

ASSOCIATION, n. act of joining together, *pagsasama-sama;* corporation, *sámahan; korporasyón*, Sp.; connection, *kaugnayan.*

ASSUME, v. to take upon oneself, *gampanán;* suppose something to be true, *akalain.*

ASSURE, v. to make sure or certain, *tiyakín; siguruhin*, Sp.

ASTONISH, see AMAZE.

AT, prep. *sa.*—at home, *sa amin; sa atin.*

ATTACH, v. to fasten, *ikabít;* add to one end, *idugtóng.*

ATTACK, v. *sumalakay, salakayin;* invade, *lumusob, lusubin.*

ATTAIN, v. to gain, *makuha, mátamó;* achieve, *maganáp;* reach, *maabót.*

ATTEMPT, v. to make an effort, *pagpilitan;* try to do, *atuhin, umato.*

ATTEND, v. to wait upon, *paglingkurán;* care for, *alagaan;* be present, *dumaló.*

ATTENDANT, n. waiter, *tagapaglingkód; sirbiyente*, Sp.; helper, *katulong.*

ATTENTION, n. careful listening, *paglilimi;* act of courtesy, *paggalang, pamimitagan.*

ATTIRE, n. clothes, *damit, pananamít.*

ATTORNEY, n. *abugado*, Sp.; *mánananggól.*

ATTRACT, v. *umakit, akitin.*

ATTRACTIVE, adj. *kaakit-akıt.*

AUDIENCE, n. *ang públikó,* Sp.;
ang mga nakikiníg; the spectators, *ang mga nanónoód.*

AUGUST, n. (month) *Agosto,* Sp.
—adj. imposing, *kapitá-pitayan.*

AUNT, n. *ale; tiyá,* Sp.

AUTHOR, n. *ang maykathâ; ang may-akdâ.*

AUTHORITY, n. power, *kapangyarihan;* person with power of government, *maykapangyarihan.*

AUTOMOBILE, n. *awto,* Lat.

AVENUE, n. *abenida,* Sp.

AVERAGE, n. a generally accepted standard, *pámantayan; pámantungan.* — adj. ordinary, *karaniwan.*

AVOID, v. *umilag, ilagan; umiwas, iwasan.*

AWAIT, v. *maghintáy, hintayin.*

AWAY, adv. far, *malayò.*

AWE, n. solemn fear, *sindák; pangingimì;* reverence, *pamimitagan.*

AWFUL, adj. frightful, *nakasísindák.*

AX, AXE, n. *palakól;* (small) *putháw.*

B

BABY, n. infant, *sanggól;* small child, *batang muntî.*

BACK, n. *likód; likurán.*

BACKWARD, adv. toward the rear, *pauróng.*

BACON, n. *tusino,* Sp.

BAD, adj. *masamâ.*

BADGE, n. mark or sign, *palátandaan;* (of metal) *tsapa;* (of ribbon) *laso,* Sp.; symbol, *sagisag.*

BAG, n. sack, *sako,* Sp., *kustál,* Sp.; pouch, *supot;* of reed, *bayóng.*

BAGGAGE, n. *dalá-dalahan; ekipahe,* Sp.

BALANCE, n. weighing apparatus, *timbangan;* what is lacking to complete something, *kakulangán;* what is added, to complete, *kapupunán.*

BAIL, n. (Law) *piyansa,* Sp., *lagak.*—v. *piyánsahán,* Sp.

BAKE, v. *lutuin sa hurnó; iihaw sa hurnó.* (*Hurnó,* Sp.)

BAKERY, n. *panaderyá,* Sp.; *tinapayan.*

BALCONY, n. *balkón,* Sp.

BALL, n. sphere, *bilog;* b. used in games, *bola,* Sp.; dance, *sáyawan; baile,* Sp.

BALLOT, n. *balota,* Sp.

BAMBOO, n. *kawayan.*

BANANA, n. *saging.*

BAND, n. that which binds, *bigkís, talì;* b. of musicians, *banda ng músikó,* Sp.

BANDAGE, n. *bindahe,* Sp.; *talì.*

BANISH, v. to condemn to exile, *itapon; idestiyero,* Sp.

BANK, n. rivershore, *pampáng;* seashore, *baybayin;* financial institution, *bangko,* Sp.

BANKER, n. *bangkero,* Sp.

BANKRUPT, adj. *hapay-puhunan;* being in want, *hikahós.*

BANNER, n. *watawat; bandilà,* Sp.

BANQUET, n. *bangkete,* Sp.; *piging; salu-salo.*

BAR, n. long piece of solid matter (as a bar of iron) *baras*, Sp.; piece (as a bar of candy), *piraso*, Sp.; a barrier, *hadláng*, *halang*; liquor counter, *bar*, Eng.; *serbeserya*, Sp.—v. to obstruct, *hadlangán*; bar (a door), *tarangkahán*; *baralán*.

BARBER, n. *barbero*, Sp.; *manggugupit*.

BARE, adj. without cover, *waláng-takíp*; bareheaded, *pugáy*; *waláng-sumbrero*; simple, unadorned, *lisdíng*.

BARGAIN, n. agreement, *kásunduan*; buying or selling at low price, *baratilyo*, Sp.

BARK, n. (of trees) *upak, talukap; balát*; (of dog) *kahól, tahól*.—v. utter a bark (as a dog), *kumahól, tumahól*.

BARLEY, n. *sibada*, Sp.

BARN, n. *kamalig*; granary, *bangán; baysá*.

BARREL, n. cask, *bariles*, Sp.; (of a gun) *baríl*, Sp.

BARREN, adj. rocky surface, without vegetation, *palanas*; infertile, *pagáng; yayát, payát*; unable to bear children, sterile, *baog*.

BASE, n. that part on which a thing rests, *patungán;* foundation, *pondo*, Sp.—v. deduce from, *ibatay, pagbatayan*.

BASEBALL, n. *beisbol*, Eng.

BASEMENT, n. equivalent to *silong*; may be exactly translated as *ilalim ng silong*.

BASIC, adj. b. principle, *pansímulain*; b. foundation, *pinagbábatayan, saligán*.

BASIS, n. *batayán, pámantungan;* principle, *símulain*; source, origin, *pinagmulán*.

BASKET, n. *basket*, Eng. (There are a number of native "baskets" named after their sizes and shapes, as, *bakol, takuyan, bilao, buslô*, etc.)

BASKETBALL, n. *basketbol*, Eng.

BAT, n. (for baseball) *bat, bet*, Eng.

BATH, n. act of bathing, *paliligò;* act of giving someone else a bath, *pagpapaligò;* bathroom, *banyo*, Sp.; *páliguán*.

BATHE, v. *maligò*.

BATTLE, n. combat, *pagbabaka;* encounter, *pagmumuók;* fight, *laban, labanán*.

BAY, n. gulf, *loók*.—at b., *nasagipít, napípigipit*.

BE, v. All forms of the verb "to be" are ordinarily translated as *ay;* to become, *maging*. (In transposed sentences, *ay* is omitted. I am a teacher, *Akó ay gurò. Gurò akó*.

BEACH, n. *baybayin; tabíng-dagat*.

BEAD, n. *abaloryo*, Sp.; (in a necklace or rosary) *butil*.

BEAM, n. rays (of the sun, etc.) *sinag;* bar of balance, *baras*, Sp.; *braso*, Sp.; supporting bar of wood or iron (in house construction), *barakilan, balakilan*.

BEAN, n. grain or legumes, *butil*. Some native beans: *sitaw, bataw, paayap, patanì, tapilán, balatong (munggó)*, etc.

BEAR, n. (animal) *oso*, Sp.—v. to endure, *matiis, mabatá;* suffer, *magtiís, magbatá;* be able to sustain, support, *maalalayan;* possess, *magtagláy, taglayín*, give birth, *manganák*.

BEARD, n. *balbas*, Sp.; *bungót*, O.T.; (thick) *yangót*, O.T.

BEARER, n. the person who bears something (as a letter of introduction) *ang maydalá.*

BEAST, n. animal, *hayop;* (wild) *halimaw, ganid.*

BEAT, v. to hit, strike with blows, *paluin, hampasín;* (with a club) *bugbugín, bambuhín;* defeat, vanquish, *talunin, daigín.*—n. throb, *tibók, kutób;* stroke of sound, *tunóg,* sometimes *pintíg.*

BEAUTIFUL, adj. *magandá;* beauteous, *marikít.*

BEAUTY, n. *gandá, kagandahan;* charm, *dikít, kariktán.*

BECOME, v. *maging;* to befit, *bumagay, mábagay.*

BECOMING, adj. of pleasing fitness, *bagay.*

BED, n. *kama, katre,* Sp.; (of bamboo) *papag;* (general) *hígaan, tulugán.*

BEDBUG, n. *surot.*

BEE, n. honey b., *laywán; pukyutan;* bumble b., *bubuyog.*

BEEF, n. *karníng-baka,* Sp.; *lamán ng baka.* — Carabao b., *karníng-kalabáw, lamán ng kalabáw.*

BEER, n. *serbesa,* Sp.

BEESWAX, u. *pagkít.*

BEFORE, prep. in front of, *sa harapán ng;* preceding (in space, time, rank, etc.) *sa unahán ng.*—adv. previously, *noóng una;* in front, *sa haráp;* formerly, *dati, dati-rati.* — conj. earlier than, *bago, bago pa.*

BEG, v. (for alms) *magpalimós;* to beseech, *mamanhík, pamanhikán.*

BEGGAR, n. *magpapalimos; pulube,* Sp.

BEGIN, v. to start doing, *magsimulá; mag-umpisá,* Sp.; *simulán, umpisahán,* Sp.

BEGINNER, n. *baguhan;* Sl. *bagitò.*

BEGINNING, n. *simulá, pasimulâ.*

BEHAVE, v. usually expressed by the prefix *magpaka-,* followed by the manner behavior meant; *magpakabuti,* to b. well; *magpakahusay,* to b. in orderly manner; *magpakasamâ,* to b. badly, —or, act like, *mag-ugalì* for good behavior and *mag-asal* for bad behavior, as, *mag-ugaling-máginoó,* act like a gentleman; *mag-asal-hayop,* act like a beast.

BEHIND, prep. at the back of, *sa likurán ng;* at the rear of, *sa hulihán ng.*—adv. late, *hulí; atrasado,* Sp.—to be left b., *maiwan.*

BEHOLD, v. to look, *tumingín, tingnán;* fix the eyes upon, *malasin, pagmalasin, magmalas.*—Behold! *Tingnán mo!*

BEING, n. person, *tao;* personality, *katauhan, pagkatao.* (For BEING, participle of "to be," see BE.)

BELFRY, n. *kampanaryo,* Sp.; *bátingawán.*

BELIEF, n. *paniniwalà;* faith, creed, *pananampalataya.*

BELIEVE, v. *maniwalà.*

BELL, n. *kampanà,* Sp.; *batingáw;* (small) *kampanilya,* Sp.; *kuliling.*

BELONG, v. does not have exact correspondence. That book belongs to me. *Ang aklát na iyán ay akin.* (That book is mine).—I belong here. *Dito akó kabilang.*

BELOVED, adj. n. *mahál, minámahál; irog, iníirog; sintá, sinísintá.*

BELOW, prep. beneath, *sa ilalim ng;* in a position below another, *sa ibabâ ng.*—adv. under, *sa ilalim;* downstairs, *sa silong, sa lupà.*

BELT, n. *sinturón,* Sp.; cloth hand around waist, *bigkís;* strip for pulleys, *korea,* Sp.

BENCH, n. *bangkô,* Sp.

BEND, v. to curve, *hubugin; hutukin;* make crooked, *baluktutin.*

BENEATH, see BELOW.

BENEDICTION, n. *bendisyón,* Sp.; *basbás,* nc.

BENEFIT, n. profit, *pakinabang;* (in someone's favor) *kapakinabangán.*

BESIDE, prep. near, *sa tabí ng; sa piling ng.*

BESIDES. adv. more, *pa;* moreover, *bukód sa roón (rito, riyán);* in addition, *at sakâ; patí, din (rin).*

BEST, adj. (sup.) *pinakamabuti; pinakamagalíng.*

BESTOW, v. to award, *ipagkaloob, pagkaloobán;* confer, *igawad, gawaran.*

BETRAY, v. *magkánuló, ipagkánuló, pagkánuluhán.*

BETTER, adj. (comp.) *lalong mabuti; lalong magalíng; lalong maigi.*

BETWEEN, prep. *sa pagitan ng* —adv. *sa pagitan.*

BEVERAGE, n. any kind of drink (but not water) *inumin;* water to drink, *inumín.*

BEWARE, v. *mag-ingat, pag-ingatan; mangilag, pangilagan.*

BEYOND, prep. on the farther side of, *sa dako pa roón ng;* on the other side of, *sa kabilâ ng;* (of a body of water, as a river) *sa ibayo ng.*

BIBLE, n. *Bíblia,* Sp.; Holy Scriptures, *Banál na Kasulatán;* Old Testament, *Matandáng Tipán;* New Testament, *Bagong Tipán.*

BICYCLE, n. *bisikleta,* Sp.

BID, v. to propose as price for something, *magturing, tumuring, turíngan;* command, *magutos, utusan, pag-utusan.*—to b. goodbye, *magpaalam.* — n. amount offered, *turing;* amount given as counter offer when buying, *tawad;* call in a card game, *tawag;* bet, *pustá,* Sp.

BIG, adj. *malakí.*

BILL, n. beak, *tukâ;* bank note, *papel-de-bangko,* Sp.; draft of a proposed law, *panukalang-batás;* statement of account, *taláutangan,* nc.; collection statement, *pasingíl;* list of merchandise purchased, *talábilihan,* nc.; poster, *kartelón,* Sp.

BIND, v. to tie together or tie up, *talian, italì;* (into a bundle) *bigkisín, bigkisán;* make into a book, *aklatín.*

BIOGRAPHY, n. *talámbuhay,* nc.

BIRD, n. *ibon.*

BIRD'S-EYE, adj. *tanáw-ibon,* nc.

BIRTHDAY, n. anniversary, *kaarawan.*

BISCUIT, n. *biskuwít,* Sp.

BISHOP, n. *obispo,* Sp.

BIT, n. a small piece, *kapyangót; munting piraso,* Sp.

BITE, v. *kumagát, kagatín.*

BITTER, adj. *mapait;* harshly b., *masakláp.*

BLACK, adj. *itím, maitím.*

BLACKBOARD, n. *pisara,* Sp.

BLACKSMITH, n. *pandáy.*

BLADDER, n. *pantóg.*

BLADE, n. (of cutting tools) *talím;* (of grass) *uhay.*

BLAME, n. reproof, *paninisi;* responsibility, *pananagót, panágutan, kapanágutan;* fault, *mali; sala.* — v. reprove, *sisihin;* place responsibility for something wrong, *papanagutín.*

BLANK, adj. free from writing or print, *waláng-sulat.* — n. spaces in which to write something (as in an objective test), *puwáng;* form to be filled, *emblangko,* Sp.; *pormularyo,* Sp.; *blangk,* Eng.

BLANKET, n. *manta,* Sp.; bed cover, *kumot; blangket,* Eng.

BLAZE, n. *liyáb; alab; dingas, ningas.*

BLEED, v. *dumugô, magdugó;* cause to b., *paduguin.*

BLESS, v. *bindisyunán,* Sp.; *magbindisyón,* Sp.; to give blessings, *magbasbás, basbasán.*

BLESSING, BLESSINGS, n. *biyayà; palà; basbás.*

BLIND, adj. *bulág.*

BLINDFOLD, n. *piríng.* — v. (self) *magpiríng;* (others) *piringán.*

BLISTER, n. (caused by burns) *paltós;* (caused by friction) *lintós.*

BLOOD, n. *dugô.*

BLOODY, adj. *madugô.*

BLOOM, n. blossom, flower, *bulaklák.*—v. to blossom, *mamulaklák, bumulaklák.*

BLOT, n. stain, *bahid; mansá,* Sp.; blemish, *dungis, lahíd.*—v. to stain, *bahiran; mantsahán,* Sp.; to dry with a blotter, *sikantihán,* Sp.

BLOTTER, n. blotting paper, *sikante,* Sp.

BLOUSE, n. *blusa,* Sp.

BLOW, n. *hampás;* (with a club) *bugbóg;* (of wind or air) *hihip;* (hammerlike) *pukpók;* (successive blows) *asód.*—v. to move (as the wind does), *humihip;* affect by blowing (as, blow the dust off, blow a bugle, etc.), *hipan.*

BLUE, adj. *asúl,* Sp.; *bugháw.*

BLUFF, n. pretense, *kabulastugán;* steep bank, *dalisdis;* precipice, *bangín.*—v. to deceive or frighten by bluffing, *mamulastóg, bulastugín.*

BLUSH, v. *mamulá.*

BOARD, n. a piece of timber, *tablá;* committee, *lupon.* — b. and l o d g i n g, *pangangasera,* Sp.; ride a vehicle, *sumakáy.*

BOAST, v. *maghambóg; magvanság; magyabáng.*

BOASTFUL, adj. *hambóg; mayabang.*

BOAT, n. *bankâ, lundáy.*

BODY, n. *katawán.* — Dead b., *bangkáy.*

BOIL, n. furuncle, *pigsá;* state of ebullition, *pagkuló.*—v. to boil or reach the boiling point, *kumuló;* to heat to the boiling point, *pakuluín;* to cook in boiling water, *pakuluán.*

BOLD, adj. daring, *pangahás;* audacious, *madaluhong;* intrepid, *mapusók.*

BOLT, n. metal pin or rod, *barál*, Sp.; threaded metal pin, *tornillyo*, Sp.; roll of cloth, *rolyo*, Sp.; *piyesa*, Sp.; *lulón. balumbón.*

BOMB, n. *bomba*, Sp.

BOND, n. anything that binds or confines, *talì, bigkís, gapos;* a binding force or influence, *kaisahán, pagkakáisá;* bail, *piyansa*, Sp.; guarantee. *akò;* pledge, *sanglâ.*

BONE, n. *butó.*—fish b., *tiník* ng *isdâ.* — f. bone stuck in the throat, *bikíg.*

BONNET, n. *bunete.* Sp.; *gora*, Sp.

BOOK, n. *aklát; libró,* Sp.

BOON, n. *utang na loób.*

BOOTBLACK, n. *limpyabota*, Sp.

BORDER, n. outer part or edge, margin, *gilid;* boundary, *hangganan;* sides, *tabihán.*

BORE, v. to pierce or drill a hole. *bumutas, magbutas; butasin.* n. hole, *butas.*

BORROW, v. *humirám. manghirám; hiramin.*

BOSOM, n. breast, *dibdíb;* the inside, innermost, *sinapupunan.*

BOSS, n. foreman, *kátiwalà;* chief, *punò;* employer, *panginoón.*

BOTANY, n. *Botániká,* Sp.; *paláhalamanan,* nc.

BOTH, pron. *kapwà.*

BOTHER, v. to annoy, *yamutín;* to trouble, *ligaligin.*—n. annoyance, *yamót, kayámutan;* trouble, *ligalig, guló;* fuss, *pagpapakaabala.*

BOTTLE, n. *bote,* Sp.; *botelya,* Sp.

BOTTOM, n. *ilalim;* ship, *bapór,* Sp.; *sasakyáng-dagat.*

BOUGH, n. a tree branch, *sangá.*

BOUNDARY, n. *hangganan; palihot, paligid: kabalantáy.*

BOUNDLESS, a d j. unlimited, *waláng-hanggán.*

BOUQUET, n. *tungkós; bukéy,* Fr.

BOW, n. forward inclination of the head, *pagtungó;* act of stooping, *pagyukô;* (in greeting or respect) *pagyukód;* weapon shooting arrows, *busog, pamanà;* string rod (for violin, etc.), *panghilis; arko,* Sp.—v. to incline the head forward, face downward, *tumungó;* to stoop, *yumukô;* (in greeting or showing respect) *yumukód.*

BOWER, n. temporary shady shelter, *habong;* arbor, *kalandóng,* O.T.; (for vegetables) *balag.*

BOWL, n. *mangkók,* Ch.; large cup, *sulyáw.*

BOX, n. *kahón,* Sp.; *kaha,* Sp.

BOXER, n. pugilist. *boksingero,* Eng.-Sp.

BOXING, n. *boksing,* Eng.

BOY, n. male child, *batang lalaki;* houseboy, *bataan, utusán; mutsatso,* Sp.

BRACELET, n. *pulseras,* Sp.; *galanggalangán,* nc.

BRAID, n. weave of reeds, *lala;* plait of hair, *tirintás,* Sp.; weave of textile, *habi.*

BRAIN, BRAINS, n. *utak.*

BRAKE, n. *preno,* Sp.; *pampatigil,* nc.; *pampahintô,* nc.

BRANCH, n. *sangá.*

BRAND, n. mark burned in, *hero,* Sp.; trade mark, *marká,* Sp.; burning piece of wood, *dupong.*

BRASS, n. *tansô.*

BRAVE, adj. *matapang;* heroic, *magiting.* See BOLD.

BREAD, n. *tinapay.*

BREADTH, n. *luwáng;* extent of width, *lapad.*

BREAK, v. *sirain*.—n. *sirà*.

BREAKFAST, n. *almusál*, Sp.; *agahan*.

BREAST, n. *dibdib*.

BREATH, n. *hiningá:* expiration of b., *hingá; paghingá*.

BREATHE, v. *humingá*.—to b. into, *hìngahán*.

BREED, n. race or strain, *lahì*. —half-b., *mestiso*, Sp.; *balugà*, O.T.

BREEZE, n. (soft) *simoy*.

BRICK, n. *laryó*, Sp.; *ladrilyo*, Sp.

BRIDE, ñ. *nobya*, Sp.

BRIDEGROOM, n. *nobyo*, Sp.

BRIDESMAID, n. *abay*.

BRIDGE, n. *tuláy*.

BRIDLE, n. (of horse) *kabisada*, Sp.

BRIEF, ad. *maikli; maigsi*.

BRIGHT, adj. shining, *makináng;* polished, *makintáb;* intelligent, *matalino*.

BRING, v. to fetch, *dalhin; magdalá*.

BRITTLE, adj. *malutóng*.

BROAD, adj. *maluwáng, malapad;* extensive, *malawak*.

BROKEN, adj. *sirâ; baság*.

BRONZE, n. yellow brass, *tansóng diláw*.

BROOK, n. *ilug-ilugan; batis; sapà*.

BROOM, n. *walis*.

BROTH, n. *sabáw;* soup, *sopas*, Sp.

BROTHER, n. *kapatíd na lalaki*. —b.-in-law, *bayáw*.

BROTHERHOOD, n. *kápatiran*.

BROW, n. forehead, *noó;* eyebrow, *kilay*.

BROWN, n./adj. (of human skin) *kayumanggí*. Shades of brown are given by *kulay* plus known brown material, as, *kulay-kapé*, coffee-brown; *kulay-kaki*, khakibrown, etc.

BRUISE, n. a black-and-blue spot on the body, caused by a blow, *pasâ*.

BRUSH, n. *sepilyo*, Sp.—tooth-b., *panghisò, sipan*.

BRUTE, adj. *hayop; halimaw; ganid*.

BUBBLE, n. *bulâ*.

BUCKET, n. pail, *baldé*, Sp.

BUD, n. *buko*.

BUDGET, n. *badyet*, Eng.

BUG, n. insect, *kulisap*, nc.

BUGLE, n. *kurnetín*, Sp.; huntsman's horn, *tambulì; alakán*, nc.

BUILD, v. *magtayô, itayô*.

BULB, n. electric b., *bombilya*, Sp.

BULK, n. mass, *lakí*.

BULL, n. *toro*, Sp.

BULLETIN, n. *buletín*, Eng.; report, *ulat;* news, *balità*.

BUMP, n. a swelling, *bukol;* a collision, *bunggô, banggá;* (of the head) *umpóg, untóg*.

BUNCH, n. (of fruits) *buwíg; langkáy;* (of flowers and leaves) *kumpól*.

BUNDLE, n. (tied) *bigkís, talì;* package, *bastâ; pakete*, Sp.; (wrapped in cloth or paper) *balutan*.

BURDEN, n. load, *dalá, dálahin; kargá*, Sp.; *kargahin*, Sp.; (on shoulder) *pasán;* (on head) *sunong;* (carried by hand) *bitbít;* (under the arm) *kipkíp*.

BURGLAR, n. *manloloób;* thief, *magnanakaw*.

BURIAL, n. interment, *paglili-bing.*

BURN, n. *paso;* scalding, *paltós.*
—v. to b., *sunugin.*

BURST, v. to break open suddenly, *tumilapon; sumambulat;* explode, *pumutók.*

BURY, v. (a dead body) *ilibíng;* (a thing) *ibaón.*

BUSINESS, n. occupation, trade, *hanapbuhay;* commercial operation, *kalakal, pangangalakal;* one's affairs, *abal, abal-abal,* nc.

BUSY, adj. *may ginágawâ; abalá.*

BUT, prep. except, *kundi.*—conj. *nguni't, subali't, dátapwá't.*

BUTCHER, n. *magpapatay;* meat vendor, *magkakarné,* Sp.; *mángangatay.*

BUTTER, n. *mantekilya,* Sp.

BUTTERFLY, n. *paruparó;* moth, *paparó, aliparó.*

BUTTON, n. *butones,* Sp.

BUTTONHOLE, n. *uhales,* Sp.

BUY, v. *bumilí;* (many things) *mamilí.*

BUYER, n. *mámimilí.*

BUZZ, n. hum, *ugong.*

BY, prep. near, *sa tabi ng;* in, on, at, *sa;* (indicating the doer of a passive), *ni ng* (pl. *niná, ng mga*); through, *sa pamamagitan ng;* because of, *dahil sa.*

C

CABARET, n. *sáyawan; kabarét,* Fr.

CABBAGE, n. *repolyo,* Sp.

CABIN, n. (native) *kubo; dampâ;* in a boat, *kamarote,* Sp.

CABINET, n. case or cupboard for keeping or displaying jewels, *eskaparate,* Sp., *estutse,* Sp.; advisory group, *gabinete,* Sp.

CABLE, n. *kable,* Sp.; cablegram, *pahatíd-kawad; kablegrama,* Sp.

CACAO, n. *kakáw.*

CACTUS, n. *hagdambató.*

CADENCE, n. rhythm, *indayog.*

CADET, n. *kadete,* Sp.

CAGE, n. *kulungán; hawla,* Sp.

CAKE, n. *keik,* Eng.—rice c., *bibingka.*—rice c. with dough, *puto.*

CALAMITY, n. *sakuná.*

CALCULATE, v. *kalkulahín,* Sp.; *tayahin.*

CALENDAR, n. *kalindaryo,* Sp.; *taláarawan.*

CALF, n. (of cattle) *guyà; bisiro,* Sp.; (of leg) *bintî.*

CALL, v. summons, *tawag;* formal visit, *dalaw.*—v. to summon, *tumawag, tawagin, tawagan;* to visit, *dumalaw.*

CALM, adj. serene, *panatag;* unexcited, *mahinahon;* quiet, *tahimik;* no noise, *waláng-ingay;* motionless, *waláng-kibô.*

CAMP, n. *kampo,* Sp.; *himpilan,* nc.

CAMPAIGN, n. *kampanya,* Sp.

CAN, n. tin cylindrical container, *lata*, Sp.—v. (aux.) to be able to, expressed by *ma-* and *maka-*, in the present tense form, as from *makuha — nakukuha*, can be obtained; from, *makabili,— nakabíbilí*, can buy.

CANAL, n. *kanál*, Sp.; ditch, *bambáng; taguling.*

CANDIDATE, n. *kandidato*, Sp.

CANDLE, n. *kandilà*, Sp.

CANDY, n. *kendi*, Eng.

CANE, n. walking stick, *bastón*, Sp.; *tungkód* —sugar c., *tubó.*

CANNON, n. *kanyón*, Sp.

CANTALOUPE, n. *nulong bilóg* (round melon).

CANVAS, n. *kanbas*, Eng., *balindáng.*

CAP, n. headgear, *gora*, Sp.; bottle cover, *panakip*; gunpowder in paper, *perminante*, Sp.; *paputók.*

CAPABLE, adj. having ability, *may-kaya.*

CAPE, n. wrap, *abrigo*, Sp.; headland (narrow) *lungos*; (short) *imus*; (high) *tangos*; (wide and long) *tangwáy.*

CAPITAL, n. amount used in running a business, *puhunan*; c. city, *ulunlunsód*; c. letter, *malaking titik.*—c. punishment, *parusang kamátayan.*

CAPITOL, n. *kapitolyo*, Sp.

CAPTIVE, n. *bihag.*

CAPTURE, v. *bumihag, bihagin.* —to be captured, *mábihag.*—to be able to c., *mabihag.*

CAR, n. *kotse*, Sp.

CARABAO, n. *kalabáw; anuwáng; damulag.*

CARD, n. stiff pasteboard, *kartón*, Sp.—Personal c., *tarheta*, Sp.— playing c., *baraha*, Sp.

CARE, n. caution, *alagà; ingat;* attention, *limi; asikaso*, Sp.

CAREER, n. *karera*, Sp.

CAREFUL, adj. *maingat; maalagà.*

CARELESS, adj. *bulagsák; waláng-ingat; pabayâ.*

CARGO, n. load, *dalá; kargá*, Sp.; *merkansiya*, Sp.

CARICATURE, n. *karikatura*, Sp.

CARPENTER, n. *karpintero*, Sp.; *anluwage.*

CARPET, n. *alpombra*, Sp.

CARRIAGE, n. vehicle, *karwahe*, Sp.; grace of movement, *bikas; tikas.*

CARRY, v. *magdalá, dalhin.*—to c. on, *magpatuloy, ipagpatuloy.* —to c. out, *isagawâ, isakatuparan.*

CART, n. *karitón*, Sp.

CASE, n. a box, *kahón, kaha;* (Law), c. in court, *usapín;* (Gram.) *kaukulán;* situation, *lagáy, tayô.*

CASH, n. ready money, *salaping hawak.*

CASHIER, n. *kahero*, Sp.; paymaster, *tagabayad.*

CASTLE, n. *kastilyo*, Sp.

CAT, n. *pusà.*

CATALOG, n. list, *tálaan; listahan*, Sp.; (of merchandise) *katálogó*, Sp.; *talákalakal*, nc.

CATCH, v. to make captive, *hulihin; bihagin;* arrest, *dakpin.*

CATHEDRAL, n. *katedrál*, Sp.

CAUSE, n. reason for, *sanhí; dahil, dahilán;* source, *pinagmulán, mulâ.*

CAVE, CAVERN, n. (natural) *yungib;* (of reptiles, etc.) *lunggâ.*

CEASE, v. *tumigil;* reduce intensity then stop altogether, *humumpáy; maghumpáy; maglubáy.*

CEILING, n. *kisamé.*

CELEBRATE, v. *magdiwang; ipagdiwang.*

CELERY, n. (Bot.) *kintsáy,* Ch.

CELL, n. room, *silíd; selda,* Sp.; (Biol.) *sélulá,* Sp. — Prison c., *piítán, bilangguan.*

CEMENT, n. *simento,* Sp.

CEMETERY, n. *libingan; sementeryo, pantiyón,* Sp.

CENSUS, n. *senso,* Sp.

CENT, n. *séntimós,* Sp.; *pera.* (One U.S. cent is equivalent to two centavos, *séntimós, pera,* in the Philippines.

CENTER, n. *gitná;* middle point, *kalágitnaan.*

CENTURY, n. *dantaón.*

CEREMONY, n. *seremonya,* Sp.; *pagdiriwang.*

CERTAIN, adj. definite, *tiyák;* true, *tunay, totoó.*—I am certain, *Akó'y nakatítiyák.*

CERTAINLY, adv. that's so, *siyangà; oo ngâ.*

CERTIFICATE, n. *katibayan; alusithâ,* O.T.; *sertipiko,* Sp.; *sertipikét,* Eng.

CHAIN, n. *tanikalâ; kadena,* Sp.

CHAIR, n. *silya,* Sp.; *úpuan, likmuan, luklukan.*

CHAIRMAN, n. *pangulo.*

CHALK, n. *yeso,* Sp.

CHALLENGE, n. *hamon.*—v. *hamunin, manghamon.*

CHAMPION, n. *kampeón,* Sp.

CHANCE, n. *pagkakátaón.*—By c., *nagkátaón.*—There's no c., *waláng pag-asa.*—To take a c., *magbakásakalì.*

CHANGE, n. alteration, *pagbabago;* variation, *pag-iibá;* amount of money (over amount of purchase), *sukli;* loose c., *baryá, muláy.*—v. to alter, *baguhin;* vary, *ibahín;* renew, replace, *palitán, halinhán.*

CHANNEL, n. passageway, *daanán;* place over which water flows, *páagusán;* rain pipe, *alulód;* ditch, *bambáng;* canal, *kanal,* Sp.

CHAOS, n. disorder, *guló;* confusion, *ligalig;* (personal) *linggatong.*

CHAPEL, n. *kapilya,* Sp.; *tuklóng, bisita,* Sp.

CHAPTER, n. *kabanatà;* (branch of a society), *sangáy, balangáy.*

CHARACTER, n. distinguishing quality, *katángian;* letter of alphabet, *titik.*

CHARGE, n. price asked for an object, *halagá; singíl;* accusation, *sakdál, hablá;* a person or thing under one's responsibility, *alagà;* responsibility, *pananágutan.*

CHARITY, n. *kawanggawâ.*

CHARM, n. *halina, panghalina; pang-akit.*

CHARMING, adj. *kahalí-halina; kaakit-akit.*

CHASE, v. to pursue, *habulin; pagatin.*

CHAUFFEUR, n. *tsupér,* Fr.

CHEAP, adj. low priced, *mura:* common, *karaniwan;* of no value, *walang-halagá.*

CHEAT, v. *magdayà, dayain.*

CHECK, n. bank order for cash, *tseke,* Sp.; mark showing something has been noted, *tsek,* Eng.; *gurlit,* nc., *tiyák.*

CHECKERBOARD, n. *damahán.*

CHECKERS, n. (game of) *dama*, Sp.

CHEEK, n. *pisngi.*

CHEER, n. gaiety, *sayá;* mirth, *tuwâ;* joy, *galák;* applause, *palakpák.*—v. to encourage, *pasiglahín;* console, *aliwín;* gladden, *pasayahín;* applaud, *pumalakpák, palakpakán.*

CHEESE, n. *keso,* Sp.

CHEMIST, n. *kímikó,* Sp.

CHESS, n. *ahedrés,* Sp.

CHEST, n. breast of fowls or animals, *pitsó,* Sp.; human breast, *dibdíb;* box, *kahón; kaha,* Sp.; wooden box with lid, *kabán, baúl,* Sp.

CHESTNUT, n. *kastanyas,* Sp.

CHEW, v. to masticate, *nguyain;* (cut or quid) *ngatain;* ("buyo") *ngumangà.*

CHICKEN, n. *manŏk.*—Wild c., *labuyò.*

CHIEF, n. *punò.*

CHILD, n. *batà.*

CHILDHOOD, n. youth, *kabataan.*

CHILL, n. gináw; (malaria) *ngiki, pangiki; kaligkíg.*

CHIN, n. *babà.*

CHOCOLATE, n. *sikulate,* Sp.

CHOICE, n. that which is chosen, *ang pinilì; ang hinirang.* — adj. selected, *pilì, hirang;* especially good, *mainam.*

CHOIR, n. *koro,* Sp.

CHOKE, v. to strangle, *sakalín;* clog, block up, *pasakan;* suppress, *timpiín.*—Be choked at the throat, *máhirinan.*

CHOKED, adj. clogged, *may-pasak.*

CHOLERA, n. *kólerá,* Sp.

CHOOSE, v. select, *pumilì, mamilì; piliin.*

CHOP, v. to cut (with an ax) *sibakín;* (into pieces) *pagpirá-pirasuhín;* (finely) *tadtarín.*

CHRIST, n. *Kristo,* Sp.

CHRISTIAN, n. & adj. *kristiyano,* Sp.; *binyagan.*

CHRISTMAS, n. *Paskó,* Sp.

CHURCH, n. *simbahan.*

CIGAR, n. *tabako,* Sp.

CIGARETTE, n. *sigarilyo,* Sp.

CIRCLE, n. *bilog; balangkát,* nc.

CIRCULAR, adj. rounded, *bilugán* —n. letter sent around, *palibotsulat.*

CIRCUMFERENCE, n. *kabilugan, paligid, palibot.*

CIRCUMFLEX, adj. (Gram.) c. accent, *tuldík na pakupyâ.*

CIRCUS, n. *sirko,* Sp.

CITIZEN, n. *mámamayán.*

CITIZENSHIP, n. *pagkamámamayán.*

CITY, n. *lunsód; siyudád,* Sp.

CIVIC, adj. *pangmámamayán.*

CIVIL, adj. *pambayan; sibil,* Sp.

CIVILIZATION, n. *kabihasnán;* culture, *kalinangán.*

CIVILIZED, adj. *may-kabihasnán;* cultured, *may-kalinangán.*

CLAIM, v. to ask, *hingín; hilingín.*—n. *hingî, hiling.*

CLAM, n. *kabibi.*

CLASH, n. conflict, *sálungatan;* fight, *labanán; paglalaban;* collision, *salpukan; banggaan;* opposition, *tunggálian.*

CLASP, n. catch to fasten things together, *ipit.*

CLASS, n. *klase,* Sp.; kind, *urì.*

CLASSMATE, n. *kaklase,* Sp.; *kaaral.*

CLAUSE, n. (Gram.) *sugnáy;* item in a document, *takdâ.*— Principal c., *punong sugnáy.*— Independent c., *sugnáy.*—Subordinate c., *sugnáy na pantulong* (or *panlangkáp.*)

CLAVICLE, n. (Anat.) *balagat.*

CLAW, n. *pangalmót;* talon, *kukó.*

CLAY, n. plastic earth, *lupang malagkít.*

CLEAN, adj. *malinis.*—v. *maglinis.; linisin.*

CLEANER, n. material or tool for cleaning, *panlinis; pampalinis.*

CLEAR, adj. (of water or explanation) *malinaw;* lighted, *maliwanag.*

CLERGYMAN, n. *parì,* Sp.; *klero,* Sp.

CLERK, n. *eskribyente,* Sp.; employee, *kawaní.*

CLEVER, adj. keen, *matalas;* intelligent, *matalino;* competent, reliable, *maáasahan.*

CLIMATE, n. *klima,* Sp.

CLIENT, n. *kliente,* Sp.

CLIMAX, n. *kasukdulán; kahayunán; katingkarán,* nc.; *karurukan.*

CLIMB, v. *umakyát; akyatín.*

CLING, v. *kumapit; kapitan; pangapitan.*

CLINIC, n. *klíniká,* Sp.; dispensary, *págamutan.*

CLOAK, n. *balabal.*

CLOCK, n. *relós,* Sp.; *orasán,* Sp.

CLOSE, v. *isará,* Sp.; *sarhán,* Sp.; *magsará,* Sp.; *ipinid.*—n. the end, *katapusán; wakás.*

CLOSED, adj. *sarado,* Sp.; *nakapinid;* covered, *may-takíp.*

CLOSET, n. (for clothes) *aparadór,* Sp.; latrine, *kumón,* Sp.; *kasilyas,* Sp.; shelved cabinet, *istante,* Sp.

CLOTH, n. *damít.*

CLOTHE, v. (oneself) *magdamít, magbihis;* (others) *damtán, bihisan.*

CLOTHES, n. (being worn) *kasuután, pananamít;* (kept ready to wear) *bihisan.*

CLOUD, n. *ulap;* (high and white) *alapaap;* (low and black) *dagím.*

CLOUDY, adj. *maulap.*

CLOWN, n. *payaso,* Sp.; *bubo,* Sp.; *lukayo,* Sp.; *pusong.*

CLUB, n. heavy stick, *pambambú;* association, *klub,* Eng.; *kapisanan, sámahan.*

CLUSTER, n. (of flowers and leaves), *kumpól;* (of bananas, lanzon, etc.) *buwíg; piling;* (of coconuts) *balaybáy,* (of other fruits) *langkáy.*

COACH, n. car, *kotse,* Sp.; trainer, *tagasanay.*

COAGULATE, v. *mamuô;* become curdled, *makurtá,* Sp.

COAL, n. *karbón,* Sp.; *batónguling.*

COARSE, adj. *magaspáng;* (of manners) *magasláw; bastós,* Sp.

COAST, n. seashore, *baybayin, baybay-dagat.*—v. to go by momentum, *magpadausdós.*

COAT, n. *amerikana,* Sp.; *sako,* Sp.

COCK, n. rooster, male bird, *tandáng.*

COCKFIGHT, n. *sabong.*

COCKPIT, n. *sabungán.*

COCKROACH, n. *ípis.*

COCOA, n. *kakáw,* Sp.

COCONUT, n. *niyóg.* — c. grove, *niyugan.*

COD, n. (fish) *bakaláw.*—c. oil, *langís ng bakaláw.*

CODE, n. *kódigo*, Sp.; system of signals, *paláhudyatan*, nc.: *kowd*, Eng.

COFFEE, n. *kapé*, Sp.

COIN, n. (loose change) *baryá*.

COFFIN, n. *kabaong; ataúl*, Sp.

COIL, n. *ikid; likaw.*—v. *umikid; ikirin; likawin.*

COLD, adj. *malamíg;* chilly, *magináw.*

COLLAR, n. (for necktie) *kuwelyo*, Sp.; neck band for animals, *kulyár*, Sp.; loop for the neck of animals, *salíig, panlíig.*

COLLECT, v. *magtipon, tipunin;* to demand payment, *maningíl; singilín;* accumulate, *maipon;* increase in number, *dumami.*

COLLECTION, n. (act of collecting) *pagtitipon; paniningil;* see COLLECT.

COLLECTOR, n. (of debts, accounts) *máningingil; kubrador,* Sp.; *mángungubrá,* Sp.; (of objects) *paláipón.*

COLLEGE, n. *koléhiyó,* Sp.; *koleds,* Eng.; *dálubhasaan,* nc.

COLONY, n. *kolonya,* Sp.; *lupang sakóp.*

COLOR, n. *kulay, kolór,* Sp.—v. *kulayan; kulurán,* Sp.

COLT, n. *bisiro ng kabayo,* Sp.

COLUMN, n. pillar, *haligi;* line, rank *hanay.*

COMB, n. (for hair) *cukláy;* crest of fowl, *palong.*—v. (the hair) *magsukláy; suklayín; suklayán.*

COMBAT, n. fight, *laban;* quarrel, *away;* duel, *duwelo,* Sp.; battle, *pagbabaka; pagpapamuók.*

COMBINATION, n. *pagsasama; kombinasyón,* Sp.; union, *pagiisá.*

COMBINE, v. *pagsamahin;* unite, *pag-isahin*

COMBUSTIBLE, adj. *masunugín.*

COME, v. to approach, *lumapit;* arrive, *dumatíng;* issue from, *manggaling sa;* attend, *dumaló.*

COMEDY, n. *komedya,* Sp.

COMET, n. *kometa,* Sp.; *bandós,* O.T.; *buntalà.*

COMFORT, n. consolation, *alíw;* ease of body, *kaalwanan;* ease of body and mind, *ginhawa.*

COMFORTABLE, adj. *maginhawa.*

COMIC, COMICAL, adj. *nakakátawá; kómiká,* Sp.

COMMA, n. (punctuation mark) *kuwít; koma,* Sp.

COMMAND, n. *utos; atas.*—v. *mag-utos; mag-atas; pag-utusan, atasan.*

COMMANDER, n. (Mil.) *komandante,* Sp.; chief, *punò.*

COMMANDMENT, n. *utos, kautusán.*

COMMENCE, v. to begin, *magumpisá,* Sp.; *umpisahán,* Sp.; *magpasimulá, pasimulán.*

COMMENCEMENT, n. beginning, *umpisá,* Sp.; *pasimulá;* graduation in, *pagtatapós.*

COMMEND, v. to praise, *purihin, papurihan.*

COMMENDATION, n. *papuri.*

COMMERCE, n. *komérsiyo,* Sp.; *pangangalakal.*

COMMERCIAL, adj. *komersiyál,* Sp.; *pangkalakal.*

COMMISSION, n. act of doing, *paggawâ, pagganáp;* a group of persons intrusted with public tasks, *komisyón,* Sp.; *lupon, kalupunan;* agent's compensation, *komisyón,* Sp.; *pursiyento,* Sp.

COMMISSIONER, n. *komisyonado,* Sp.

COMMIT, v. to do something wrong, *magkásala; magkámalî;* give over for safekeeping, *ipagkátiwalà; ilagak.*

COMMITTEE, n. *lupon; kumité,* Sp.

COMMON, adj. ordinary, *karaniwan;* general, *panlahát;* for the public, *pangmadlâ.* — c. article (Gram.), *pantukoy na pambálaná.*—c. noun (Gram.), *pangngalang pambálaná.*

COMMONWEALTH, n. the whole body of people organized into a government, *sampámahalaán; komonwels,* Eng.

COMMUNICATE, v. to tell, *sabihin;* impart, *ipatalós, ipabatíd;* make known, *ipagbigáy-alám.*

COMMUNION, n. close intimacy, *pagtatalamitam;* (the Holy Sacrament) *Komunyón, Pakinabáng.*

COMMUNITY, n. *komunidád,* Sp.; the people in general, *ang madlâ;* a whole town, *ang sambayanán.*

COMPANION, n. *kasama.*

COMPANY, n. corporation, *samahan;* business house, *bahay-kalakal;* attendance, *pagdaló.*

COMPARE, v. to liken, *ihambíng; itulad; iwangis; iparis*

COMPARISON, n. *paghahambíng; pagtutulad; pagwawangis; pagpaparis;* (Gram.) *púnuluran; pagpapánularan.*

COMPEL, v. *pilitin.*

COMPENSATION, n. salary, *sahod; suweldo,* Sp.; service fee, *upa;* reward, *gantimpalà;* remuneration, *gantimpagál; bigáy-palà.*

COMPETE, v. enter into rivalry, *makiagaw, makipagpang-agaw;* enter a contest, *makipagtimpalák.*

COMPETENT, adj. able, *maykaya.*

COMPETITION, n. contest, *timpalák;* rivalry, *pángagawán.*

COMPETITOR, n. (in contest) *katimpalák;* opponent, *kalaban;* rival, *kaagaw; karibál,* Sp.

COMPLAIN, v. *dumaíng; magreklamo,* Sp.; *maghinakdál.*

COMPLAINT, n. *daíng; reklamo.* Sp.; *hinakdál.*

COMPLEMENT, n. (Gram.) *kagánapan; pamunô; layon.*— subjective c., *panaguríng pansimunò.*—objective c., *karagdagang layon.*

COMPLETE, adj. *buô;* fully done or finished, *yarì na; tapôs na.* —v. *buuín;* to finish, *tapusin, yariin.*

COMPLEX, adj. intricate, *masikot;* involved, *pasikut-sikot.*— c. sentence (Gram.), *pangungusap na langkapan.*

COMPLEXION, n. *kutis,* Sp.; skin coloring, *kulay ng balát.*

COMPOSE, v. to form, *magbuô;* create, *lumikhâ.*

COMPOSITION, n. things making a whole, *kabuuán, kayarián;* school exercise, *komposisyón,* Sp.

COMPOUND, adj. *tambalan.*—c. sentence (Gram.), *pangungusap na tambalan.* — c. subject, *simunong tambalan.* — c. predicate, *panaguríng tambalan (panabing tambalan).*

COMPREHEND, v. *máintindihán,* Sp.; *máunawaan, máwatasan.*

COMPUTATION, n. *pagtutuós; katuusán.*

COMRADE, n. companion, *kasama;* friend, *kaibigan;* intimate friend, *katoto.*

COMPUTE, v. *magtuós; tuusín.*

CONCAVE, adj. *malukóng.*

CONCEAL, v. to hide something, *itagò;* keep secret, *maglihim: ilihim.*

CONCEIVE, v. to surmise, *akalain;* be in the early stage of pregnancy, *maglihí;* (in the fetal stage) *magbuntís.*

CONCENTRATE, v. (upon) *pagduruhan,* Sp.; fix one's attention to, *paglimiin; pag-isiping matamán.*

CONCERN, n. *anxiety, pag-aalálalá;* business firm, *bahay-kalakal.*—It's no c. of yours. *Walâ kang dapat pakialamán.*

CONCERNING, prep. relating to, *ukol sa;* regarding, *hinggíl sa;* about, *tungkól sa.*

CONCERT, n. (musical) *konsiyerto,* Sp.; harmony, *pagtutugmaan; tugmaan.*

CONCLUDE, v. to finish, *tapusin; magtapós;* bring to an end, *wakasán; magwakás;* deduce, *hinuhain; maghinuhà.*

CONCRETE, adj. actual, *tunay;* tangible, *nádaramá, konkreto,* Sp.—n. hardened mixture of cement and sand with gravel, etc., *konkreto,* Sp:; *sementong binubò, binubò;* solid mass, *buô.*

CONDEMN, v. to sentence, *hatulan;* punish, *parusahan.*

CONDITION, n. state of being, *lagáy;* circumstances, *kalágayan;* situation, *katáyuan;* a stipulation, *kondisyon,* Sp.; *takdâ;* a limitation in time, *taning.*

CONDUCT, n. personal behavior, *ugalì, pag-uugalì.*

CONDUCTOR, n. (in a public vehicle) *konduktór,* Sp.; (in a musical group) *patnugot.*

CONFER, v. to grant, bestow, *igawad,* (upon) *gawaran;* · consult, *sumanggunì; isanggunì.*

CONFERENCE, n. meeting, *pulong;* interview, *panayám;* consultation, *sanggúnian.*

CONFESS, v. to admit as true, *pananggapán; m a n a n g g á p;* (Eccl.) *mangumpisál, magkumpisál,* Sp.

CONFIDENCE, n. faith, *pananalig;* hope, *pag-asa;* trust, *pagtitiwalà.*

CONFINE, v. to keep within boundaries, *ipaloób, ikulóng;* imprison, *ibilanggô.*

CONFISCATE, v. *samsamín; manamsám.*

CONFLICT, n. See CLASH.

CONFUSION, n. *guló;* entanglement, *gusót, kagúsutan;* amazement, *pagkagulat, pagkagitlá; kagitlahanan.*

CONGRESS, n. *kongreso,* Sp.; *kapulungan.*

CONNECT, v. to join together, *pagdugtungín;* link together, *pagkabitín;* r e l a t e together, *pag-ugnayín.*

CONNECTION, n. relation, *kaugnayan.*

CONQUER, v. to overcome, subdue, *malupig, lupigin;* defeat, *talunin;* occupy by force, *masakop, sakupin.*

CONQUEROR, n. *manlulupig; mánanakop.*

CONSCIENCE, n. *konsiyénsiya,* Sp.; *budhî.*

CONSENT, v. to agree, *pumayag, payagan.*—n. *pagpayag.*

CONSEQUENCE, n. (past) *ang kinálabasán, ang kináuwián;* (future) *ang kálalabasán, ang káuuwián;* what did happen, *ang nangyari;* what would or will happen, *ang mangyayari.* —Of no c., *waláng bagay.*

CONSIDER, v. to think over carefully, *pag-isipin; liripin;* to esteem, *ıtangì;* to regard, *ipalagáy; isaalang-alang.*

CONSIDERABLE, adj. large in extent, *malawak;* important, *mahalagá;* large in amount or quantity, *di-gágaanó; di-gayón lamang.*

CONSIDERATION, n. careful thought, *paglilirip;* respect, *paggalang, pamimitagan;* esteem, *pagpapalagáy, pagtingín;* regard, *pagsasa-alang-alang.*

CONSIST, v. to c. of, *binubuô ng.*

CONSONANT, n. letter of the alphabet, not vowel, *katinìg.*

CONSPICUOUS, adj. visible, *kita;* obvious, *halatâ;* remarkable, *kapuná-puná.*

CONSTABLE, n. *kustable,* Sp.

CONSTABULARY, n. *kustabularyo,* Sp.; *tanod-bansá.*

CONSTANT, adj. *matimtiman;* unchanging, *waláng-bago, waláng-pagbabago.*

CONSTITUTION, n. structure, *kayarián;* (Law) *Saligáng-Batás.*

CONSTRUCT, v. to build, *magtayô, itayô;* form, *magbuô, buuin.*

CONSULT, v. *sumanggunì.*

CONSUME, v. use up, exhaust, *ubusin;* eat, *kainin, kanin.*

CONTAGIOUS, adj. *nakakáhawa; nakakálalin.*

CONTAIN, v. to hold within, *malamán; maglamán.*

CONTAINER, n. (small size) *sisidlán;* (any) *lalagyán.*

CONTEMPT, n. *paghamak;* disdain, *pagpalibhasà.*

CONTEMPTIBLE, adj. *hamak;* meriting disdain, *kapalí-palibhasà.*

CONTEND, v. *makipaglaban;* argue, dispute, *makipagtalo;* assert in argument, *ikatwiran, ipangatwiran;* maintain in argument, *igiit, ipanindigan.*

CONTENTED, adj. *nasisiyahán.*

CONTEST, n. conflict, *laban, paglalaban; sálungatan;* competition, *páligsahan;* artistic competition, *timpalák.*

CONTINENT, n. one of the great divisions of land on earth, *kontinente,* Sp.; *sanlupain; daigdíg.*

CONTINUATION, n. (act of) *pagpapatuloy;* the thing carried on after an interruption, *karugtóng.*

CONTINUE, v. *magpatuloy, ipagpatuloy; itulóy.*

CONTINUED, to be c., *itútulóy.*

CONTINUOUS, adj. *patuluytuloy;* unbroken, *waláng-lagót; waláng-patíd;* unceasing, *waláng-tigil.*

CONTRABAND, n. *kontrabando,* Sp.; *bagay na bawal.*

CONTRACT, n. formal agreement.—n. *kontrato,* Sp.; *kásunduan;* agreement to build, *kontrata,* Sp.

CONTRACTOR, n. *kontratista,* Sp.

CONTRADICT, v. *salansangín; salungatín.*

CONTRARY, adj. *salungát; laban.*

CONTRAST, n. *kaibahán (kaibhán).*—v. *pag-ibahin.*

CONTRIBUTE, v. *umambág, mag-ambág; ambagán;* supply articles for publication, *magpalathalà.*

CONTRIBUTION, n. *ambág;* help, *tulong;* aid, *abuloy.*

CONTROL, v. to restrain, *pigilin;* dominate, subdue, *supilin.*

CONVENIENT, adj. (in time) *nápapanahón;* (in comfort) *maginhawa;* (in ease) *magaán;* (in handiness) *madalî;* (in nearness) *malapit.*

CONVERSATION, n. *pag-uusap, pagsasálitaan; sálitaan;* interview, *pagpapanayám.*

CONVICT, v. *mahatulan.* — n. prisoner, *bilanggô.*

CONVICTION, n. firm belief, *paniniwalà.*

CONVINCE, v. to cause to believe, *papaniwalaın.*

COOK, n. *kusinero,* Sp.; *tagapaglutò.*—v.*maglutò; lutuin.*

COOKED, adj. *lutò; nilutò.*

COOL, adj. somewhat cold, *malamíg-lamíg;* not warm, *di-mainit;* fresh, *presko,* Sp

COOPERATE, v. to help, *tumulong;* join others in doing, *makitulong, makipagtulungán;* (together) *magtulungán.*

COOPERATIVE, adj. — n. *túlungan; úsungan; kooperatiba,* Sp.

COORDINATION, n. *túwangan.*

COPPER, n. *tansô.*

COPRA, n. *kalibkib; kopra,* Eng.

COPY, n. *kopya,* Sp.; *salin;* (of a book) *sipì;* imitation, *huwád.* —v. *kumopya;* imitate, *kumuwád, huwarán; manghuwád.*

COQUETRY, n. flirtatiousness, *kalimbangán; pagkamalimbáng.*

CORD, n. string, *pisì; leteng* (Ch.) ; twine, *panalì, talì;* rope, *lubid.*

CORDIAL, adj. hearty, *taós-pusò; buóng-pusò.*

CORK, n. stopper, *tapón,* Sp.; *pasak, siksík.*

CORN, n. *maís,* Sp.

CORNER, n. *sulok.*

CORPORATION, n. *korporasyón,* Sp.; *sámahan.*

CORPS, n. *pulutóng; pangkát.*

CORPSE, n. *bangkáy.*

CORRECT, adj. *wastô;* right, *tumpák, tamà.* — v. *magwastô. iwastô; magtumpák, itumpák.*

CORRECTION, n. *pagwawastô.*

CORRESPOND, v. to be like or equal to something else, *mákatumbás;* suit, agree, or fit, *mákaayon;* communicate by means of letters, *sumulat, lumiham; makipagsulatán, makipaglihamán.*

CORRESPONDING, adj. *katumbás; kaayon; katuwáng.*

CORRUPT, adj. rotten, *bulók;* spoiled, *sirâ;* depraved, *mahalay.*

CORSET, n. *kursét.* Fr.

COST, n. price, *halagá;* amount paid, *bayad.*

COSTLY, adj. expensive, *mahál.*

COT, n. light, movable bed, *kama;* canvas folding c., *tiheras,* Sp.

COTTAGE, n. (on a hill or in a forest) *amák;* small nipa hut, *kubo;* shanty, *barongbarong.*

COTTON, n. *bulak.*

COUCH, n. sofa, *supá,* Sp.

COUGH n. *ubó.* — v. *umubó;* to suffer from c., *ubuhín.*

COUNCIL, n. *kapulungan; konseho,* Sp.

COUNCILOR, n. *konsehál,* Sp.; *kagawad ng kapulungan.*

COUNSEL, n. *payo.* — v. to give advice, *magpayo; payuhan, pagpayuhan.*

COUNT, n. a reckoning, *bilang.*—v. to reckon by units, *bumilang; magbiláng; bilangin.*

COUNTENANCE, n. the expression of the face, *pagmumukhâ.*

COUNTER, n. table in a store, *despatso,* Sp.; apparatus or machine for counting, *pambilang.*

COUNTRY, n. native land, *lupang-tinubuan; bayan:* rural parts, *kabukiran.*

COUPLE, n. a pair, *isáng paris;* the two, *ang dalawá;* a married c., *ang mag-asawa.*

COURAGE, n. *tapang, katapangan.*

COURSE, n. line of motion, *daán; pinagdáraanan, pagdáraanan;* series of lessons, *kaaralán; kurso,* Sp.; part of a meal served at one time, *putahe,* Sp.; procedure, *paraán.*

COURT, n. hall of justice, *húkuman;* a sovereign and his retinue, *korte,* Sp.—v. to woo, *manligaw, mangibig.*

COURTEOUS, adj. respectful, *magalang.*

COURTESY, n. *paggalang.*

COUSIN, n. *pinsan.*

COVER, n. *takíp.*—v. *takpán.*

COW, n. *baka.*

COWARD, adj. *duwág.*

COZY, adj. *maginhawa.*

CRAB, n. (large) *alimango;* (smaller) *alimasag;* (tiny) *talangkâ.*

CRACK, n. snapping noise, *pamumutók; lagutók;* a break on glassware, *lamat, basag.*—v. to snap, *mamutók, lumagutók.*

CRADLE, n. *duyan; uyayi.*

CRAFTY, adj. *suwitik,* Ch.; *tuso;* tricky, *mahibò.*

CRAMP, n. (Med.) *pulikat.*

CRANK, n. bent handle for turning a shaft, *pihitán.*

CRASH, v. to fall, *lumagpák; bumagsák.*

CRATE, n. *bastâ; empake,* Sp.

CRAYON, n. *krayon,* Eng.

CRAWL, v. to creep, *gumapang.*

CRAZY, n. *loko,* Sp.; *balíw, hibáng.*

CREAM, n. rich, oily part of milk which gathers at top, *halagap;* cosmetic ungu.nt, *pumada,* Sp.; light yellow color, *krema,* Sp.; the best part of anything, *anɡ pinakaubod; ang kakanggatá.*

CREATION, n. act of creating, *paglikhâ; paglaláng;* thing created, *ang nilikhâ; ang nilaláng;* the universe,, *sansinukob: santinakpán; sangkalikasán.*

CREATOR, n. *manlilikhâ;* God, *ang Lumikhâ; Bathalà; Diyós,* Sp.; *ang Maykapál.*

CREATURE, n. thing created, *ang nilikhâ; ang nilaláng;* a human being, *tao.*

CREDENTIAL, n. *katibayan.*

CREDIBLE, adj. *mapaniniwalaan.*

CREDIT, n. *kréditó,* Sp.; one's deserved right to be praised, *kapurihán;* honor, *dangál, karángalan.*

CREDULOUS, adj. *mapaniwalain.*

CREEK, n. rivulet, *ilúg-ilugan.*

CREEP, v. *gumapang;* (continuously) *maggapáng.*

CREW, n. group, *pulutóng; pangkát; kawan.*

CRIB, n. manger, *sabsaban; labangán;* baby's bed, *kamita,* Sp.

CRICKET, n. *kamaksî, túrurukan.*

CRIME, n. *krimen,* Sp.; sinful conduct, *pagkakásala; sala.*

CRIMINAL, n. *kriminál,* Sp.; *salarín.*

CRIPPLE, n.-adj. *lumpó.*

CRITIC, n. *mánunurì.*

CRITICISM, n. *pagsusurì; pagpuná.*

CRITICIZE, v. *magsurì, suriin; pumuná, punahín.*

CROOKED, adj. bent, *kilô;* curved, *likô, baluktót;* twistéd, *kilú-kilô: balú-baluktót.*

CROP, n. harvest, *ani;* (Zool.) gizzard, *balúmbalunan.*

CROSS, n. *kurús, krus,* Sp.—v. To mark with a c., *kurusán.*— To move to the opposite side. *tumawíd; tawirín.*—To make the sign of the c., *mag-antandâ.*— adj. ill-tempered, *mainit ang ulo.*

CROSS-EYED, adj. *dulíng.*

CROW, n. black vulture, *uwák;* the cry of a rooster, *tilaok.*—v. to make the loud shrill sound that a rooster makes, *tumilaok.*

CROWBAR, n. *bareta,* Sp.

CROWD, n. throng, *lipumpón; libumbón.*

CROWN, n. *korona,* Sp.; *putong.* —v. *koronahan,* Sp.; *putungan.*

CRUEL, adj. *malupit.*

CRUELTY, n. *kalupitán.*

CRUMB, n. (of bread or rice) *mumo.*

CRUSH, v. to break into pieces or flatten by pressure, *pisaín;* grind to powder, *ligisín;* squeeze with the fingers or the hand, *pisilín;* pulverize, *durugín.*

CRUST, n. hard outer covering or surface layer, *pangibabaw.*

CRY, v. to shout, *sumigáw; humiyáw;* weep, *umiyák;* of an animal, to utter its call (bird), *humuni;* (horse) neigh, *humalinghíng;* (cattle) *umungâ;* (dog) *tumahól, kumahól; umaw-aw;* (cat) *umingáw; ngumiyáw;* (goat) *umumì.*

CRYSTAL, n. *krıstál,* Sp.; *bubog.*

CUCUMBER, n. *pipino,* Sp.

CUFF, n. (of shirt) *punyós,* Sp.

CULTIVATE, v. to till, *maglináng; linangín;* prepare (the soil) for crops, *bungkalín, maghungkál;* improve or develop by care, labor, or study, *linangín.*

CULTURE, n. tillage, *paglilináng;* result of training of mental or moral powers, *kalinangán.*

CULTURED, adj. *may-kalinangán.*

CUNNING, adj. crafty, *suwitik,* Ch.; *tuso;* astute, *matalas.*

CUP, n. *kopa;* Sp.; *tagayán;* (for coffee or tea) *tasa,* Sp.

CUPBOARD, n. *páminggalan;* (attached to kitchen window) *banggerahán.*

CURE, n. *lunas; gamót; kagámutan.*—v. *lunasan; gamutín.*

CURIOUS, adj. *mausisà.*

CURL, v. *kulutín.*

CURRENT, n. flow, *agos;* (of water from tap) *tulò;* (of electricity) *koryente,* Sp.; *dagitab,* nc.—adj. present, *kasalukuyan.*

CURSE, n. imprecation, *sumpâ.*— v. *sumpain.*

CURTAIN, n. *kurtina,* Sp.; *tabing.*

CURVE, n. *kurba,* Sp.; *kilô.*—v. *pakurbahán, pakurbahín; ikilô.*

CUSHION, n. pillow, *unan.* — Chair, c., *.almuwadón,* Sp; bed c., *kutsón.*

CUSTOM, n. habit, *ugalì;* behavior, *asal.*

CUSTOMER, n. *mámimili; sukì.*

CUT, v. *putulin;* to slice, *hiwain.*

CUTLERY, n. *mga panghiwà.*

D

DAB, v. to strike or touch lightly, *pikpikín.*

DAD, DADDY, n. a child's name for father, *tatay, tatang, itáy.*

DAGGER, n. *balaráw; daga.*

DAILY, adj. *pang-araw-araw.—* adv. *araw-araw.*

DAINTY, adj. delicious, *malinamnám;* choice, *pilì.*

DALE, n. *labák, lambák.*

DAM, n. a barrier across a watercourse, (specially in rice fields and fishponds), *pilapil.*

DAMAGE, n. injury, *sirà;* act of willfully harming, *paninirà;* calumny, *paninirang-puri.*

DAMN, v. *sumpáin.*

DAMP, adj. moist, *halumigmíg; basá-basâ.*

DANCE, v. *sumayáw, magsayáw,* n. *sayáw;* a dancing party, *sáyawan.*

DANDRUFF, n. *balakubak.*

DANGER, n. *panganib.*

DANGEROUS, adj. *mapanganib.*

DANGLE, v. to hang or swing loosely, *ilawít, palawitín; ibitin.*

DANGLING, adj. hanging, *nakalawít; nakabitin.*

DARE, v. to be bold enough, *maglakás-loób;* venture, *mangahás.*

DARING, adj. fearless, *walángtakot;* venturous, *pangahás.*

DARK, adj. *madilím.*

DARLING, n. *irog, giliw.*

DARN, v. *magsulsí,* Sp.; *sulsihán,* Sp.

DATA, n. *bagay-bagay; datos,* Sp.

DATE, n. *petsa,* Sp.

DAUGHTER, n. *anák na babae.* —d.-in-law, *manugang na babae.*

DAWN, n. *bukáng-liwaywáy; liwaywáy.*

DAY, n. *araw.*—Christmas D., *kapaskuhán.*—New Year's D., *Baguntaón.*

DAYLIGHT, n. *araw.*—It's still d., *Araw pa.* It's already d., *Araw na.*

DAZE, v. to confuse, stupefy, *tuligín,* de confused, stupefied, *matulíg.*

DAZZLE, v. *silawin;* be dazzled, *masilaw.*

DAZZLING, adj. *nakasísilaw.*

DEAD, adj. *patáy.*

DEADLY, adj. causing death, *nakamámatáy (makamámatáy).—* d. enemy, *mahigpít na kaaway.*

DEAF, adj. *bingí.*

DEAFENING, adj. *nakabíbingí.*

DEAF-MUTE, n. *bingí't-pipí.*

DEAL, v. to d. in, *magbili ng, magtindá ng.*

DEALER, n. *mag-*plus the goods dealt in, with the first syllable doubled, as, fish-dealer, *mag-iisdá;* rice-dealer, *magbibigás,* etc.

DEAN, n. *dekano,* Sp.

DEAR, adj. *mahál.*

DEATH, n. *kamátayan.*

DEBATE, n. *pagtatalo; pakikipagtalo.*

DEBILITY, n. *kahinaan.*

DEBONAIR, adj. genial, *magiliw.*

DEBT, n. *utang.*

DEBTOR, n. *may-utang.*

DEBUT, n. *debyú, debú,* Fr.

DECADE, n. *sampúng taón.*

DECALOG, n. *Sampúng Utos.*

DECAY, v. *mabulók.*

DECAYED, adj. *bulók.*

DECEIT, n. *dayà.*

DECEMBER, n. *Disyembre,* Sp.

DECENCY, n. respectàbility, *kapamitaganan;* moral cleanliness, *kalinisang-budhi.*

DECENT, adj. respectable, *desente,* Sp.; *kapitá-pitagan;* free from obscenity, *di-mahalay.*

DECEPTIVE, adj. *madayà.*

DECIDE, v. *magpasiyá; pagpasiyahán.*

DECISION, n. *pasìyá; pasyá.*

DECISIVE, adj. definite, *tiyák;* final, *pangwakás.*

DECLAIM, v. *bumigkás.*

DECLARATION, n. *saysáy; badyá.*

DECLARATIVE, adj. (Gram.) *paturól.*

DECLARE, v. *magsaysáy, isaysáy.*

DECOY, n. *pangatì.*

DECREASE, v. *magbawas, bawasan;* diminish, *lumiít.—n. pagbabawas; paglíit, pag-untì.*

DECREE, n. *utos, batás.*

DEDICATE, v. *maghandóg, ihandóg.*

DEDICATION, n. *handóg.*

DEDUCT, v. *bawasin.*

DEED, n. *gawâ.*

DEEM, v. *isìpin, akalain.*

DEEP, adj. *malalim.*

DEEPEN, v. *palaliman.*

DEER, n. *usá.*

DEFEAT, v. to vanquish, *talunin.* —n. overthrow, *pagkatalo.*

DEFEATED, adj. *talo; talunan.*

DEFECATE, v. *dumumí;* vul. *tumae.*

DEFECT, n. *kasiraán; depekto,* Sp.

DEFEND, v. *magtanggól.*

DEFENSE, n. *pagtatanggól.*

DEFER, v. *ipagpaliban.*

DEFIANCE, n. resistance, *paglaban.*

DEFICIENT, adj. *kulang.*

DEFICIT, n. *dépisit,* Eng.; *lugi.*

DEFINE, v. *magturing, turingan.*

DEFINITE, adj. *tiyák.*

DEFINITION, n. *turing; katuringan.*

DEFY, v. *lumaban.*

DEGREE, n. *digrí,* Eng.; *antás.*

DEJECTED, adj. *malumbáy, nalúlumbáy.*

DELAY, n. *abala, balam.*

DELEGATE, n. *kinatawán, sugò.*

DELICIOUS, adj. *masaráp; malinamnám.*

DELIGHT, n. *lugód; galák.*

DELIRIOUS, adj. *nahíhibáng.*

DELIVER, v. to set free, *palayain;* save from, *iligtás;* give, *ibigáy;* carry and hand to an owner, *iabót; dalhin.*

DELUGE, n. *dilubyo,* Sp.; *malaking bahâ; gunaw.*

DELUSION, n. false idea or theory, *talimuwáng,* nc.

DEMAND, v. *hingín, hilìngin.—* In d., *maraming nangángailangan.*

DEMOCRACY, n. *demokrasya,* Sp.

DEMOCRAT, n.-adj. *demókratá,* Sp.; *makádemokrasya,* Sp.

DEMOCRATIC, adj. *demokrátikó,* Sp.

DEMONSTRATE, v. to exhibit, *ipakita; itanghál.*

DEMONSTRATION, n. *pakita.*

DEMONSTRATIVE, adj. (Gram.) *pamatlíg, panurò.*

DEN, n. cave or lair of beast, *lunggâ;* cavern, *yungíb; kuweba,* Sp.

DENIAL, n. refusal, *pagtanggí;* negation, *pagkakailâ.*

DENY, v. *tumanggi, tanggihán.*

DEPARTMENT, n. (of government) *kágawarán;* branch (of business, study, science), *sangáy; sangá.*

DEPEND, v. to rely on, *umasa;* trust, *magtiwalà.*

DEPENDENT, n. a person who relies upon another for his food, *pákainín.*

DEPORT, v. *itapon; idestyero,* Sp.

DEPOSIT, v. *ilagak; idepósitó,* Sp.—n. money kept in a bank, *lagak; depósitó,* Sp.; sediment, *latak, tining.*

DEPOSITION, n. removal from office, *pagtitiwalág;* (Law) act of giving testimony, *pagsaksí, pananaksí.*

DEPOT, n. warehouse, *pintungan;* railway station, *himpilan ng tren* (*tren,* Sp.); *istasyón ng tren* (*istasyón, tren,* Sp.)

DEPRIVE, v. to take away from, *alisán;* to stop from having, (be deprived of) *mawalán.*

DEPTH, n. *lalim.*

DERIVE, v. to come from a certain source, *manggaling;* to draw from, *kunin* (*sa*); *hanguin* (*sa*).

DESCEND, v. *bumabá; lumusong.*

DESCRIBE, v. *maglarawan, ilarawan.*

DESCRIPTION, n. *paglalarawan.*

DESERT, v. to forsake, *lisanin;* abandon, *neglecs, pabayaan;* leave, *iwan.*—n. *iláng.*

DESERVE, v. to be worthy, *magindapat.*—You d. it, *Sadyáng dapat sa iyó.*

DESIGN, n. project, *panukalà;* drawing, *dibuho,* Sp.; intention, *tangká; hangád.*

DESIRE, n. *nais, nasà;* craving, *pita.*—v. *magnais, naisin; magnasà, nasain; pitahin.*

DESK, n. *pupitre,* Sp.; table, *mesa,* Sp.

DESOLATE, adj. having no inhabitants, *waláng tao;* gloomy, *mapangláw;* in a neglected condition, *pinabayaan.*

DESPAIR, n. loss of hope, *pagkawalá ng pag-asa.*

DESPISE, v. *masuklám, kasuklamán; alimurahin; alipustaín.*— n. *pagkasuklám; pag-alimura; pag-alipustá.*

DESTINE, v. *iukol;* to settle the future use of, *itaán; ilaán; italagá.*

DESTROY, v. *iwasák; igibâ.*

DESTRUCTION, n. *pagkawasák: pagkagibâ.*

DETAIL, n. *sangkáp;* a part of something, *bahagi, kabahagi.*

DETAIN, v. *pigilan; antalahin.*

DETECTIVE, n. *tiktík; batyáw; detektib,* Eng.; *sekreta,* Sp.

DETERMINE, v. to decide, *magpasiyá;* resolve to do, *magtika, pagtikahan;* find out for oneself, *alamin;* fix or establish, *tiyakin.*

DETERMINED, adj. *nátatalagá; handá: disidido,* Sp.

DEVELOP, v. to grow, *tumubò;* become better, *bumuti, gumaling;* cultivate, *linangín;* reveal, *ilahad.*

DEVELOPMENT, n. *pagtubò; paglakí; paglagó;* act of unfolding, *paglalahad.*

DEVICE, n. *paraán;* invention, *kathà;* emblematic design, *sagisag.*

DEVIL, n. *diyablo,* Sp.

DEVOTE, v. to set apart for a special purpose, *ilaán; italagá; iukol;* dedicate, *ihandóg; itungód;* give onself up to some occupation, *magtamán, pagtamanán.*

DEVOTION, n. *pagsasakit;* piety, *pagbabanál, kabánalan;* strong affection, *pagmamahál.*

DEVOUR, v. *lamunin; sakmalin; silain.*

DEW, n. *hamóg.*

DIAGRAM, n. *balangkás.*

DIALOGUE, n. conversation, *paguusap; sálitaan:* (in a play, book, etc.) *diyálogô,* Sp.; *pálitang-usap.*

DIAMETER, n. *bantód,* O.T.

DIAMOND, n. *diyamante,* Sp.

DIARRHEA, n. *kursó; bululós.*

DIARY, n. *talásarili,* nc.

DICTATE, v. *idiktá,* Sp.

DICTION, n. *pananalitâ.*

DICTIONARY, n. *diksiyonaryo.* Sp.; *talátinigan.*

DIE. v. *mamatáy.*

DIFFER, v. to be unlike, (dual) *magkáibá;* disagree, *di-umayon: di-sumang-ayon.*

DIFFERENCE, n. *kaibahán. kaibhán.*

DIFFERENT, adj. *ibá;* distinct, *kaibá;* not similar, *di-katulad.*

DIFFICULTY, n. *hirap, kahirapan.*

DIG, v. *humukay, maghukáy, hukayin.*

DIGNITY, n. (of manner) *kabinihan;* honor, *dangál, karángalan.*

DILIGENCE, n. *sigsá; sikap; sipag.*

DILIGENT, adj. *masigsá: masikap; masipag.*

DIM, adj. hazy, vague. *malabò;* dark, *madilím.*

DIMPLE, n. *biloy.*

DINE, v. (at noon) *mananghalian;* (at night) *maghapunan;* to eat. *kumain.*

DINNER, n. (at noon) *tanghalian;* (at night) *hapunan.*

DIP, v. to put something into a liquid, *isawsáw;* (using a ladle or any other instrument for dipping) *isalok, sumalok, salukin.*

DELEGATE, n. *kinatawán.*

DIRECTION, n. address, *direksiyón,* Sp.; *kinátitirahán;* instruction, *turò,* (Instructions for using: *paggamit*); act of managing, *pamamatnugot; pa-mamahalà.*

DIRECTOR, n. *patnugot.*

DIRT. n. *dumi.*

DIRTY, adj. *marumi.*

DISAPPEAR. v. *mawalâ.*

DISAPPOINT, v. *biguín;* be disappointed, *mabigô.*

DISAPPOINTMENT, n. *kabiguán.*

DISAPPROVE, v. *masamaín;* not to approve, *di-pagtibayin.*

DISASTER. n. *sakunâ.*

DISCHARGE. v. to free, *palayain;* remove from office. *itiwalág.*

DISCONTENT, n. *pagkawaláng kasiyaháng loób.*

DISCOURAGE, v. *pahinain ang loób;* be discouraged, *manghinà ang loób.*

DISCOVER. v. *tumuklás, tuklasín. mátuklasán.*

DISCRIMINATION, n. *pagtatangî.*

DISCUSS, v. *talakayin, pagtalakayan, magtalakay.*

DISEASE. n. *sakít.*

DISGRACE, n. ignominy, *kaayupan, kadustaán.*

DISGUISE, n. (the costume) *balatkayô;* act of, *pagbabalatkayô.* v. *magbalatkayô.*

DISH, n. *pinggán; plato,* Sp.; food served, *pagkain; putahe,* Sp.

DISILLUSION, n. *talugimpán,* nc.

DISOBEDIENT, adj. *suwaíl.*

DISOBEY, v. *sumuwáy; suwayín.*

DISORDERLY, adj.-adv. *maguló.*

DISPLAY, v. to exhibit, *itanghál;* unfold, *iladlád.*

DISPLEASE, v. to vex, *galitin;* annoy, *yamutín.*

DISPUTE, n. *pagtatalo.*—v. *maki-pagtalo.*

DISSOLVE, v. *tunawin; lusawin;* be dissolved, *matunaw, malusaw.*

DISTANCE, n. remoteness, *layò;* (between two points) *agwát; pagitan.*

DISTANT, adj. remote, *malayò.*

DISTINCT, adj. different, *ibá;* marked off, *tangì, bukód-tangì.*

DISTINCTIVE, adj. *katangi-tangì.*

DISTINGUISH, v. to consider as different from others, *ibahín;* mark off, separate, *ibukód.*

DISTINGUISHED, adj. eminent, *bunyî, mabunyî.*

DISTRESS, n. anguish, *pighatî;* suffering, *pagdurusa.*

DISTRIBUTE, v. to apportion, *ipamahagi;* give away, *ipamigáy, mamigáy.*

DISTRIBUTION, n. *pamamahagi; pamimigáy.*

DISTRICT, n. *purók; distrito,* Sp.

DISTURB, v. to throw into disorder or confusion, *guluhín, mangguló;* to unsettle, *tigatígin;* to interfere with, *makialám, pakialamán.*

DITCH, n. *kanál,* Sp.; *bambáng.*

DIVE, v. *sumisid.*

DIVIDE, v. (in two) *hatiin; maghatì.*

DIVINE, adj. *dibino,* Sp.; *bathalaín.*

DIVORCE, n. *dibórsiyó,* Sp.

DIZZY, adj. *nahíhilo; nalíliyó.*

DO, v. to perform, make, *gawín;* carry out, *tuparín.*

DOCK, n. *dáungan.*

DOCTOR, n. *doktór;* Sp.

DOCTRINE, n. *doktrina,* Sp.; *aral.*

DOG, n. *aso.*

DOLL, n. *manikà,* Sp.

DOLLAR, n. *dolar, dolyar,* Eng.

DOME, n. *bubóng na bilóg.*

DOMESTIC, adj. (of the house) *pantáhanan;* (of a nation) *panariling-bansá.*

DOMINION, h. authority, *kapangyarihan; dominyo,* Sp.

DONE, adj. finished, completed, *yarì na.*

DONKEY, n. *buriko,* Sp.

DOOM, n. Last Judgment, *Huling Paghuhukóm;* the end, *ung wakás;* ang *katapusán;* destiny, fate, *kapalaran.*

DOOR, n. *pintô.*

DOSE, n. *dosis,* Sp.

DOT, n. *tuldók.*

DOUBLE, adj. *ibayo; dublé,* Sp.; in pairs, *parís, parís-parís.*

DOUBT, n. *alinlangan; duda,* Sp.

DOUBTFUL, adj. *álanganin;* hesitant, *urong-sulong.*

DOVE, n. *kalapati.*

DOWN, adv. *pababâ, sa ibabâ.*

DOWNFALL, n. *pabagsák.*

DOWNSTAIRS, adv. *sa lupà; sa silong.*

DOWNWARDS, adv. *pababâ.*

DOZEN, n. *dusena,* Sp.; twelve, *labindalawá.*

DRAFT, n. current of air, *hanginan;* an outline, *balangkás; bangháy.*

DRAG, v. to haul along, *kaladkarín.*

DRAGONFLY, n. *tutubî.*

DRAMA, n. *dulà; drama,* Sp.

DRAW, v. to pull, *hilahín; batakin;* pull out, *bunutin; hugutin;* d. a picture, *gumuhit ng larawan.*

DRAWER, n. (of desk) *kahón,* Sp.; (undergarments) *kalsunsilyo, Sp.*

DREAD, v. to fear greatly, *mahintakutan; m a s i n d á k ;* be afraid, *matakot.*—n. *takot; pangambá.*

DREADFUL, adj. *nakasísindák; nakatátakot.*

DREAM, n. *pangarap; panaginip.*
—v. *mangarap, managinip.*

DRESS, n. clothes, *barò; damít.*
—v. to put on clothes, *magbarò, magdamít: magbihis.*

DRIFT, v. to float, *lumutang;* be driven along, *matangáy.*

DRILL, n. tool for boring holes, *balibol; pambutas,* military exercises, *dril,* Eng.

DRINK, v. *uminóm, inumín.*—n. beverage, *inumín.* (Water for drinking, *inumín*).

DRIP, v. to all in drops, *pumaták-paták; tumulò; kumayat.*

DROOP, v. *manlupaypáy.*

DROP, n. *paták.*—v. *pumaták.*

DROWN, v. to sink and perish in water, *malunod;* kill by plunging into water, or other liquid, *lunurin.*

DROWSY, adj. *nag-áantók; ináantók.*

DRUG, n. *gamót, droga,* Sp.

DRUGGIST, n. *magbibili ng gamót; butikaryo(a),* Sp.

DRUGSTORE, n. *butika,* Sp.; *parmasya,* Sp.

DRUNK, adj. *lasing; langó.*

DRUNKARD, n. *maglalasing; lasenggo.*

DRY, adj. *tuyô.*—v. *tuyuin.*

DUAL, adj. *dálawahan.*

DUCK, n. *itik; pato,* Sp.; *bibe.*

DUE, adj. owed, owing, *utang;* fit, suitable, *bagay; tumpák;* scheduled to arrive, *nakatakdáng dárating.*

DULL, adj. not sharp, *mapuról;* uninteresting, *nakaíinip.*

DUMB, adj.-n. *pipi; apáw, umíd.*

DUNGEON, n. *bartulina,* Sp.; prison cell, *bilangguan; piitan.*

DUPLICATE, n. *salin; pangalawáng salin.*

DURATION, n. *tagál.*

DURING, prep. *habang, samantalang.*

DUST, n. *alikabók.*

DUSTY, adj. *maalikabók.*

DUTY, n. *tungkulin: katungkulan;* tax, *buwis.*

DWARF, n. *unano,* Sp.

DWELL, v. *tumirá; tumahán; mamahay. manirahan.*

DWELLING, n. house, *bahay;* home, *táhanan;* residence, *tírahan.*

DYE, n. *dampól; tina.*

DYNAMITE, n. *dinamita,* Sp.

DYNAMO. n. *dinamo,* Sp.

DYSENTERY, n. (Med.) *iti; pagiiti.*

E

EACH, pron. *bawa't isá.*

EAGER, adj. *sabík, nasásabík.*

EAGLE, n. *ágilá,* Sp.

EAR, n. organ of hearing, *tainga;* seed-bearing spike, as of corn, *pusò ng maís.*

EARLY, adv. *maaga.*

EARN, v. to get for service rendered, *kitain, kumita.*

EARNEST, adj. fervent, *maalab;* assiduous, *masigasig.*

EARNINGS, n. *kita, kinikita.*

EARRING, n. *hikaw.*

EARTH, n. the globe on which we live, *daigdíg; mundó,* Sp.; dry land, soil, *lupà.*

EARTHQUAKE, n. *lindól.*

EARTHWORM, n. *bulati.*

EASE, n. *alwán, kaalwanán.*
EAST, n. *silangan.*
EASTER, n. *Kuwaresma,* Sp.;
Mahál-na-araw.
EASTERN, adj. *sílanganán.*
EASY, adj. *maalwán; magaán;*
madalî.
EAT, v. *kumain, kanin (kainin).*
ECHO, n. *alingawngáw; ulyáw.*
ECLIPSE, n. *lahò; paglalakò;*
eklipse, Sp.
ECONOMIC, adj. *pangkabuhayan.*
ECONOMICAL, adj. *matipíd, ma-*
simpán.
ECONOMIZE, v. *magtipíd.*
EDGE, n. thin cutting side of a
knife, ax, etc., *talím;* verge of
a cliff, *gulod; gilid.*
EDIBLE, adj. *makákain, nakáka-*
in.
EDIFICE, n. *gusalî.*
EDITOR, n. *editór,* Sp.
EDUCATE, v. to develop by teach-
ing or training, *ipanuto;* in-
struct, *turuan.*
EDUCATION, n. *pagpapanuto;*
pagtuturò.
EEL, n. *duhól; palós.*
EFFECT, n. outcome (past), *ki-*
nálabsán; (future) *kálalabsán.*
EFFECTS, n. possessions, *ari-*
arian.
EFFECTIVE, adj. *mabisâ.*
EFFICACY, n. *bisâ.*
EFFORT, n. *pagpupunyagî; si-*
kap, pagsisikap; pagsasakit.
EGG, n. *itlóg.*
EGGPLANT, n. *talóng.*
EIGHT, n.-adj. *waló.*
EIGHTEEN, n.-adj. *labingwaló.*
EIGHTY, n.-adj. *walumpû.*
EITHER, pron. *alinmán sa dala-*
wa.
ELASTIC, adj. *napaháhabà.*
ELBOW, n. *siko.*
ELECT, v. to choose, *pumilì, pi-*
liin; select by voting, *maghalál,*
ihalál.

ELECTION, n. process of voting,
paghahalál; general elections,
hálalan.
ELECTOR, n. *manghahalal; bu-*
tante, Sp.
ELECTRICIAN, n. *elektrisista,*
Sp.
ELECTRICITY, n. *elektrisidád,*
Sp.; *dagitab,* cw.
ELEGANT, adj. *makisig; mabi-*
kas.
ELEMENT, n. *sángkáp;* a part,
bahagi.
ELEMENTARY, adj. *panimulâ;*
pasimulâ.
ELEPHANT, n. *elepante,* Sp.;
gadyá.
ELEVATE, v. *itaás, magtaás.*
ELEVATOR, n. *pantaás; elebe-*
tor, Eng.; *timbawan,* nc.
ELEVEN, n.-adj. *labíng-isá.*
ELF, n. *duwende,* Sp.
ELIMINATE, v. *alisín.*
ELOPE, v. *magtanan; lumayas.*
ELSE, adj. other and different,
ibá pa.—adv. *pa.*—conj. *at kung*
hindî'y.
ELSEWHERE, adv. *sa ibáng da-*
ko; sa ibáng poók.
EMBER, n. *baga.*
EMBLEM, n. *sagisag.*
EMBRACE, v. to hug, *yakapin;*
comprise, *masakláw.*
EMBROIDERY, n. *burdá,* Sp.
EMERALD, n. *esmeralda,* Sp.
EMERGENCY, n. pressing neces-
sity, *kagípitan.*
EMIGRATE, v. *mandayuhan.*
EMINENT, adj. *mabunyi.*
EMOTION, n. *damdamin.*
EMPEROR, n. *Emperador,* Sp.
EMPHASIS, n. (Rhet.) *kapamiga-*
tán; stress, *diín.*
EMPLOYER, n. *maypagawâ.*
EMPLOYMENT, n. occupation,
gáwain; empleo, Sp.

EMPTY, adj. *waláng-lamán.*
ENCIRCLE, v. *palibutan; paligi-ran, ipaligid.*
ENCLOSE, v. *ilakip.*
ENCOUNTER, v. *mákatagpô; mákasalubong.*
ENCOURAGE, v. *palakasín ang loób; pasiglahín.*
END, n. extreme or last part of anything, *dulo, duluhan;* conclusion, *wakás; katapusán;* object aimed at, *túnguhin, puntahin.*
ENDEAVOR, n. *pagsasakit; pagsusumakit.*
ENDLESS, adj. *waláng-wakás; waláng-katapusán.*
ENDURANCE, n. *tatág; tagál.*
ENEMY, n. *kaaway.*
ENFORCE, v. *magpatupád, ipatupád.*
ENGINE, n. *mákiná,* Sp.
ENGINEER, n. man skilled in engineering, *inhinyero,* Sp.
ENGLISH, n.-adj. *Inglés.*
ENGRAVE, v. *mag-ukit, ukitin, iukit.*
ENJOY, v. *magtamasa, pagtamasahan.*
ENOUGH, adj.-adv. *kainaman: sapát.*
ENROLL, v. *magpatalâ.*
ENSLAVE, v. *alipinin, busabusin.*
ENTER, v. *pumasok, pasukin.*
ENTERTAIN, v. to amuse, divert, *libangín;* (self) *maglibáng.*
ENTHUSIASM, n. *siglá.*
ENTIRE, adj. *buô.*
ENTRAILS, n. internal parts of animal bodies, *lamáng-loób;* the intestines, *kaliliitan.*
ENTRANCE, n. means or place for entering, *pasukán.*
ENTREAT, v. *makiusap, pakiusapan; mamanhík, pamanhíkán.*
ENUMERATE, v. *isá-isahín; baybaying isá-isá.*
ENVELOPE, n. *sobre,* Sp.

ENVIOUS, adj. *mainggitin; mapanaghili.*
ENVY, n. *inggít; hilì; pangimbuló.*
EQUAL, adj. (in measure) *kasukát;* (in amount) *kasindami;* (in degree) *kasintayog;* (in value) *kasinghalagá;* (in size) *kasinlakí;* alike, *kawangis, katulad.*
EQUIPMENT, n. *mga kagamitán.*
ERA, n. *panahón.*
ERASE, v. *payiin, pawiin, burahín,* Sp.
ERECT adj. *patayô; patindíg;* straight up and down, *tuwíd.*—v. to build, *magtayô, itayô.*
ERROR, n. *kamálian.*
ERUPT, v. *pumutók.*
ESCAPE, v. *magtanan, tumakas.*
ESCORT, n. *abay.*—v. *umabay, abayan.*
ESOPHAGUS, n. *lalamunan.*
ESPECIALLY, adv. *lalò na.*
ESSAY, n. literary composition, *sanaysáy,* cw.
ESSENCE, n. quality of a thing, *kakaniyahán;* substance made from plant. drug, etc., *kakanggatâ.*
ESTABLISH, v. *magtatág, itatág; magtayô, itayô.*
ESTEEM, n. *pagtatangì; pagtingín.*
ETERNAL, adj. *waláng-hanggán.*
ETERNALLY, adv. *magpakailán pa man.*
EULOGY, n. *papuri.*
EVAPORATE, v. *sumingáu; maigá.*
EVEN, adj. level, *pantáy* regular, *matining;* not odd, *paris.*—adv. at the very time, *noon pa man;* still (more), *lalò pa.*
EVENING, n. *gabí.*—e. star, *talang panggabí.*

EVENT, n. *pangyayari.*
EVER, adv. *kailanmán.*
EVERY, adj. *bawa't.*
EVERYBODY, pron. *bawa't tao;* all, *lahát.*
EVERYONE, pron. *bawa't isá;* all, *lahát.*
EVERYWHERE, adv. *saanmán.*
EVIDENCE, n. *katunayan.*
EVIDENT, adj. *kita; halatá.*
EVIL, adj. harmful, *nakasásamâ;* bad, *masamâ.*
EXACT, adj. *tumpák;* correct, *wastô; sukát na sukát.*
EXAGGERATION, n. *pagmamalabís.*
EXAMINATION, n. *pagsubok; pagsusúlit; iksamen,* Sp.
EXAMINE, v. to test, *subukin; iksaminin,* Sp.; investigate, *siyasatin.*
EXAMPLE, n. *halimbawà;* a pattern, *tularán.*
EXCEED, v. *lumampás, humigit.*
EXCELLENCE n. *kagalingán.*
EXCELLENT, adj. *magaling.*
EXCEPT, prep. *kundî; máliban sa; liban sa.*
EXCEPTION, n. *taliwás; kataliwasan.*
EXCESS, n. *kalabisán.*—adj. *labis.*
EXCHANGE, n. *pálitan.*
EXCLAIM, v. *bumulalás.*
EXCLAMATION, n. *bulalás.* — e. point, *bantás na pandamdám.*
EXCURSION, n. *pagliliwalíw.*
EXCUSE, v. to offer an apology for something done, *humingî ng paumanhín;* let a fault forgiven, *patawarin, pagpapaumanhínán.*—n. act of, *pagpapaumanhín;* apology, *paghingî ng paumanhín.*
EXECUTIVE, adj. *mapanupád;* having to do with the application of laws, *tagapagpatupád.*
EXEMPT, adj. free, *malayà.*

EXERCISE, n. *pagsasanay;* program, *palátuntunan.*
EXHAUSTION, n. fatigue, *kapagalán, hapò.*
EXHIBIT, v. *ipakita; itanghál.*
EXHIBITION, n. *pakita; tanghál;* (place of) *tanghalan.*
EXIST, v. to live, *mabuhay.*
EXIT, n. departure, *pag-alís, pagyao;* a passage out, *lábasan.*
EXPAND, v. *lumakí; lumapad; mangalat.*
EXPEDITION, n. a march, or voyage by a group of persons for a purpose, *pandadayuhan; espedisyón,* Sp.
EXPENSE, n. *gugol; gastos,* Sp.
EXPENSIVE, adj. costly, *mahál; mahalagá; magastos,* Sp.
EXPERIENCE, n *karanasan; esperyénsiyá,* Sp.
EXPERIMENT, n. trial, *pagtitikím;* test, *pagsubok.*
EXPERT, n.-adj. *dalubhasà.*
EXPIRE, v. *matapos;* to die, *mamatáy.*
EXPLAIN, v. *magpaliwanag; magpalinaw; ipaliwanag; linawin.*
EXPLANATION, n. *paliwanag.*
EXPLICABLE, adj. *máipaliliwanag.*
EXPLODE, v. *pumutók; sumambulat.*
EXPLOSION, n. *putók.*
EXPLOSIVE, n. *paputók.*
EXPORT n. *luwás.*—v. *magluwás.*
EXPORTATION, n. *pagluluwás.*
EXPOSE, v. to make known, *ihayag; ilahad.*
EXPOSITION, n. *paglalahad; pagsasaysáy.*
EXPRESS, v. *ipahayag;* to assert, *ibadyá; ipagbadyá.*
EXPRESSION, n. *pahayag; pagpapahayag.*
EXPRESSIVE, adj. *malamán.*
EXQUISITE, adj. *marikit.*

EXTEMPORANEOUS, adj. *panandalî; panandalian; biglaan.*

EXTEND, v. *paabutín;* (in length) *pahabaın;* (in time) *patagalán.*

EXTENT, n. (in space) *lawak. kalawakan;* (in time) *tagál, lawig;* measure, *sukat;* limit, *hanggán;* size, *lakí;* compass, *sakláw.*

EXTERMINATE, v. *lipulin;* to annihilate, *puksaín.*

EXTRA, adj. *karagdagan; ekstra,* Sp.

EXTRACT, n. *estrakto,* Sp.; *katás; gatâ.*—v. to pull by the roots, *bunutin;* obtain juice by pressing, *katasın, katasán.*

EXTRAORDINARY, a d j. *dipangkaraniwan.*

EXTRAVAGANT, adj. excessive, *labis:* wasteful, *mapag-aksayá.*

EXTREME, adj. farthest away, *kálayú-layuan;* last, *hulí;* final, *katapusán.*

EXTREMITY, n. the very end, *dulo;* the very edge, *duyo, tangwâ:* the very tip, *dunggót.*

EXULT, v. *magsayá; magalák.*

EYE, n. *matá.*

EYEBROW, n. *kilay.*

EYEGLASS, n. *salaming pangmatá.*

EYELETS, n. *uhetes,* Sp.

EYELID n. *takipmatá; talukap ng matá.*

F

FAIR, adj. pleasing to the eye, *marikít;* beautiful, *magandâ;* satisfactory, *nakasísiyá;* just, *makatárungan.*—n. bazaar, *perya,* Sp.; exhibition, *tanghalan.*

FAITH, n. *pananampalataya;* trust, *pagtitiwalà;* belief, *paniniwalà;* reliance, *pananalig.*

FAITHFUL, adj. *tapát na loób;* constant, *matimtiman.*

FALL, v. *mahulog; malaglág.*

FALSE, adj. not real, *di-tunay;* imitation, *huwád;* untrue, *di-totoó;* disloyal, *taksíl; lilo;* lying, *sinungaling, bulaan;* dishonest, *waláng-dangál.*

FALSEHOQD, n. *kasinungalingan, kabulaanan.*

FAME, n. *kabantugán; kabunyián.*

FAMILIAR, adj. acquainted, *kilalá;* known, *alám.*

FAMILY, n. *pamilya,* Sp.; *anák, magaanak;* clan, *angkán.*

FAMINE, n. *pagkakagutom, taggutom, gutom.*

FAMOUS, adj. well known, *bantóg;* known about, *balità; kilalà;* popular, *populár.*

FAN, n. (folding) *abaniko; pamaypáy.*

FANCY, n. *guniguni;* phantasmagoria, *kinikitá;* whim, *kagustuhán.*

FANG, n. *pangil.*

FAR, adv. *malayò.*

FARE, n. sum paid for a journey, *pasahe,* Sp.; *bayad.*

FAR EAST, n. *Dulong Silangan.*

FAREWELL, n. *paalam; pamamaalam.*

FARMER, n. *magbubukíd.*

FASCINATING, adj. *nakabibighanì; kabighá-bighanì.*

FASCINATION, n. *kabighanian;* state of being fascinated, *pagkabighanì.*

FASHION, n. mode, vogue, *moda,*
Sp.; *karaniwan, palasak.*
FAST, adv. rapidly, *mabilís;*
swiftly, *matulin.*
FASTEN, v. to tie, *italì, talian;*
attach, *ikabít.*
FASTIDIOUS, adj. *maselang.*
FAT, adj. *matabâ.*
FATAL, adj. fateful, *nakasásawî,*
mortal, *nakamámatáy.*
FATE, n. *palad, kapalaran; des-
tino,* Sp.; *tadhanà.*
FATHER. n. *amá.*
FAULT. n. *kapintasan;* flaw, defect, *depekto,* Sp.; *sirà.*
FAVOR, v. *mabutihin, magalingín;* to approve, *sang-ayunan,
pagtibayin;* support, *tangkili-
kin, katigan.*—n. granting of a
request, *pairog;* appreciation,
esteem, *pagtatangì;* approving
regard, *pagtingín.*
FAVORABLE, adj. harmonious,
kaayon, katugmâ; convenient,
maluwág; timely, *nápapanahón;*
advantageous, *mabentaha,* Sp.
FAVORITE, n. one preferred, *hirang, pilì;* one particularly es-
teemed, *tangì, itinátangì; kina-
gígiliwan, kinalúlugdán.*
FEAR, n. *takot.*—v. *matakot, ka-
takutan.*
FEARFUL, adj. inspiring dread,
nakatátakot.
FEARLESS, adj. *waláng-takot.*
FEAST, n. *pistá,* Sp.; an elabo-
rate repast, *handaan;* banquet,
pigíng, bángkete, Sp.
FEATHER, n. tiny hairs, *balahibo;* plumage, *plumahe,* Sp.;
pakpák.
FEATURE, n. distinctive character, *katangian;* characteris-
tics of facial expression (features), *pagmumukhâ;* prominent item (as in a program),
tampók, pinaka-tampók.

FEBRUARY, n. *Pebrero,* Sp
FEDERAL adj. *pederál* Sp.;
sang-isahan, nc.
FEE, n. (for service) *upa, de:et-
sos,* Sp.; (for admission or
membership in an association)
butáw; (for license) *bayad;* ti)
pabuyà; gratuity, *gantimpagál;*
(for rental service) *paupa.*
FEEBLE, adj. weak, *mahinà;* in-
firm, *masasaktín.*
FEEL, v. *damdamín, dumamdám;*
ne able to f., *máramdamán; ma-
káramdám;* become aware of,
madamá, damahin.
FEELING, n. *pakiramdám;* emotion, *damdamin.*
FELLOW, n, companion, *kasama;*
(of the same faith) *kapanalig;*
one of a pair, *kaparis;* the other
half, *kabiyák;* member of a society, *kasapì, kaanib.*
FEMALE. n. & adj. *babae.*
FEMININE, adj. *pambabae.*
FENCE, n. *bakod.*
FERN. n. (common & edible)
pakô.
FERRY, n. *bantilan, táwiran.*
FERTILE, adj. fruitful, *mabu-
nga;* luxuriant, *malagô;* rich,
mayaman; (of soil) *matabâ.*
FERTILIZER, n. *abono,* Sp.; *pa-
tabâ.*
FESTIVAL, n. *pagdiriwang;* feast,
pistá, Sp.
FETCH, v. to go after and bring,
sunduin, kaunin; carry, *dalhín.*
FEVER, n. *lagnát;* (slight) *say-
nát, sinat.*
FEVERISH, adj. *nilálagnát; si-
násaynát; maysinat, sinísinat.*
FIBER, n. *labayin, himaymáy.*
FICKLE, adj. *sálawahan.*
FICTION, n. *kathâ.*
FIDELITY, n. *katapatán; pag-
kamatapát.*

FIELD, n. land cleared for tilling, *lináng;* plowed land, *araruhan;* land intended for farming, *bukid;* uncultivated land, *parang;* a field of action (in science, arts, or letters) *larangan.*

FIERCE, adj. *balawís;* savage, *mabangís.;* intense, *masidhî.*

FIERY, adj. *maapóy;* ardent, *maalab.*

FIFTEEN, n. & adj. *labinlimá.*

FIFTH, n. & adj. *ikalimá; panlimá.*

FIFTY, n.-adj. *limampû.*

FIG, n. (Bot.) *igos,* Sp.

FIGHT, v. to contend in battle, *makibaka, bumaka;* war against, *mandigmâ;* meet in combat, *lumaban, labanan;* contend against each other, *maglaban.*

FIGHTER, n. *manlalabán.*

FILE, n. *kikil.*

FILL, v. *punuín.*

FILTER, n. *salaán.* — v. *salain, magsalà.*

FINAL, adj. *wakás, pangwakás.*

FINALLY, adv. *sa wakás.*

FINANCE, n. *palásalapian;* pl., *pananalapí.*

FIND, v. *mátagpuán, mákita;* to discover, *mátuklasán.*

FINE, n. *multa,* Sp.—adj. delicate, *mainam.*

FINERY, n. *parikít.*

FINGER, n. *dalirì.*

FINISH, v. to complete, *yariin;* bring to an end, *tapusin, wakasán.*

FIRE, n. *apóy.*

FIREFLY, n. *alitaptáp.*

FIREMAN, n. (of fire department) *bumbero,* Sp.

FIRM, adj. hard, *matigás;* compact, *pipís;* stable, *matibay;* rigid, *hapít, maigtíng;* enduring, *matatág.*

FIRST, adj. *una,* Sp.

FISH, n. *isdâ.*

FISHERMAN, n. *mángingisdâ; mámamalakaya.*

FISHERY, n. a fish pond, *pángisdaan, paláisdaan.*

FIT, adj. proper, *dapat;* suitable, *bagay, angkóp, tumpák.*

FIVE, n.-adj. *limá.*

FIX, v. to make stable, *patibayin;* repair, *gawín.*

FIXED, adj. firm, *pirmí, nakapirmí;* stable, *matibay, matatág;* unchangeable (irreducible), *dimabábago, waláng-pagbabago.*

FLAG, n. *watawat, bandilà,* Sp.

FLAME, n. *lingas, ningas, dingas.*

FLASH n. *kisláp, dikláp.*

FLAT, adj. level, *pantáy;* even, *patag;* having breadth and evenness but little thickness, *lapád.*

FLATTER, v. *manghibò; hibuin; manghibok, hibukin.*

FLATTERY, n. *panghihibò, panghihibok; hibò, hibok.*

FLAVOR, n. taste, *lasa.*

FLEE, v. *tumakas, magtanan.*

FLEET, adj. swift, *matulin.* — n. navy, *plota,* Sp.

FLESH, n. *lamán;* meat for food, *lamán, karné,* Sp.

FLESHY, adj. *malamán.*

FLICKER, v. *umandáp-andáp.*

FLIGHT, n. *paglipád.*

FLING, v. *ipukól; ibató; iitsá,* Sp.

FLIRT, v. *manlimbáng; makipaglimbangan.*—n. *manlilimbáng.*

FLIRTATIOUS, adj. *mapanlimbáng.*

FLOAT, v. *lumutang.*

FLOCK, n. (of animals) *kawan;* (of birds) *langkáy.*

FLOOD, n. *bahá.*—v. *bumahâ.*

FLOOR, n. *sahíg.*

FLORID, adj. *mabulaklák.*

FLOUR, n. *arina,* Sp.; (of cassava) *gawgáw.*

FLOURISH, v. to prosper, *lumagô; yumabong; umunlád.*

FLOW, v. *umagos;* (in small quantities) *dumaloy;* to stream, as from a faucet, *tumulò.*

FLOWER, n. *bulaklák.*

FLOWERY, adj. *mabulaklák.*

FLUENT, adj. (of speech) *matatás.*

FLUID, adj. *tunáw, lusáw.*

FLUTTER, v. to wave in the wind (as a flag), *wumagaywáy;* cause to f., *pawagaywayín.*

FLY, v. *lumipád.*—n. house f.. *langaw.*

FOAL, n. *bisiro,* Sp.

FOAM, n. *bulâ, kapa,* Sp.; froth, *halagap, halipawpáw.*

FOCUS, n. *katumbukán.*—v. *itumbók.*

FODDEL, n. *kumpáy.*

FOE, n. *kaaway; kalaban.*

FOG, n. *ulap, alapaáp.*

FOLD, v. to double up (as paper or cloth), *tiklupín;* bend over a part, *ilupî, lupián.*

FOLDED, adj. *tiklóp; nakatiklóp.*

FOLK, n. people (in general), *mga tao;* relatives, *kamag-anak.*

FOLKLORE, n. *alamát.*

FOLLOW, v. *sumunód, sundín.*

FOLLOWER, n. *kasunód;* disciple. *alagád;* one of the same sect or party, *kapanalig.*

FOLLY, n. *kabaliwan;* foolishness, *kaululán.*

FOND, adj. *mairugín; mawilihín, maıbigín.*

FOOD, n. *pagkain.*

FOOL, n.-adj. *hangál; ulól;* idiot, *tangá.*

FOOLISH, adj. *ulól; uslák; loko,* Sp.; *ungás.*

FOOT, n. *paá.*

FOOTBALL, n. *putból,* Eng.

FOOTPRINT, n. *bakás ng paá.*

FOOTSTEP, n. *hakbáng;* footfall, *yabág.*

FOR, prep. intended for, *pará sa, pará kay; ukol sa, ukol kay;* because of, *dahil sa.*—conj. because, *sapagká't.*

FORBID, v *ipagbawal, magbawal.*

FORCE, n. *lakás;* violence, *dahás;* power. *kapangyarihan.*

FORCED, adj. compulsory, *sápilitán.*

FOREFATHER, n. *ninunò;* pl., *mga pinagnunuan.*

FOREHEAD, n. *noó.*

FOREIGN, adj. (things, ideas, customs) *banyagà;* (persons) *dayuhan; tagaibáng bansá.*

FOREMAN, n. *kapatás,* Sp.; *kátiwalà.*

FOREMOST, adj. *káuná-unahan; pángunahín.*

FOREST, n. *gubat;* woodland, *kakahuyan.*

FORESTER, n. *manggugubát.*

FORESTRY, n. (science of) *palágubatan,* nc.

FOREVER, adv. *magpakailanmán.*

FOREVERMORE, adv. *magpakailán pa mán.*

FORGE, n. smithy, *pandayan.*—v. *pandayín.*

FORGET, v. *kalimutan, limutin;* to fail to recall, *mákalimutan, makimutan;* leave behind through oversight, *maiwan; mákaligtaán.*

FORGIVE, v. *patawarin, magpatawad.*

FORGIVENESS, v. *kapatauarán.*

FORK, n. (of table silver) *renedor,* Sp.; (of road) *sambát.*

FORM, n. *anyô; hugis.*

FORMAL, adj. *pormál,* Sp.

FORMER, adj.-pron., *ang náuná, náuuná;* previous, *dati.*

FORMERLY, adv. *dati;* in past time, *noóng una; noóng araw.*

FORMULA, n. *pórmulá,* Sp.

FORSAKE, v. *pabayaan:* leave, *iwan;* desert, *layasan: iumayas.*

FORT, n. *muóg; kutà.*

FORTIFY, v. *patibayan; palaka-sín.*

FORTUNATE, adj. *mapalul.*

FORTUNE, n. *portuna,* Sp.; *palad, kapalaran.*

FORTY, n.-adj. *apatnapû.*

FORWARD, adv. onward, *patuloy.*

FOUL, adj. dirty, *marumí;* morally offensive, *mahalay;* loathsome, *nakapandidiri, nakasúsuklám.*

FOUNDATION, n. basis, *batayán; pábatayán.*

FOUNDER, n. *maytatág.*

FOUNTAIN, n. *bukál; balong.*

FOUR, n.-adj. *apat.*

FOURTEEN, n.-adj. *labíng-apat.*

FOURTEENTH, n.-adj. *ikalabíng-apat.*

FRAGMENT, n. *kapútol; kapiraso,* Sp.

FRAGRANT, adj. *mabangó; mahalimuyak.*

FRAIL, adj. *mahinà.*

FRAME, n. *bastág;* (for pictures) *kuwadro,* Sp.; (for embroidery) *bastidór,* Sp.; *bastagan.*

FRATERNAL, adj. *pangkapatíd. pangkápatiran.*

FRATERNITY, n. *pagka-kapatíd: kápatiran.*

FRAUD, n. *praude,* Sp.; deceit, *dayà;* artifice, *laláng, linláng.*

FRAYED, adj. *nisnís.*

FRECKLE, n. *pekas,* Sp.

FREE, adj. *malayà;* gratuitous, *waláng-bayad;* licentious, *layâ;* loose (of animals), *alpás.*—v. to liberate, *palayain;* be free, *lumayà.*

FREEDOM, n. *kalayaan.*

FREIGHT, n. cargo, *dalá, lulan, kargá,* Sp.

FRENCH, n.-adj. *Pransés.*

FREQUENT, adj. *malimit, madalás.*

FRESH, adj. *sariwà;* new, *bago;* cool, refreshing, *malamíg.*

FRETFUL, adj. irritated, *nayávamót;* captious, *maligalig.*

FRIAR, n. *prayle,* Sp.

FRICTION, n. *pingkí, pingkian.*

FRIDAY, n. *Biyernes,* Sp.

FRIED, adj. *prito,* Sp.; *pinirito,* Sp.

FRIEND, n. *kaibigan.*

FRIENDLY, adj. *palákaibigan;* affable, *magiliw.*

FRIENDSHIP, n. *pagkakaibigan.*

FRIGHTEN, v. *sindakín; takutin.*

FRIGHTFUL, adj. *kasindák-sindák, nakasísindák; katakot-takot. nakatátakot.*

FRILLS, n. *pleges, pilyeges,* Sp.

FRINGE, n. *lamuymóy; palawít.*

FRIVOLITY, n. (of persons) *kaparakán.*

FRIVOLOUS, adj. (of persons) *parák;* (of things) *waláng-kapararakan.*

FROG, n. *palakâ.*

FROLICSOME, adj. playful, *malarô;* gamboling, *malikót.*

FROM, prep. *sa;* coming of, out of, *galing sa, mulá sa;* beginning at, *buhat sa, magmulâ sa.*

FRONT. n. forepart, *unahán; van, bungad;* position directly before or facing, *harapán.*

FRONTIER, n. *duluhan; hangganan.*

FRONTISPIECE, n. *pultada; unang panig, unang mukhâ.*

FROWN, v. *magkunót-noó; to* scowl, *sumimangot.*

FRUGAL, adj. sparing, *mapagárimuhunán;* economical, *masimpán;* thrifty, *matipíd.*

FRUIT, n. *bunga;* pl. *prutas,* Sp., *mga bungang-kahoy.*

FRUITFUL, adj. *mabunga.*

FRUITLESS, adj. *waláng-bunga;* barren, *pahát;* sterile, *kutad;* (of persons) *baog.*

FRY, n. tiny fish, *gunó; dulóng;* small f., *muntíng isdâ.*—v. to cook with fat in a pan, *magpirito, ipirito,* Sp.

FUEL, n. *panggatong.*

FULFILL, v. to carry out, *gawín; tuparín;* execute, perform, *ganapín.*

FULL, adj. *punô;* saturated, *lipós, puspós;* satiated, *busóg.*

FUME, n. *asbók;* smoke, *asó, usok.*

FUMIGATE, v. *pausukan, magpausok;* (with incense or herbs), *suubin.*

FUN, n. *kasáyahan; kátuwaan.*

FUNCTION, n. *tungkulin.*

FUND, n. *pondo,* Sp.; capital, *puhunan;* money set apart for expenses, *laáng-gugulín.*

FUNDAMENTAL, adj. *pábatayán;* serving as foundation, *pámantungan;* primary, *pánimulaan.*—n. primary principle, *simulain;* basis, *batayán;* foundation, *pámantungan.*

FUNERAL, n. *libíng, paglilibíng.*

FUNEREAL, adj. *panlibíng.*

FUNNY, adj. *katawá-tawá.*

FURIOUS, adj. *nagngangalit.*

FURNACE, n. *kaldera,* Sp. *ápuyan.*

FURNISH, v. *pagkaloobán; bigyán.*

FUROR, n. *guló;* stir, *balasaw.*

FURROW, n. *tudlíng; bagbág ng araro.*

FURTHER, adj. *karagdagan;* more distant, *lalong malayo.*— adv. *lalò na, lalô pa.*

FURUNCLE, n. boil, *pigsá;* abscess, tumor, *bagâ.*

FURY, n. *pagngangalit.*

FUSE, n. (Elect.) *pusible,* Sp.

G

GAIETY, n. *kasáyahan; kasiglahán.*

GAILY, adv. *masayá;* gleefully, *tuwáng-tuwá.*

GAIN, v. to make a profit, *magtubò;* obtain a benefit, *makinabang;* obtain an advantage, *magkabentaha,* Sp. — n. profit, *tubò;* benefit, *pakinabang;* advantage, *kapanáigan, bentaha,* Sp.

GAINFUL, adj. yielding profit, *mapagtútubuan;* beneficial, *mapakikinabangan.*

GALE, n. strong wind, *hanging malakás.*

GALL, n. bile, *apdó;* rancor, *galit, yamót.*

GALLANT, adj. chivalrous, *butihin; mairugín.*

GALLERY, n. platform on side and end walls of a theatre, *pal-*

ko, Sp.; exhibition building for works of art, etc., *tanghalan.*

GALLOP, v. to run with a succession of springs or leaps, *kumabíg;* cause to g., *magpakabíg.*

GALLOWS, n. *bibitayán.*

GAMBLE, v. tô play a game for money, *maghuwego*, Sp.; play cards for money, *magsugál*, Sp. —n. game for money, *huwego, sugál.*

GAMBLER, n. *hugadór*, Sp.; *magsusugal, mánunugal*, Sp.; *sugaról*, Sp. colloq.

GAME, n. *larô.*

GARAGE, n. *garahe*, Eng.

GARBAGE, n. *basura*, Sp.; *sukal.*

GARDEN, n. *halamanan; hardín*, Sp.

GARDENER, n. *hardinero*, Sp.; *maghahalamán.*

G .RGLE, n. *magmumog; n ₁gkalagkág.*

GARLAND, n. wreath of flowers, *koronang bulaklák.*

GARLIC, n. *bawang.*

GARMENT, n. *damít; barò.*

GARRULOUS, adj. *matabíl;* talkative, *masalitâ.*

GARTER, n. *ligas*, Sp.; *garter*, Eng.

GAS, n. *gas;* petroleum, *petrolyo*, Sp.; gasoline, *gasolina*, Sp.

GASKET, n. *sapín, pansapín.*

GATE, n. *tárangkahan; pasukán.*

GATHER, v. to bring together, *tipunin;* collect, *magtipon.*

GATHERING, n. *pagtitipon; katipunan.*

GAUDY, adj. *maringal.*

GAUZE, n.⁄*gasa*, Sp.

GAVEL, n. *malyete*, Sp.

GAY, adj. *masayá;* lively, *masiglá.*

GAZE, *tumitig, titigan.*—n. *titig.*

GEAR, n. wheels with adjusted parts to each other, *engranahe*, Sp.

GEM, n. jewels, *hiyás* (Sp. *joyas*) ; pearl, *perlas*, Sp., *mutyâ.*

GENDER, n. (Gram.) *kasarian.*— Femínine g., *kasariang pambabae.*—Masculine g., *kasariang panlalaki.*

GENERAL, adj. relating to a whole, *panlahát.*—n. title above colonel, *henerál*, Sp.

GENERATION, n. of the steps in a line of descent, *saling-angkán; salinlahì*, nc.

GENEROSITY, n. *kagandahanyloób;* liberality, *pagkabukás-kamáy, pagkamapagbigáy.*

GENEROUS, adj. *magandángloób;* liberal, *bukás-kamáy, mapagbigáy.*

GENIAL, adj. *magiliw; mairugín;* cordial, *bukás-pusò;* friendly, *palákaibigán.*

GENIUS, n. a very gifted person, *talining*, nc.; great natural ability, *kataliñingan*, nc.

GENTLE, adj. *mabinì; mahinhín;* docile, *masúnurin;* soft, *banayad.*

GENTLEMAN, n. *máginoó; ginoó.*

GENUINE, adj. *tunay;* pure, *dalisay; lantáy.*

GEOLOGY, n. *heolohiya*, Sp.

GEOGRAPHY, n. *heograpya*, Sp.

GEOMETRY, n. *heometriya*, Sp.

GERM, n. seed, *binhî;* sprout, *paltók*, (of mongos, *toge, tawge*, Ch.) ; microbe, *mikrobyo*, Sp.; origin, *pinagmulán.*

GERMAN, n. *Alemán*, Sp.

GERMICIDE, n. *pamatáy-mikrobyo*, Sp.

GERUND, (Gram.) verbal noun, *pandiwang makangalan.*

GESTICULATE, v. *magkikiyâ; magkukumpás.*

GESTURE, n. action, *kilos*, *galáw*.

GET, v. to obtain, *makuha* (unintentional, *mákuha*); *kunin*; acquire, *matamó* (unintentional, *mátamó*).

GHOST, n. *multó*, (Sp. *muerto*).

GIANT, n. *higante*, Sp.

GIDDY, adj. feeling dizzy, *nahihilo*, *nalíliyó*; whirling rapidly, *nag-íinikót*, *nag-íinog*.

GIFT, n. *bigáy*; something bestowed, *gawad*; a present, *ala-ala*, *regalo*, Sp.; donation, *kaloób*; benefaction, *biyayà*.

GIFTED, adj. *matalino*, *matalas*.

GILD, GUILD, n. mutual aid association, *samaháng-damayán.*— v. to overlay or wash with gold, *gintuán*, *duraduhin*, Sp.

GIN, n. *hinyebra*, Sp.; wine, *alak*.

GINGER, n. (Bot.) *luya*.

GIPSY, n. *hitano*, (fem. *hitana*), Sp.

GIRDLE, n. *bigkís*; belt, *sinturón*, Sp.

GIRL, n. *batang babae*.

GIST, n. substance, *kakanggatâ*; main point, *buód*; theme, *paksâ*.

GIVE, v. *magbigáy*, *ibigáy*, *bigyán*; to bestow, *igawad*; donate, *ipagkaloob*.

GIZZARD, n. *balumbalunan*.

GLAD, adj. pleased, *nalúlugód*, *natutuwâ*; joyful, *nagágalák*.

GLADNESS, n. *lugód*, *tuwâ*; ·*galák*.

GLAMOR, n. *halina*; witchery, *lamuyot*.

GLAMOROUS, n. *mapanghalina*; bewitching, *mapanlamuyot*.

GLANCE, n. *sulyáp.*—v. *sumulyáp.*—To g. at, *sulyapán*.

GLARE, v. to look fiercely, *umirap*, *irapan*; shine with a dazzling light, *magningning.*·— n. fierce look, *irap*; dazzling

brightness, *ningníng na nakasisilaw*.

GLASS, n. *bubog*; mirror, *salamín*.

GLASSWARE, n. *babasagín*.

GLEAM, n. *banaag*; flash of light, *kisláp*, *sinag.*—v. *bumanaag*, *mamanaag*; to flash, *kumisláp*.

GLIMMER, v. *umandáp-andáp*; *kumuráp-kuráp*; *kumisáp-kisáp*.

GLIMPSE, n. *sigláw*; *biglóng tingín*; glance, *sulyáp*.

GLITTER, n. *kináng*.

GLOAMING, n. *takipsilim*.

GLOBE, n. *globo*, Sp.; a spherical body, *bilo*.

GLOOM, n. *lagím*; obscurity, *karimlán*; melancholy, *kalumbayan*.

GLORIFY, v. *paluwalhatian*.

GLORIOUS, adj. *maluwalhatì*.

GLORY, n. *luwalhatì*.

GLOTTIS, n. (Anat.) *lalamunan*.

GLOVE, n. *guwantes*, Sp.; (in baseball) *glab*, Eng.

GLOW, v. to give out a bright light, *magliwanag*.

GLUE, n. *kola*, Sp.; *pandigkít*; *pangkola*, *pangolǫ*, Sp.

GLUTTONOUS, adj. greedy, *matakaw*; voracious, *masibà*.

GNAT, n. *nikník*.

GNAW, v. *ngatngatín*; *pang-itín*.

GO, v. to proceed, *magpatuloy*; move forward, *sumulong*; take steps, as in walking, *lumakad*; depart, *umalís*.

GOAL, n. *túnguhin*, *puntahin*; (in games as football) *gol*, Eng.

GOAT, n. *kambíng*.

GO-BETWEEN, n. *bugaw*; *tuláy*, fig.; intermediary, *tagapamagitan*.

GOD, n. *Diyós,* Sp.; *Bathalà;* Creator, *Lumikhá, Maykapál.*

GODCHILD, n. *ináanák.*

GODDESS, n. *diyosa,* Sp.; *diwatà.*

GODFATHER, n. *ninong* (cor. Sp., *padrino*).

GODHOOD, n. *pagka-Diyós,* Sp.; *pagka-Bathalà.*

GOLD, n. *gintô.*

GOLDEN, adj. *ginintuán; gintô.*

GOLDSMITH, n. *pandáy-gintô; platero,* Sp.

GOLF, n. *golp,* Eng.

GOOD, adj. *mabuti; magaling.*

GOODBY, GOODBYE, n.-inter. (Said by person departing) *Paalam na pô;* (said by person left) *Adyós pô.*—n. act of farewell, *pamamaalam.*

GOODNESS, n. *kabutihan; kagálingan.*

GOOSE, n. *gansâ.*

GORGEOUS, adj. *marilág;* glittering in various colors, *marikít, maringal.*

GOSPEL, n. *Ebanghelyo,* Sp.

GOSSIP, n. talebearing, *sitsít; tsismes,* Sp.; idle talk, *satsát, daldál; yapyáp,* sl.

GOVERN, v. to control by authority, *makapangyayari;* execute, *magpaganáp, magpatupád;* manage, *mamahalà, pamahalaan.*

GOVERNMENT, n. *pámahalaán, gubyerno,* Sp.

GOVERNOR, n. *gubernadór,* Sp.; *punò ng lalawigan.*

GRAB, v. *sunggabín; sunggabán; agawin, mang-agaw.*

GRACE, n. *kariktán;* elegance of manner, *tikas, bikas;* good-will, *mabuting kaloobán, magaang kaloobán;* favor, *palà; grasya,* Sp.

GRACEFUL, adj. *marikít;* elegant (manner, demeanor), *mati-*

kas, mabikas; beautiful, *magandá.*

GRACIOUS, adj. affable, *magiliw.*

GRADE, n. *grado,* Sp.; *antás;* (at school) *grado,* Sp., *baitáng;* mark obtained at school, *nota.*

GRADUAL, adj. *untí-untî, utáy-utáy;* step by step, *hakbánghakbáng; bai-baitáng.*

GRADUATE, n. one who completed studies at. school, *gradwado,* Sp., *nagtapós.*

GRADUATION, n. (from school) *pagtatapós.*

GRAIN, n. *butil.*

GRAM, n. *gramo,* Sp.

GRAMMAR, n. *balarilà; gramátiká,* Sp.

GRAMMATICAL, adj. *pambalarilà, makabalarilà; panggramátiká,* Sp.

GRANARY, n. barn, *baysá, bangán.*

GRAND, adj. large, *malakí;* great, *dakilà.*

GRANDCHILD, n. *apó.*

GRANDEUR, n. greatness, *kadakilaán.*

GRANDFATHER, n. *nunong lalaki; lolo,* Sp.; *lelong,* Sp.; *ingkóng.*

GRANDMOTHER, n. *nunong babae; lola,* Sp.; *lelang,* Sp.; *impó.*

GRANT, v. to bestow, *ipagkaloob;* give, *ibigáy.*

GRANULAR, adj. *butíl-butíl.*

GRAPE, n. *ubas,* Sp.

GRAPEFRUIT, n. (Bot.) *kahíl.*

GRAPH, n. *guhit-bangháy.*

GRASP, v. to seize and hold by clasping, *sunggabán.*

GRASS, n. *damó.*

GRASSHOPPER, n. *luktón, balang.*

GRASSY, adj. *madamó.*

GRATEFUL, adj *kumikilala ng utang na loób.*
GRATITUDE, n. *pagkilala ng utáng na loób.*
GRAVE, n. place of burial, *libingan.*—adj. serious in sickness, *malubhâ.*
GRAY, adj. *gris,* Sp.; ashy, *abuhin, kulay-abó.*
GRAZE, v. to eat grass (said of animals), *manginain.*
GREASE, n. *grasa,* Sp.
GREASY, adj. *magrasa,* Sp.; fatty, *matabá;* oily, *malangís.*
GREAT, adj. *dakilà.*
GREED, n. *katakawan;* gluttony, *kasibaan;* covetousness, *kayamuan.*
GREEN, n.-adj. *luntî, luntián; berde,* Sp.
GREENHORN, n.-adj. *baguhan.*
GREET, v. *bumatì, batiin.*
GRENADE, n. *granada,* Sp.
GRIEVE, v. to be in sorrow, *mahapis, maqdalamhatì;* suffer woe, *mamighatí.*
GRIM, adj. stern, *mahigpít;* relentless, *waláng-badlíng.*
GRIND, v. *gilingin.*
GRINDER, n. *gilingán.*
GRIP. n. firm hold, *hawak, kapit.*
GROAN, n. *daíng; hinaíng.*
GROUP, n. *pulutóng; pangkát;* a small crowd, (staying the while) *umpók, umpukan.*
GROW, v. *tumubò; sumiból.*

GROWL, v. *umungol.*—n. *ungol.*
GROWTH, n. *tubò, siból; pagtubò, pagsiból.*
GUARANTEE, n. *garantiya,* Sp.; promise, *pangakò;* pledge, *akò;* something given in pledge, *sanglâ.*
GUARD, v. *bumantáy, magbuntáy; bantayán.*—n. *bantáy.*
GUAVA, n. (Bot.) *bayabas.*
GUESS, v. to predict, *humulà, hulaan.*—n. *hulà.*
GUEST, n. *panauhin, bisita,* Sp.; *dalaw.*
GUIDANCE, n. *pamamatnubay;* leading by the hand, *pag-akay.*
GUIDE, v. *patnubayan;* to lead by the hand, *akayin.*—n. *giya,* Sp.; *tagahatíd, patnubay.*
GUILTY, adj. *maysala; may kasalanan.*
GUITAR, n. *gitara,* Sp.
GULF, n. *loók.*
GULLET, n. *lalaugan.*
GUN, n. *baríl,* Sp.
GUST, n. (of wind) *hihip;* sudden rush of wind with rain, *siqwá.*
GUTTER, n. *alulód;* roadside canal. *bambáng, kanál.* Sp.
GUTTURAL, GLOTTAL, adj. (Gram.), *impít, paimpít.*
GYMNASIUM, n. *himnasyum,* Lat.
GYRATE, v. *uminog, mag-iinog.*

H

HA, inter. *Ha!*
HABIT, n. behavior, *ugalì, paguugalì;* vice, *bisyo,* Sp.
HABITABLE, adj. *matítirahán.*
HABITUAL, adj. *pangkaugalián; pinagkaugalián.*

HACIENDA, n. *asyenda,* Sp.
HAIR, n. *buhók;* tiny h., *balahibo.*
HAIRPIN, n. *talsók, aguhilya,* Sp.
HALF, adj. *kalahatì.*
HALFBREED, n.-adj. *mestiso,* Sp.; (of Negritoes) *balugà.*

HALL, n. *bulwagan.*

HALO, n. *sinag sa ulo.*

HAM, n. *hamón,* Sp.

HAMLET, n. *nayon; baryo,* Sp.

HAMMER, n. *martilyo,* Sp.; *pamukpók.*

HAMMOCK, n. *duyan.*

HAND, n. *kamáy.*

HANDBAG, n. *hanbag,* Eng.

HANDBOOK, n. *hanbuk,* Eng.; *polyeto,* Sp. (*muntaklát*), nc.)

HANDFUL, adj. *sandakót, karakót;* a few, *iilán.*

HANDICAP, n. *handikap,* Eng.; hindrance, *sagabal, balakid.*

HANDKERCHIEF, n. *panyô,* Sp.; *panyolito,* Sp.

HANDLE, n. *hawakán, tatangnán.*—v. to touch or feel with the hand, *hipuin, hawakan, tangnán.*

HANDMADE, adj. *yarì sa kamáy.*

HANDSAW, n. *sarutsó,* Sp.

HANDSOME, adj. well-formed, *mabikas, matipunò;* beautiful, *magandá;* elegant, *makisig.*

HANDWRITING, n. *sulat-kamáy;* characteristic writing, *sulat, pagsulat.*

HANG, v. to attach to something above, *isabit;* suspend, *ibitin;* put to death on the gallows, *bitaytn.*

HANGMAN, n. *berdugo,* Sp.; *tagabitay.*

HAPHAZARD, adv. at random, *pasumalá.*

HAPPEN, v. *mangyarı.*

HAPPENING, n. *pangyayari.*

HAPPILY, adj. *masayá;* fortunately, *sa kabutihang palad.*

HAPPINESS, n. *ligaya, kaligayahan;* Joy, *lugód, galák.*

HAPPY, adj. *maligaya.*

HARBOR, n. *doongán, sadsaran.*

—v. to shelter, *magsanggalány, mag-adyá;* entertain, cherish (as designs), *magtaglay.*

HARD, adj. *matigás;* stern, *mahigpít;* difficult of accomplishment, *mahirap.*

HARDEN, v. *manigás;* to become solid, *mamuô.*

HARDLY, adv. *bahagyá.*

HARDNESS, n. *katigasán.*

HARDSHIP, n. privation, *kasalatán, kadahupán;* oppression, *kaapihan;* severe labor, *paghihirap;* suffering, *pagdurusa.*

HARDY, adj. *matatág;* robust; *matipunò.*

HARELIPPED, adj. *bingót.*

HARM, v. to hurt, *saktán;* damage or injure, *sirain, manirà.*

HARMFUL, adj. *nakasísirá; nakasásamâ, makasásamâ.*

HARMLESS, adj. *di-makaáanó.*

HARMONICA, n. *silindro,* Sp.

HARMONIOUS, adj. *magkatugmâ.*

HARMONY, n. *pagkatugmâ; tugmaan.*

HARNESS, n. *guwarnisyón,* Sp.

HARP, n. *alpá,* Sp.; lyre, *lira,* Sp.; *kudyapî.*

HARSH, adj. *mabagsík.*

HARVEST, n. *ani;* (act of) *pagaani.*—v. *mag-ant.*

HASTE, n. hurry, *pagmamadalî, pag-aapurá,* Sp.

HASTY, adj. hurried, *nagmámadalî, mádalian;* precipitate, *dalás-dalás; apurado,* Sp.

HAT, n. *sumbrero,* Sp.; *kupyâ.*

HATCHET, n. *putháw.*

HATE, v. *mapoót, kapootán.*

HATRED, n. *poót, kapootán.*

HAUGHTY, adj. *mapagmataás;* proud, *palalò.*

HAUL, v. *batakin, hilahin.*

HAUNCH, n. *pigî.* — To sit on one's haunches, *naningkayád.*

HAVE, v. *magkaroón*. The prefix *magka-* expresses "to have" and takes the thing held, possessed, felt, suffered, experienced, as *magka-bahay*, to h. a house; *magka-lagnát*, to h. fever. The general sense of having is expressed by *may* or *mayroón*.

HAWAIIAN, n. *Hawayano*, Sp.

HAWK, n. *lawin*.

HAY, n. *dayami;* fodder, *kumpáy.*

HAZARDOUS, adj. dangerous, *mapanganib.*

HAZY, adj. dim, *malabò, kulimlím.*

HE, pron. *siyá.*

HEAD, n. *ulo;* chief, *punò.*

HEADACHE, n. *sakít ng ulo.*

HEADING, n. title, *pamagát.*

HEADLAND, n. promontory, *lungos;* cape (sharp), *tangos;* (slight) *imus;* peninsula, *tangwáy.*

HEADQUARTERS, n. *himpilan;* *kuwartél,* Sp.

HEAL, v. to cure, *pagalingín;* become well, *gumaling.*

HEALTH, n. *kalusugan,* colloq.; soundness of body, *kagálingan ng katawán.*

HEALTHY, adj. *malusóg,* colloq.; strong, *malakás.*

HEAP, n. *buntón,* Sp. (montón). —v. to pile up, *ibuntón, magbuntón.*

HEAPING, adj. overfull, *paulo.*

HEAR, v. to perceive by the ear, *márinig;* attend or listen to, *makinig, pakinggán;* note well by listening, *dinggín.*

HEARING, n. (sense of) *pandiníg.*—Judicial h. *paglilitis.*

HEARSAY, n. rumor, *balità, balí-balità;* common report, *sabí-sabí.*

HEART, n. (Anat.) *pusò.*

HEARTBEAT, n. *tibók ng pusò.*

HEARTBROKEN, adj. *may pusong windáng.*

HEARTLESS, adj. *waláng-pusò.*

HEARTY, adj. *buóng pusò;* cordial, *magiliw, mairog.*

HEAT, n. *init;* ardor, *alab.*

HEATHEN, n., *di-binyagan.*

HEAVEN, n. *kalangitán;* sky, *langit.*

HEAVENLY, adj. *makalangit;* glorious, *maluwalhatì.*

HEAVY, adj. *mabigát.*

HECTARE, n. *ektarya,* Sp.

HEDGE, n. *pimpín,* nc.

HEED, v. *pansinín;* to take care, *maa-ingat, pag-ingatan.*

HEEL, n. (of foot) *sakong;* (of shoes) *takóng,* Sp.

HEIGHT, n. *taás;* altitude, *tayog:* stature (of man), *tangkád, hagwáu:* elevation, *timbáw,* nc.

HEIGHTEN, v. to raise, *itaás,* *elevate, itimbáw.*

HEINOUS, adj. *kalait-lait;* hateful, *kapoót-poót.*

HEIR, n. *tagapagmana.*

HELL, n. *impiyerno,* Sp.

HELLO, inter. *Haló!*

HELM, n. *ugit;* timón, Sp.

HELMSMAN, n. *tagaugit.*

HELP, n. *tulong:* — v. *tumulong, tulungan.*

HELPFUL, adj. *matulungin, pulátulóng.*

HELPLESS, adj. unable to do for oneself, *waláng-kaya;* unable to do anything about, *waláng-magawà.*

HEMISPHERE, n. half of the terrestial globe, *hating-daigdíg,* nc.; half a sphere, *hating-bilo.*

HEMP, n. *abaká.*

HEN, n. female, egg-laying fowl, *inahín.*

HENCE, adv. from this time on, *mulá ngayón;* from this place, *mulá rito;* for this reason, *dahil dito; kayâ.*

HENCEFORTH, adv. *mulâ ngayón.*

HENPECKED, adj. *talusaya*, O.T.

HER, pron. (prepositive) *kanyá;* (postpositive) *niyá.*

HERB, n. *damó.*

HERD, n. flock, *kawan.*

HERE, adv. *dito.*

HEREAFTER, adv. from this time forth, *mulâ ngayón.* — n. the life after death, *kabiláng buhay.*

HEREBY, adv. by virtue of this, *sa bisà nitó.*

HEREIN, adv. here, *dito.*

HEREOF, adv. of this, *nitó;* about this, *ukol dito;* from this, *mulâ rito.*

HERETOFORE, adv. up to this time, *hanggá ngayón.*

HEREWITH, adv. *kalakip dito.*

HERNIA, n. (Med.) *luslós.*

HERO, n. *bayani; taong magiting;* chief character in a story, play, etc., *bida*, Sp.; *pángunahing tauhan.*

HEROIC, adj. *magiting; báyanihín*, nc.

HEROISM, n. *kabayanihan; kagitingan.*

HERON, n. *tagák; kandangaok.*

HESITANT, adj. *nag-áalangán; nag-áalanganin; nag-áatubilì; paulik-ulik.*

HESITATE, v. to vacillate, *magalangán;* waver, *mag-atubilì; mag-ulik-ulik, magpaulik-ulik.*

HEW, v. to cut, as with an axe, *sibakín; palakulín.*

HICCOUGH, HICCUP, n. (Med.) *sinók.*

HIDDEN, adj. *tagô, nakatagò.*

HIDE, v. to conceal (something) *itagò;* (self) *magtagò.*—n. animal skin, *katad, kuwero*, Sp.

HIDEOUS, adj. ugly, *pangit;* h o r r i b l e, *nakapangíngilabot;* shocking, ghastly, *nakapanghihilakbót;* repulsive, *kasuklámsuklám.*

HIGH, adj. *mataás;* elevated in location, *matayog;* exalted, *bunyî, mabunyî.*

HIGHWAY, n. *daáng-bayan.*

HIKE, v. *maglakád.*—n. *paglalakád.*

HILL, n. *buról.*

HILLY, adj. *burúl-buról; maburól.*

HILLSIDE, n. *dahilig.*

HILT, n. *puluhan.*

HIM, pron.—To or for him, *sa kaniyá.*

HINDER, v. to obstruct, *hadlangán;* block, *harangan.*

HINGE, n. (of door) *bisagra*, Sp.

HINT, n. *pahiwatig;* indirect suggestion, *paramdám; parinig.*

HIP, n. (Anat.) *balakáng.*

HIRE, v. to employ for wages, *upahan;* lease for temporary use, *alkilahín*, Sp.; *upahan.*

HIS, pron. (prepositive) *kaniyá;* (postpositive) *niyá.*

HISS, n. *singasing.*

HISTORIAN, n. *mánanaysáy; mánanalaysáy.*

HISTORIC, adj. *makasaysayan.*

HISTORY, n. *kasaysayan;* a narrative or tale of events, *salaysáy.*

HIT, v. to give a blow to, *hampasín;* strike, *patamaan.*

HITHER, adv. to (toward) this place, *paparitó;* to this point, *hanggáng dito.*

HIVE, n. beehive, *bahay-pukyutan.*

HIVES, n. (Med.) urticaria, *tagulabáy; pamamantál.*

HOARSE, adj. *pagáw; paós; malát.*

HOBBY, n. *libangan; hobi,* Eng.

HOCK, n. back part of the human knee joint (popliteal space), *alakalakán.*

HOE, n. *asaról,* Sp.; *asada,* Sp

HOG, n. pig, *baboy.*

HOLD, v. to grasp and keep in the hand, *hawakan; pigilan; tu-banan;* retain, keep, *itagò.*

HOLDER, n. possessor, *mayha-wak;* owner, *may-arì;* container, *lalagyán, sisidlán.*

HOLDUP, n. an attack with intent to rob, *panghaharang; pang-aabát.*

HOLE, n. *butas.*

HOLIDAY, n. festival day, *pistá,* Sp.; a day of freedom from labor, *araw na pahingá;* a day of abstinence. *araw na pangilin;* vacation, *bakasyón,* Sp.

HOLINESS, n. sanctity, *kasantu-hán,* Sp.; piety, *kabánalan;* divineness, *kabathalaán.*

HOLLOW, adj. *guwáng, guáng.*

HOLY, adj. pious, *banál;* blessed, *pinagpalà;* sacred *sagrado,* Sp.

HOMAGE, n. *pintuhò;* allegiance, *pagkatig.*

HOME, n. *táhanan.*

HOMELY, adj. simple, plain, *lis-díng;* cozy, *maginhawa.*

HOMEMADE, adj. *yaring-sarili.*

HOMICIDE, n. *pagpatáy sa ká-puwá; omisidyo,* Sp.

HONEST, adj. honorable, *mara-ngál;* straightforward, *tapát.*

HONESTY, n. *karangalan;* straightforwardness, *katápatan.*

HONEY, n. *pulót, pulút-pukyutan.*

HONEYBEE, n. *pukyutan.*

HONEYMOON, n. *pulutgatá; lú-nademyél,* Sp.

HONOR,' n. *dangál, karángalan; puri, kapurihán.*

HONORABLE, adj. *marangál;* illustrious, *bunyî, mabunyî.*

HONORARY, adj. *pandangál.*

HONORIFIC, adj. *pamitagan; panggalang.*

HOOD, n. soft covering for head and neck, *pandóng;* head covering attached to cloak, *kaput-sa,* Sp.; shoulder covering of a graduation gown, *museta,* Sp.

HOOF, n. *kukó* (of horse, *ng ka-bayo*).

HOOK, n. *kawit, pangawit; kala-wit.*

HOOKED, adj. curved like a hook, *baluktót.*

HOOP, n. *aro,* Sp.; *buklód.*

HOP, v. to leap or jump over on one leg, *magkandirít.*

HOPE, n. *pag-asa.*

HOPEFUL, adj. *umáasa; may-pag-asa.*

HOPELESS, adj. *waláng-pag-asa.*

HORIZON, n. *kagiliran,* nc.

HORIZONTAL, adj. *pahigá.*

HORN, n. *sungay;* trumpet made of h., *tambulì.*

HORNET, n. (Entom.) *putakti.*

HORRIBLE, adj. *nakapangingila-bot;* dreadful, *naksisindák.*

HORRID, adj. obnoxious, *nakasú-suklám.*

HORRIFY, v. to fill with great fear, *sindakín, manindák.*

HORROR, n. *kasindakán, kataku-tan.*

HORSE, n. *kabayo,* Sp.-Mex.

HOSE, n. socks, *medyas,* Sp.; flexible tube for conveying water from a faucet, *balindáng,* nc.

HOSPITAL, n. *ospitál,* Sp.; *bahay-págamutan.*

HOST, n. one who entertains another, *ang may-anyaya, punong-abala.*

HOSTAGE, n. *prenda,* Sp.

HOSTILE, adj. antagonistic, *laban, salungát.*

HOSTILITY, n. *pagka-kalaban; pagka-salungát.*

HOT, adj. *mainit;* fiery, *maapóy;* passionate, ardent, *mapusók.*

HOUR, n. *oras,* Sp.

HOUSE, n. *bahay;* place of abode, *tírahan.*

HOUSEHOLD, n. *pamamahay.*

HOW, adv. in what manner, *papaanó;* to what degree or extent, *gaanó.*—How good? *Gaanóng kabuti?*—How bad? *Gaanóng kasamá?*—How many? *Ilán?*—How much? *Magkano?*—How far? *Gaanóng kalayò?*—How near? *Gaanóng kalapit?*—How long? *Gaanóng kahabà?*—How long? (time) *Gaanóng katagál?* —How soon? *Gaanóng kadali?*

HOWEVER, adv. in whatever manner, *sa papánumán.*—conj. vet, notwithstanding, *gayunmán.*

HOWL, v. *umungal;* to utter a loud, wailing cry (as, dogs), *tumambáw;* utter a prolonged cry of pain or distress, *umangal;* roar, as the wind, *umugong, umungol.*

HUB, n. *ehe,* Sp.

HUG, v. to embrace, *yapusán; yapusín.*

HUGE, adj. *malaking-malaki.*

HUM, n. buzzing, *haging;* sound through closed lips, *higing;* rumble, *ugong.*—v. to buzz, *humaging;* sing with closed lips, *humiging; higingin.*

HUMAN, adj. *pantao.*—h. being, *tao.*—h. race, *sangkatauhan.*

HUMANE, adj. *makatao;* compassionate, *mahábagin, maawaín;* sympathetic, *madamayín.*

HUMANITARIAN, adj. *makatao.*

HUMANITY, n. mankind as a whole, *sangkatauhan;* state or quality of belonging to mankind,

pagkatao; human nature, *katauhan.*

HUMBLE, adj. lowly of feeling, *mababang-loób;* lowly in condition, *abâ, hamak:* mean, *imbí.*—v. to abuse, *abaín, hamakin;* humiliate, *hiyain, iringin.*

HUMID, adj. damp, *halumigmíg,* moist, *basábasà.*

HUMIDITY, n. *kahalumigmigán.*

HUMOR, n. state or temper of mind, *lagáy ng loób;* wit, *katalasan;* the funny side of things, *katatawanán;* the power to see or tell the funny side of things, *pagkamapagpatawá.*

HUMOROUS, adj. *nakakátawá.*

HUNCH, n. *kutób; kutób ng loób.*

HUNCHBACK, n. *kubà.*

HUNDRED, n. adj. *sandaán;* one hundred, *isáng daán.*

HUNGER, n. *gutom.*

HUNGRY, adj. *gutóm.*

HUNT, v. to search after, *paghanapin.*

HURL, v. to throw violently, *ihagis, ibanggít;* cast down, *ipukól.*

HURRAH, inter. *Mabuhay!*

HURRY, v. to press on, *magmadali; magdalás-dalás.*

HURT, v. to inflict pain upon, *manakit, saktán;* wound, *sugatan.*

HUSBAND, n. *asawa.* (*Asawa,* however, is of common gender.)

HUSK, n. *upak, talupak; bunót.*

HYMN, n. *imno,* Sp.

HYPHEN n. (Gram.) *gitlíng.*

HYPOCRISY, n. *pagkamalábigâ.*

HYPOCRITE, adj. *malábigâ.*

HYPODERMIC, adj. *pambalambán.*

HYPOGASTRIUM, n. (Anat.) *pusón.*

HYPOTHESIS, n. theory, *hakà;* supposition, *palagáy.*

I

ICE, n. *yelo*, Sp.
ICED, adj. *elado*, Sp.; *may-yelo*.
ICEMAN, n. *magyeyeló*.
ICING, n. *tumpáng*, nc.
ICY, adj. *parang yelo;* cold, *mala-míg*.
IDEA, n. *hagap;* mental pattern, *kuru-kurò;* plan, intention, *hinagap, bantâ;* general notion, *hakà, harayà;* vague thought, *warí-warì;* supposition, *sapantahà, akalà*.
IDEAL, adj.-n. embodying the perfect example or type, *ulirán*.
IDEALISM, n. *idealismo*, Sp.; *pangungulirán*, nc.
IDEALISTIC, adj. *maka-ideál*, Sp.; *kauliranán*, nc,; *mapangarapín*.
IDEALIZE, v. *uliranín*, nc.
IDIOM, n. language of a people, *wikà;* characteristic method of expressing a thought, *wikaín, sálitaín*.
IDIOMATIC, adj. *pangwikaín, pansálitaín*.
IDIOSYNCRASY, n. *kagayunán;* oddity, *pagka-kakatwâ*.
IDIOT, n. *utô;* stupid person, *hangál;* senseless person, *ungás;* an imbecile, *tulalâ*.
IDLE, adj. not occupied or employed, *waláng-ginágawâ;* not used, *di-ginágamit;* indolent, *batugan;* worthless, futile, *waláng-kapararakan*.
IDOL, n. *ídoló*, Sp.; *anito*.
IF, conj. *kung*.
IGNOBLE, adj. mean, *imbí; marawal*.
IGNOMINY, n. *pagkadustâ, kadustaán*.
IGNORANCE, n. *kamangmangán; kamaangán*.

IGNORANT, a d j. uneducated, *mangmáng;* uninstructed, *mangá*.
ILL, adj. *may-sakít; may-karamdaman*.
ILLEGAL, adj. *labág sa batás*.
ILLEGIBLE, adj. *di-mabasa*.
ILLITERATE, n.-adj. unable to read, *di-makabasa;* unable to write, *di-makasulat;* ignorant, *mangmáng*.
ILLNESS, n. *sakít; karamdaman*.
ILLOGICAL, adj. *walâ sa katwiran*.
ILLUSION, n. *tagimpán, harayà*, nc.; mistaken perception, *maling-damá;* delusion, *talimuwáng*.
ILLUSTRATE, v. to make intelligible by concrete examples, *isahalimbawà, maghalimbawà*.
ILLUSTRATION, n. picture, *larawan*.
ILLUSTRIOUS, adj. *mabunyî, bunyî*.
IMAGE, n. *larawan; imahen*, Sp.
IMAGERY, n. *kaharayaan*, nc.
IMAGINATION, n. picture-forming power, *panlalarawan;* a notion, *hakà; harayà*.
IMAGINATIVE, adj. *maharayà, mapagharayà;* inventive, *mapanlikhâ; mapangathâ*.
IMAGINE, v. to form a mental picture of, *maglarawan (ilarawan)* sa *diwà;* form an idea of, *hagapin, kuruin, hakain;* 'think, *isipin*.
IMBUE, v. *lipusín;* to permeate, *tiqmakin*.
IMBUED, adj. *lipos;* permeated, *tiqmák*.
IMITATE, v. *tumulad. tularan;* to mimic, *manggagád, gagarín;*

counterfeit, *manghuwád, huwarán;* follow the example of, *manggaya, gumaya, gayahan.*

IMITATION, n. (act of) *panunulad;* counterfeit, *huwád.*

IMITATOR, n. *mánunulad; manggagaya;* counterfeiter, *manghuhuwád.*

IMMEDIATE, adj. instant, *daglî, daglian.*

IMMEDIATELY, adv. *agád; agád-agád.*

IMMENSE, adj. vast *malawak;* huge, *malakíng-malakí.*

IMMERSE, v. *ilubóg, palubugín;* to dip, *isawsáw; itubóg.*

IMMIGRANT, n. *mandadayunan; dapo.*

IMMIGRATE, v. *mandayuhan.*

IMMIGRATION, n. *pandadayuhan.*

IMMORAL, adj. *mahalay.*

IMMORTAL, adj. *waláng-kamátayan.*

IMMUNE, adj. *di-talbán.*

IMPART, v. to give, *ibigáy, ipagkaloób;* give knowledge of, *ipabatíd;* reveal, *ibunyág, ihayág;* teach, *iturò.*

IMPARTIAL, adj. *waláng-kinikilıngan.*

IMPATIENT, adj. *maínipin.*

IMPEACH, v. to call in question, *ipalitis;* arraign for misconduct in office, *taluwalagín,* nc.

IMPEACHMENT, n. *pagtatalso-walág,* nc.

IMPEDIMENT, n. *hadláng; sagabal.*

IMPENDING, adj. imminent, threatening, *nagbábalà.*

IMPENETRABLE, adj. *di-matagusán.*

IMPERATIVE, adj. *makaharì;* (Gram.) *pautós.*

IMPERFECT, adj. *di-ganáp.*

IMPERIL, v. *ibungad sa panganíb.*

IMPERTINENT, adj. disrespectful, *waláng-pitagan, waláng-galang;* intrusive, *pang-abala, pakialám;* insolent, rude, *bastós.*

IMPETUOUS, adj. hasty and rash, *gahasà, magahasà.*

IMPLORE, v. *mamanhik, lumuhog, manikluhód.*

IMPLY, v. *ipahiwatig; ipakahulugán.*

IMPOLITE, adj. rude, *bastós;* disrespectful, *waláng-pitagan, waláng-galang.*

IMPORTANCE, n. value, *halagá;* weight, *bigát.*

IMPORTANT, a d j. *mahalagá;* weighty, *mabigát.*

IMPORTUNITY, n. *kasugirán.*

IMPOSSIBLE, adj. *imposible,* Sp.; cannot be, *di-maáarì;* cannot happen, *di-mangyáyari.*

IMPRESS, v. *ikintál.*

IMPRISON, v. *ibilanggô.*

IMPROBABLE, adj *di-maáarì.*

IMPROMPTU, adj. *di-handâ; biglaan.*

IMPROVE, v. to make better, *pabutihin; pagalingín;* grow better, *bumuti, gumaling, umigi.*

IMPRUDENT, adj. rash, *pabiglábiglâ.*

IMPUDENT, adj. offensively forward, *waláng-pakundangan.*

IN, prep. *sa;* within, *sa loób ng.*

INASMUCH AS, adv. *yayamang; dahil sa.*

INAUDIBLE, adj. *di-máriníg.*

INAUGURATION, n. *pasinayà.*

INCAPABLE, adj. *waláng-kaya.*

INCENDIARISM, n. *panununog.*

INCENSE, n. *insenso,* Sp.

INCH, n. *dalì; pulgada,* Sp.

INCISE, v. (Med.) *tistisín, hiwain.*

INCISION, n. (Med.) *tistís, hiwà.*

INCITE, v. to spur on, *ibuyó;*

instigate, *upatán; magpaabong, paabungan;* abet, *sulsulán.*

INCLINE, v. to lean, *humilig, kumiling; lean* (on the back of a chair), *sumandál.*

INCLINED, adj. sloping, *hilíg, kilíng; nakahilig, nakakiling.*

INCLOSE, v. to shut within, *kulungín,* insert, *ilakip.*

INCLUDE, v. *isama;* to be included, *mápasama.*

INCOME, n. *kita, kiníkita.*

INCOMPARABLE, adj. *waláng-kawangis; waláng-kaparis.*

INCONCEIVABLE, adj. *di-malirip.*

INCONVENIENT, adj. causing trouble, *pangguló, pang-abala.*

INCORRECT, adj. *di-wastó; malî.*

INCREASE, v. to become bigger, *lumakí;* multiply, *dumami;* enlarge, *lakihán;* augment, *dagdagán, damihan.*

INCUBATOR, n. *pámisaan.*

INCUR, v. *mápalá.*

INCURABLE, adj. *waláng-lunas.*

INDECENT, adj. *mahalay.*

INDEED, adv. *ngâ;* in fact, in truth, *sa katunayan.*

INDEFINITE, adj. *di-tiyák;* vague, *di-malinaw.*

INDELIBLE, adj. *di-mapapawì.—* I. ink, *tintang indeleble,* Sp.

INDEPENDENCE, n. *kasarinlán; pagsasarilí;* freedom, *kalayaán.*

INDEPENDENT, adj. *nagsásarilí;* free, *malayà.*

INDEX, n. *indeks,* Eng.; *talátuntunan.—*I. finger, *hintuturò.*

INDICATE, v. to point out, *iturò;* show, *ipakita;* make known, *ipakilala.*

INDICATIVE, adj. *nagpápakilala; pinagkákilanlán.—* (Gram.) i. mood, *panaganong paturól.*

INDIFFERENCE, n. *pagwawaláng-bahalà;* want of zeal or interest, *pagkawalang-siglá.*

INDIGENT, adj.-n. destitute, *dukhâ, abâ;* needy, *salát, dahóp, hikahós.*

INDIGESTION, n. *impatso,* Sp.

INDIGNANT, adj. *galit, nagágalit;* having a rising feeling of anger, *nagngingitngit.*

INDIGNATION, n. *galit, pagkagalit;* rising anger, *ngitngít, pagnginyitngít.*

INDISTINCT, adj. faint, *malabò;* indiscernible, *di-maaninaw, di-maaninag;* indefinite, *di-tiyák.*

INDIVIDUAL, adj. pertaining to or characteristic of one, *sarili, panarili;* existing as a single and distinct thing, *nag-iisá, bukód.—*n. a person, *isáng tao.*

INDOLENT, adj. *batugan;* lazy, *tamád.*

INDORSE, v. *endusahán,* Sp.; to sign, *lagdaán, pirmahán,* Sp.; in government offices, to send to another official for action, comment, information, etc., *ilipat, itagubilin.*

INDORSEMENT, n. *endoso,* Sp.; *paglilipat, pagtatagubilin.*

INDUCE, v. to prevail upon, persuade, *hikayatin;* infer, *hinunahin, maghinuha;* form a general principle from particulars, *magbuód, buurín.*

INDUCEMENT, n. attraction, *pang-akit;* incentive, *pampasiglá.*

INDUCTIVE, adj. *pasakláw.—*i. reasoning, *pangangatwirang pasakláw.*

INDULGE, v. *palayawin, magpalayaw;* to humor, *magpairog, pairugan.*

INDULGENCE, n. *pagpapalayaw.*

INDULGENT, adj. *mápagpalayaw;* liberal, *mapagbigáy.*

INDUSTRIAL, adj. *industriál,* Sp.; *pangkapamuhayán.*

INDUSTRIOUS, adj. *masipag;* diligent, *masiglá, masikap;* assiduous, *masikháy.*

INDUSTRY, n. *industriyá,* Sp.; *kapamuhayán;* quality of being hard working, *kasipagan;* diligence, *kasiglahán, kasikapan;* assiduity, *kasikhayán.*

INEFFABLE, adj. *di-maulatan:* inexpressible, *di-masaysáy, di-maabót-sabi.*

INEFFECTUAL, adj. inefficacious, *waláng-bisà;* weak, *mahinà.*

INEFFICIENT, adj. *waláng-kaya;* unskilled, *di-sanáy.*

INERT, adj. *tiníng;* motionless, *waláng-kilos; waláng-galáw.*

INERTIA, n. *katiningan; pagkawaláng-kilos; pagkawaláng-galáw.*

INEVITABLE, adj. unavoidable, *di-mailagan;* unpreventable, *di-masawatà; di-mapigilan.*

INEXCUSABLE, adj. unpardonable, *di-mapatátawad.*

INEXHAUSTIBLE, adj. *walángpagkasaíd; di-masásaíd.*

INEXORABLE, adj. unyielding, *waláng-tinag, di-matinag;* unrelenting, *waláng-higkát.*

INFALLIBLE, adj. *di-maáaring magkámali.*

INFAMY, n. public disgrace, *kadustaán, kaayupan;* an infamous deed, *kawaláng-hiyaán, kabuhungán.*

INFANCY, n. *kasanggulán; kumusmusán.*

INFANT, n. *sanggól.*—ad¹. *musmós; murang-isip.*

INFANTRY, n. *hukbóng-lakád; impanteriya,* Sp.

INFATUATED, adj. *haling; naháhaling.*

INFATUATION, n. *pagkahaling; kahalingán.*

INFECT, v. to become infected, *máhawa; málalinan.*

INFECTIOUS, adj. *nakakáhawa:* contagious, *nakakálalin.*

INFERIOR, adj.-n. *mababà.*

INFERIORITY, n. *kababaan.*

INFIDELITY, n. *kaliluhan; kataksilán.*

INFINITE, adj. *waláng-hanggán.*

INFINITESIMAL, adj. *napakakatiting; katiting na katiting.*

INFINITIVE, adj. (Gram.) *pawatás.*

INFIX, n. (Gram.) *gitlapì.*

INFLAMMABLE, adj. *siklabin; madaling masunog; masunugin; madaling magdaig.*

INFLAMMATION, n. (Med.) redness, *pamumulá;* swelling, *pamamagâ.*

INFLATE, v. to puff up, *pabintugín;* to raise unduly, as prices, *pataasán, pataasín.*

INFLICT, v. to cause to be suffered, *ipabatá;* impose as a punishment, *iparusa.*

INFLUENCE, v. to have sway over, *makapangyari;* modify or affect the condition of, *makapagpabago* (or, *makapagpa-* plus the appropriate root-wood).
—n. energy, *lakás;* power, *kapangyarihan.*

INFLUENTIAL, adj. *makapangyarihan; malakás.*

INFORM, v. to give to (a person) definite knowledge of, *ipaalam;* tell, *sabihin;* enlighten, *pagpatalastasán;* acquaint with a fact, *ipabatíd, pabatirán, magpabatíd, ipagbigáy-alam.*

INFORMAL, adj. *impormál,* Sp.; not allowing the rules or customs accepted as good form, *wa-*

láng-tuto; not ceremonious, as an i. party, *panarili.*

INFORMATION, n. knowledge given, *pabatíd, patalastás;* knowledge acquired, *kabatirán;* news, *bulità.*

INGENIOUS, adj. having inventive skill, *mapangathâ.*

INGROWN, adj. *pasalingsíng.*

INHABIT, v. *tumirá, manirahan, tirahán.*

INHABITANT, n. *máninirahan; ang nakatirá.*

INHALE, v. *lumangháp, langhapín.*

INHERENT, adj. *katutubò; likás.*

INHERIT, v. *magmana, manahin; makámana, makápagmana.*

INHERITANCE, n. *mana.*

INHUMAN, adj. merciless, *walâng-awà, walâng-habág;* unfeeling, *walâng-pandamdám.*

INIQUITY, n. *katampalasanan; kabalakyután.*

INITIAL, n. first letter of a word, *unang titik.*—adj. starting, *pansimulâ, pasimulâ.*

INITIATE, v. to introduce into a secret society or the like, *turumulán,* nc.; set on one's feet or into the first principles of anything, *ituntón, itúto.*

INJECT, v. (Med.) (hypodermically), *iturók; iiniksiyón,* Sp.

INJECTION, n. (Med.) *iniksiyón,* Sp.

INJURE, v. to cause to be injured, *ipanganyayà, ipahamak;* hurt, *saktán;* spoil, *sirain.*

INJURY, n. *kapinsalaán;* damage, *sirà;* hurt, *sakít.*

INJUSTICE, n. unfairness, *paykawaláng-katárungan;* a b u s e suffered, *kaapihán.*

INK, n. *tintá,* Sp.; *dinsól,* nc.

INNER, adj. internal, *panloób;* interior, *paloób, sa loób.*

INNOCENCE, n. freedom from guilt or sin, *kawaláng-kasalanan;* lack of acquaintance with evil, *kawaláng-malay;* youthful guilelessness, *kamusmusán.*

INNOCENT, adj. sinless, guiltless, *walâng-kasalanan;* guilelessly young, *musmós;* unaware of any evil, *walâng-malay.*

INNOVATION, n. *pagbabayo, kabaguhán.*

INORGANIC, adj. *tulagáy,* nc., O.T.

INQUIRE, v. to ask a question, *magtanóng, itanóng;* seek information, knowledge, *mag-usisà, usisain.*

INQUIRY, n. asking of a question, *pagtatanóng;* seeking of information, *pag-uusisà.*

INQUISITIVE, adj. *matanóng; mausisà.*

INSANE, adj. *loko,* Sp.; *sirâ ang ulo; sirâ ang bait;* crazy, *baliw, hibáng;* mad, *bangâw, ulól.*

INSANITARY, adj. (person) *masamláng; salaulà;* dirty, *marumí.*

INSECT, n. *kulisap,* nc.

INSECTICIDE, n. *pamatáy-kulisap,* nc.

INSERT, v. to introduce into (between) *isíngit;* cause to be included, *ilakip, isama.*

INSIDE, n. interior, *loób.*—adv. *sa loób.*—adj. *panloób.*

INSINUATION, n. *pamarali, parali; pasaringíg,* nc.

INSIPID, adj. *mayapá;* tasteless, *walâng-lasa;* uninteresting, *nakaíiníp.*

INSIST, v. *ipilit, igíit.*

INSISTENT, adj. *mapilit, mapagpumilit.*

INSPECT, v. to examine closely and critically, *suriin, magsurì;* investigate, *siyasatin, magsiyasat;* review and survey officially, *siyasigin, maniyasig; balayagin, mamalayag,* nc.

INSPECTOR, n. *ispektór,* Sp.; *tagasurì; tagasiyasat.*

INSPIRATION, n. *pamukaw-siglá;* act of drawing air into the lungs, *paglangháp.*

INSPIRE, v. to animate, *bigyángbuhay, bigyáng-siglá;* arouse, *pukawin, gisingin;* encourage, *palakasin ang loób.*

INSTALMENT, n. *hurnál,* Sp.

INSTANCE, n. something offered as an illustration, *paliwanag;* or example, *halimbawà;* of the present month, *ng buwáng kasalukuyan.*

INSTANTLY, adv. *agád.*

INSTEAD OF, prep. *sa halíp ng, sa halíp ni.*

INSTITUTE, n. a place of education, *páturuan, pásanayan;* an organization devoted to scientific, artistic, professional or literary investigations, *surián, pásurian;* or researches *pásaliksikan; Instituto,* Sp.

INSTRUCT, v. to teach, *turuan, magturò;* educate, *parunungin.*

INSTRUCTOR, n. *tagapagturò;* teacher, *gurò, maestro* (*maestra*), Sp., *titser,* Eng.; professor, *propesór,* Sp.; *gurò.*

INSTRUMENT, n. *instrumento,* Sp.; *kasangkapan.*

INSUBORDINATION, n. *pagkasuwaíl.*

INSUFFICIENT, adj. *di-sapát.*

INSULT, v. to abuse by word, *laitin, manlait; tungayawin, manungayaw;* treat with gross contempt, *alipustaín, mang-alipustâ; duhagihin, manduhagi.—*

n. *panlalait, panunungayaw; pang-aalipustâ, panduruhagi.*

INSURANCE, n. *seguro,* Sp.

INTACT, adj. unimpaired, *di-naáanó;* whole, *buô.*

INTANGIBLE, adj. *di-masaláng.*

INTEGRITY, n. *kalinisang-budhî.*

INTELLECT, n. *katalusán;* mind, *diwà;* intelligence, *katalinuhan.*

INTELLIGENCE, n. *katalinuhan.*

INTELLIGENT, adj. *matalino.*

INTEND, v. to have in mind as a purpose or aim, *mag-isip, isipin.*

INTENSE, adj. *masidhî;* aggravated, *malubhâ.*

INTENSIVE, adj. deep and thorough, *maikay.*

INTENTION, n. purpose, *hángarin;* design, *tangkä;* object, *luyon.*

INTENTIONAL, adj. *sinadyâ; tinikís.*

INTERCEDE, v. *mamagitan, ipamagitan.*

INTEREST, n. that which causes excitement of feeling, *pangwili;* rate paid for use of borrowed money, *interés,* Sp.;*tubò.*

INTERESTED, adj. *náwiwili; nakakágustó.*

INTERESTING, adj. *nakawíwili.*

INTERFERE, v. *makialám, pakialamán; manghimasok, panghimasukan.*

INTERIOR, n. *loób.*—adj. *sa loób.*

INTERMEDIATE, adj. *panggitnâ.*

INTERPRET, v. to translate, *isalin;* give or deduce a meaning for, *pakahuluganán.*

INTERPRETER, n. *tagasalin; interpreté,* Sp.

INTERRUPT, v. to interfere with an action, *gumambalà, manggambalà, gambalain;* break into a conversation, sumabád. pumaklí.

INTERVAL, n. pagitan.

INTERVIEW, n. pakikipanayám. —v. kapanayamín.

INTESTINE, n. bituka.

INTRODUCE, v. to conduct or bring in, ipasok; present in a formal manner, iharáp, (socially) ipakilala.

INTRODUCTION, n. payhaharáp, pagpapakilala; beginning, pasimulâ, pambungad.

INTRUST, v. ipagkátiwalà.

INTUITION, n. salagimsím; instantaneous understanding, kawatasán; comprehension, kalutasán, katalastasán.

INUNDATION, n. flood, bahâ.

INVADE, v. lumusob, lusubin; sumalakay, salakayin.

INVASION, n. paglusob; pagsalakay.

INVENT, v. kumathô, kathain, mangathâ.

INVENTION, n. pagkathâ; kathâ.

INVENTOR, n. mángangathâ.

INVEST, v. to put money in some venture, mamuhunan, pamuhunanan.

INVESTIGATE, v. surtín, siyasatin.

INVESTIGATION, n. pagsusurí, pagsisiyasat.

INVINCIBLE, adj. di-mapasukò; waláng-talo.

INVISIBLE, adj. di-mákita; maysalikmatà.

INVITATION, n. anyaya, paanyaya.

INVITE, v. mag-anyaya, anyayahan.

INVOLUNTARY, adj. di-kusà;

di-pakusâ; unintentional, di-sinásadyâ.

INVOLVED, adj. complex, langkapan; intricate, salimuót; confused, guló; tangled, gusót.

INVULNERABLE, adj. di-talbán, di-tablán.

IRASCIBLE, adj. mayagalitín.

IRON, n. bakal.

IRONICAL, adj. pabalintunâ.

IRONY, n. balintunà, balintunay.

IRREGULAR, adj. disorderly, gulú-guló; waláng-kaayusan; not straight (crooked), kilu-kilô, likú-likô.

IRRESISTIBLE, adj. di-mapaglabanan.

IRRESPONSIBLE, adj. alibughâ; waláng-kapanágutan.

IRREVERENT, adj. lapastangan; waláng-pakundangan; waláng pitagan.

IRRIGATION, n. patubig; (Med.) pagsusumpit.

IS, see BE, v.

ISLAND, n. puló.

ISSUE, n. (Law & Pol.) isyu. Eng.; (Arg.) Point of contention, ang pinagtátalunan; a printing of a book, newspaper, etc., palimbág, palathalà.

ISTHMUS, n. tangwáy; see CAPE.

IT, pron. (Not commonly translated.) What is it? Anó iyón? Anó iyán?—I have it. Nasa-akin.

ITEM, n. bagay; sum entered in an account, talâ; a newspaper paragraph, balità.

ITS, pron. (prepositive) kaniyá; (postpositive) niyá.

IVORY, n. garing.

IVY, n. (Bot.) galamáy-amò.

J

JAB, n. sapók.—v. sapukín, manapók.

JAIL, n. bilangguan; kalaboso, Sp.; piitán.

JAM, n. a thick, sweet, fruit preserve, *halea*, Sp.

JANITOR, n. *diyánitór*, Eng.; *tagalinis*.

JANUARY, n. *Enero*, Sp.

JAPAN, n. *Hapón*, Sp.

JAPANESE, n.-adj., *haponés*, Sp.

JAR, n. *saro.*—earthen j., *bangâ; tapayan.*

JAVANESE, n.-adj. *habanés*, Sp.

JAW, n. *pangá.*

JAWBONE, n. *sihang.*

JEALOUS, adj. *naninibughô;* prone to jealousy, *mapanibughô.*

JELLY, n. *halea*, Sp.; *huyá*, Sp.

JERK, n. *labtík.*—v. *labtikín.*

JEST, n. joke, *birò.*

JESUIT, n. *Heswita*, Sp.

JEW, n. *Hudyó*, Sp.

JEWEL, n. *hiyás*, Sp.; *alahas*, Sp.

JEWELER, n. *mag-aalahás.*

JOB, n. a piece of work, task, *gáwain;* employment, *empleo*, Sp.; *trabajo*, Sp.

JOCKEY, n. *hinete*, Sp.

JOIN, v. to unite together, *pagisahin;* connect together, *pagdugtungín, paglikawin;* unite with, *makisama, makiisá;* come together as one, *magkáisá.*

JOINT, n. (Anat.) *kasúkasuán.*— adj. joined, put together, *magkasama.*

JOKE, n. *birò; sistí.* Sp.

JOLLY, adj. *masayá; masiglá.*

JOT, v.—j. down, *italâ; isulat.*

JOURNALISM, n. *pamamahayag.*

JOURNEY, n. trip, travel, *paglalakbáy.*

JOY, n. *tuwà;* gladness, *galák;* happiness, *ligaya;* pleasure, *lugód.*

JUDGE, n. *hukóm; huwés*, Sp.

JUDGMENT, n. *hatol, kahatulán;* decision, *pasiyá.*

JUDICIAL, adj. *panghúkuman.*

JUICE, n. *katás.*

JUICY. adj. *makatás.*

JULY, n. *Hulyo*, Sp.

JUMP, v. *lumuksó; lumundág;* to leap downward, *tumalón.*

JUNE, n. *Hunyo*, Sp.

JUNIOR, n.-adj. *diyunyor*, Eng.

JURISDICTION, n. *ang nasasaklawán.*

JURY, n. *tagahatol;* board of judges in a contest, *inampalan.*

JUST, adj. equitable, *maká-katárungan;* based on reasonable grounds, *makatwiran.*

JUSTICE, n. *katárungan;* rectitude, *katwiran;* a magistrate, *mahistrado*, Sp.

JUSTIFY, v to make right, *ituwíd, iwastô;* show or prove to be right, *ipakilalang may katwiran.*

JUVENILE, adj. suitable to the young, *pambatà.*

JUXTAPOSE, v. *pag-ipingin;* to place near each other, *pagtabihín.*

K

KAPOK, n. *kapók*, Mal.; *buboy.*

KEEN, n. *matalas;* sharp, *matalím.*

KEEP, v. to have the care of, *ingatan, alagaan;* hide, *itagò.*

KEEPER, n. *tagapag-ingat; tagapag-alagà.*

KERNEL, n. *butil.*

KEROSENE, n. *gas*, Sp.

KETTLE, n. *kaldero*, Sp.

KEY, n. *susì.*

KEYBOARD, n. *teklada*, Sp., *túpaan.*

KICK, n. *sipà, sikad.*—v. *sumipà, manipà; sumikad, manikad.*

KID, (colloq.), n. child, *batà.*
KIDNAP, v. (a girl) *gabutin;* (a child) *agawin;* (an adult) *dukutin.*
KIDNEY, n. (Anat.) *bató.*
KILL, v. *pumatáy, patayín;* slay, *kumitíl, kitilín.*
KILOGRAM, n. *kilo,* Sp.
KILOMETER, n. *kilómetró,* Sp.
KILOWATT, n. *kilowat,* Eng.
KIN, n. *angkán; hinlóg,* relatives, *kamag-anak.*
KIND, n. class, *klase,* Sp.; *urì,* —adj. *mabaít;* gracious, *mapagbigáy-loób;* considerate, *maalalahanín.*
KINDLE, v. to set fire to, *palingasin;* ignite, *sindihán,* Sp.
KINDNESS, n. *kabáitan;* graciousness, *pagka-mapagbigáy-loób.*
KING, n. *harì.*
KINGDOM, n. *kaharian.*

KISS, n. *halík.*—v. *humalík, halkán, hagkán.*
KITCHEN, n. *kusinà,* Sp.
KITE, n. *buladór,* Sp.; *sapi-sapi; saranggola,* Sp.
KITTEN, n. *kutíng.*
KNEE, n. *tuhod.*
KNEECAP, n. *bayugo ng tuhod.*
KNEEL, v. *lumuhód;* to use something to k. on, *luhurán.*
KNIFE, n. *lanseta, laseta,* Sp.
KNIT, v. *magniting,* Eng.
KNOCK, v. to rap, as on a door, *tumuktók, tuktukán.*
KNOCKER, n. *panuktók, tuktukan.*
KNOT, n. *buhól*—v. *ibuhól.*
KNOW, v. *málaman, máalaman.*
KNOWLEDGE, n. *kaalaman;* learning, *karunungan;* cognition, *katalusán.*
KNUCKLE, n. *bukó ng dalirì.*

L

LABEL, n. *etiketa,* Sp.; inscription, *taták.*
LABOR, n. work, *gawà;* task, *gáwain.*
LABORATORY, n. *laboratoryo,* Sp.
LABORER, n. *manggagawà;* trabahador, Sp.
LACE, n. ornamental fabric, *puntás,* Sp.; string or cord to hold something together, as in shoes, *talì;* or in chemises, *laso.*
LACK, n. *kakulangán, kasalatán,* —v. to need, *mangailangan;* be without, *mawalán.*
LACKING, adj. *kulang; kapós.*
LAD, n. a boy, *batang lalaki;* a youth, *binatilyo* (colloq.).
LADDER, n. *hagdán.*
LADY, n. woman, *babae.*—Ladies

and gentlemen, *Mga kababaihan at kaginoohan.*
LAKE, n. *lawà; dagat-dagatan.*
LAMB, n. *kurdero,* Sp.; sheep, *tupa.*
LAME, adj. *piláy;* halt, *hingkód.*
LAMENT, v. to bewail, *managhóy;* weep, wail, *manangis.*
LAMENTATION, n. *taghóy, panaghóy.*
LAMP, n. *ilaw, ilawán; lampará,* Sp.
LAND, n. ground, soil, earth, *lupà.*
LANDMARK, n. *muhón,* Sp.; any mark, *tandá, palátandaan.*
LANDSCAPE, n. *tánawin.*
LANE, n. *landás;* trail, path, *bulaos.*
LANGUAGE, n. *wikà; salitâ.*

LANGUID, adj. drooping, *unsya-mî*.

LANGUISH, v. *maunsyamî;* to fade, *mangupas.*

LANTERN, n. *paról,* Sp.

LAP, n. *kandungan, kalungan—* v. to lick up with the tongue, *humimod, himurin.*

LAPEL, n. *sulapa,* Sp.

LARD, n. *mantikà,* Sp.

LARGE, adj. big, *malakí.*

LARYNX, n. (Anat.) *gulunggu-lungán.*

LARVA, n. (Zool.) *kitíkití; uód.*

LAST, adj. final, at the end, *hulí.* —at l., *sa wakás.*

LATE, adj. tardy, *hulí.*

LATELY, adv. *kailán lamang; kaí-kailán lamang.*

LATER, adv. *mámayâ; kinamá-mayaán.*

LATRINE, n. *pálikuran.*

LAUDABLE, adj. *kapuri-puri.*

LAUGH, n. *tawa.*—v. *tumawa.*

LAUGHABLE, adj. *nakakátawá.*

LAUGHTER, n. *pagtatawá.*

LAUNDRY, n. *pálabahan.*

LAW, n. *batás, ley,* Sp.

LAWN, n. *damuhán.*

LAWYER, n. *abugado,* Sp.; de-fender, *mánananggól.*

LAY, v. to place, put or deposit, *ilagáy.*

LAYER, n. one thickness, stra-tum, coating, etc., *susón, pa-tong.*

LAZY, adj. *tamád.*

LEAD, n. *tingâ.*

LEAD, v. to guide by the hand, *akayin;* guide by going ahead, *manguna, pangunahan.*

LEADER, n. *lider,* Eng.

LEAF, n. *dahon.*

LEAFY, adj. *madahon, malabay.*

LEAGUE, n. *liga,* Sp.; alliance, *buklód;* association, *samahán, kapisanan.*

LEAK, n. (liquid) *tulò.*— v. *tu-mulò.*

LEAN, v. to incline, *humilig, su-mandál; kumiling.*

LEAP, v. *lumundág;* to jump downward, *tumalón.*—n. *lundág, talón.*

LEARN, v. to acquire knowledge of, *mátuto;* he informed about, *mabatíd, matalós.*

LEARNED, adj. *marunong;* eru-dite, *matalisik;* scholarly, *pan-tás.*

LEARNING, n. *karunungan;* act or process of acquiring knowl-edge, *pag-aaral, pagkakátuto;* knowledge, *kaalaman,* erudi-tion, *katalisikan;* scholarliness, *kapantasán.*

LEAST, adj.-n. the least, *ang pi-nakamaliít.*—At l., *man lamang.*

LEATHER, n. *katad; kuwero,* Sp.

LEAVE, v. to depart, *umalís;* al-low to remain behind, *iwan;* not to take along something upon departure, *iwanan.*

LECTURE, n. *panayam.*

LEECH, n. *lintâ.*

LEFT, adj. (side) *kaliwâ.*

LEG, n. *paá; bintî.*

LEGEND, n. *alamát.*

LEGISLATIVE, adj. *pambatás.*

LEGION, n. *Lehiyón,* Sp.

LEGISLATOR, n. *mambabatás.*

LEGISLATURE, n. *bátasan.*

LEMON, n. *dayap.*

LEMONADE, n. *limunada,* Sp.; *dinayapan.*

LEND, v. *magpahirám, pahira-mín.*

LENGTH, n. *habà;* (of time) *ta-gál.*

LENGTHEN, v. *pahabain, paha-baan;* (in time) *patagalán.*

LENIENT, adj. indulgent, *ma-pagpasunód;* not severe, *di-ma-hiqpít.*

LENS, n. *lente*, Sp.

LENT, n. *Kuwaresma*, Sp.; *Mahál na Araw*.

LEPER, n. *kétungin; leproso*, Sp.

LEPROSY, n. *ketong; lepra*, Sp.

LESSON, n. *aralín; liksiyón*, Sp.; *lisyón*, Sp.

LEST, conj. *bakâ*.

LET, v. to permit, *pahintulutan, tulutan;* allow, *bayaan, hayaan*.

LETTER, n. epistle, note, missive, *liham, sulat;* (of alphabet) *titik, letra*, Sp.

LETTUCE, n. *letsugas*, Sp.

LEVEL, adj. *pantáy, patag*.

LEVER, n. *panimbáng*.

LIABILITY, n. obligation, *ságutin*.

LIAR, n. *sinungaling; bulaan*.

LIBEL, n. *libelo*, Sp.; *paninirangpuri*.

LIBERAL, adj. *mapagbigáy*.

LIBERTY, n. *kalayaán*.

LIBRARY, n. *aklatan*.

LICENSE, n. *lisénsiya*, Sp.

LIE, v. to tell a falsehood, *magsinungaling, magbulaan*.

LIE, v. to l. down, *humigâ*.

LIEUTENANT, n. *tenyente*, Sp.

LIFE, n. *buhay;* manner of living, *pamumuhay;* biography, *talambuhay*.

LIFT, v. to raise with the hands, *buhatin;* place in a higher position, *itaás*.

LIGAMENT, n. (Anat.) *litid*.

LIGATURE, n. (Gram.) *pangangkóp*.

LIGHT, n. illumination, *liwanag*, lamp, *ilaw*.

LIGHTEN, v. to reduce in weight, *pagaanín, pagaanán*.

LIGHTER, n. a device for lighting, *panindí, pansindí*.

LIGHTNING, n. (the flash) *kidlát;* the electric charge, *lintík*.

LIKE, v. (root-verbs only) *gustó, ibig.*—adj. *katulad, kapara, kawangis*.

LIKELY, adj. seeming like, *animo* (with *'y* i.e., *animó'y*); *para* (with *-ng* form of *na*, i.e., *parang*).

LIKEWISE, adv. in like manner, *gayundín;* also, too, *din, rin; man, namán*.

LILT, n. rhythm, *indayog*.

LIME, n. *apog* (ocailum oxide).

LIMIT, n. border, boundary, *hanggá, hanggahan, hangganan.*—v. *hangganán*.

LINE, n. *guhit*.

LINEN, n. *linen*, Eng.

LINGER, v. to delay, *magtagál*.

LINIMENT, n. (Med.) *panghaplás*.

LINK, n. *likaw; kawing*.

LION, n. *león*, Sp.; *liyón*, Sp.

LIP, n. *labì*.

LIQUEFY, v. *tunawin*.

LIQUID, n. *tubig.*—adj. *tunáw, lusáw*.

LIQUOR, n. *alak*.

LIST, n. roll of names, items, etc., *talaán; listahan*, Sp.

LISTEN, v. *makiníg, pakinggán*.

LITER, n. *litro*, Sp.

LITERACY, n. *karunungang bumasa't sumulat*.

LITERARY, adj. *panliteratura*, Sp.; *pampánitikán; pampánulatan*.

LITERATURE, n. *literatura*, Sp.; *pánitikán; pánulatan*.

LITIGATION, n. *usapín*.

LITTLE, adj. *maliít; muntî*.

LIVE, v. *mabuhay;* to spend or pass one's life (in a certain manner), *mamuhay*.

LIVE, adj. alive, *buháy;* flaming, *naglílingas;* of present interest, *nangkasalukuyan*.

LIVELY, adj. animated, *masiglá*.

LIVER, n. *atáy.*

LIZARD, n. (grass) *bubulí, him-bubulí;* (river) *bayawak;* (house) *butikî;* gekko, *tukô.*

LOAD, n. (on head) *sunong;* (on shoulders) *pasán;* (in hand) *bitbít, dalá;* (on vehicles) *lulan, kargá,* Sp.; charge of a gun, *tangáy, kargá,* Sp.

LOAN, n. money lent, *pautang;* money borrowęd, *utang;* money granted for temporary use, *pahirám.*

LOBE, n. (of brain) *umbók;* (of ear) *dunggót.*

LOBSTER, n. *uláng.*

LOCAL, adj. *pampoók;* for "this" place only, *pandito lamang;* for "that" place only, *pandoón lamang;* for "us" only, *pang-atin lamang.*

LOCALITY, n. place, *poók, lugál,* Sp.; district, *purók.*

LOCATION, n. *kinalálagyán;* residence, *kinatítirahán;* site, *kinatátayuán.*

LOCATIVE, adj. (Gram.) *kalaanán, pangkalaanán.*

LOCK, n. *susì; seradura,* Sp.; *trangká,* Sp.; *kandado,* Sp.

LOCKET, n. *laket,* Eng.

LOCKSMITH, n. *pandáy-kabán.*

LOCOMOTIVE, n. *mákiná,* Sp.

LOCUST, n. *balang, luktón.*

LOFTY, adj. high, *mataás;* towering, *matayog.*

LOG, n. *kalap;* tree trunk, *punò ng kahoy.*

LOGIC, n. *lóhiká,* Sp.

LONELY, adj. lonesome, *nagíisá;* depressed, *nalúlumbáy.*

LONG, adj. (in measurement) *mahabà;* (in time) *matagál, malaon.*

LOOK, v. *tumingín, tingnán.*

LOOSE, adj. *maluwág; talihabsô.*

LOOSEN, v. *paluwagín, paluwagán, luwagán.*

LOOT, v. *mandambóng.*

LORD, n. *poón;* master, *panginoón.*

LOOTER, adj. *mandarambóng; luter,* Eng.

LOSE, v. to mislay or miss, *mawalâ;* stray, *máligáw.*

LOSS, n. *pagkawalâ;* failure to win, *pagkatalo;* pl., *kapinsalaán;* (in business), *kalugihán.*

LOT, n. plot of land, *lote,* Sp.; fortune, fate, *kapalaran*—a l. of, *marami.*

LOTTERY, n. *loteriya,* Sp.

LOUD, adj. noisy, *maingay;* full sounding, *malakás.*

LOUSE, n. *kuto.*

LOVABLE, adj. *kaibig-ibig.*

LOVE, n. *pag-ibig;* affection, *pagmamahál.*

LOVELINESS, n. *kariktán.*

LOVELY, adj. *marikít; kaibig-ibig.*

LOVER, n. one who pays court to a lady, *manliligáw; mángingibíg;* a betrothed, *katipán, kasintahan.*

LOW, adj. *mababà.*

LOWLY, adj. *hamak, abâ.*

LOYAL, adj. *tapát na loób.*

LOYALTY, n. *katapatáng-loób.*

LUCK, n. *suwerte,* Sp.

LUCKY, adj. *masuwerte,* Sp.; *ginágaling.*

LULLABY, n. *alò.*

LUMBER, n. board, *tablá,* Sp., *kahoy.*

LUMINOUS, adj. *makináng.*

LUMP, n. a mass, *bugál;* a swelling, *bukol;* protuberance, *umbók,* collection of things, *tumpók.*

LUNGS, n. (Anat.) *bagà.*

LUSTER, n. *kináng.*

LUXURY, n. *luho,* Sp.

LYE, n. *lihiya*, Sp.

LYRE, n. *lira*, Sp.; *kudyapî*.

LYRIC, n. *awit.*—love l., *kundiman.*

MACHINE, n. *mákiná*, Sp.

MAD, adj. *hibáng, halíng.*

MADAM, n. (married lady) *ginang;* (unmarried lady, honorific, *gining*).

MAGAZINE, n. *mágasin*, Eng.

MAGIC, n. *máhiyá*, Sp.; *balaghán,* nc.—adj. *mabalaghán*, nc.

MAGICIAN, n. *mambabalaghán; mago*, Sp.; conjurer, *salamangkero*, Sp.

MAGISTRATE, n. *mahistrado*, Sp.: *iudge, hukóm.*

MAGNET, n. *batu-balanì; imán,* Sp.

MAGNIFICENT, adj. *marilág;* brilliant. *maningning.*

MAH-JONGG, n. *madyong*, Ch.

MAID, n. *dalaga;* female servant, *utusáng babae; mutsatsa*, Sp.

MAIDEN. n.-adj. *dalaga.*

MAIDENHOOD, n. *pagkadalaga.*

MAIDENLY, adj. modest, *mahinhín;* gentle, *mayumì.*

MAIL, n. *koreo*, Sp.; *meil*, Eng.

MAIN, adj. most important, *pinakamahalagá.*

MAINTAIN, v. to sustain, *sustinihán*, Sp.; *ipanindigan;* bear the expense of, *gastahán; susténtuhín*, Sp.

MAJESTIC, adj. regal, *makaharì;* magnificent, *marilág.*

MAJOR, adj. greater, (in number, extent, etc.) *lalong malakí,* —n. the m. subject (in college), *medyor*, Eng.

MAJORITY, n. *ang nakarárami.*

MAKE, v. to compose, fashion, *gumawâ, gawín;* prepare for use, *maghandâ, ihandâ;* create, *lumikhâ; likhaín.*

MAKER, n. God, *Diyos*, Sp.; *Bathalà, Maylikhâ, Maykapál;* one who composes, fashions, *tagagawâ, tagayarì.*

MAKESHIFT, n.-adj. *pansamantalá.*

MALARIA, n. *pangiki, malarya,* Sp.

MALAY, n. *Maláy, Malayo*, Sp.

MALE, n.-adj. *lalaki.*

MALEDICTION, n. curse, *sumpâ;* profanity, *tungayaw.*

MALICE, n. *malisya*, Sp.

MALTREAT, v. *mang-apí, apihin.*

MAMMA, n. *Mamá*, Sp.; *Ináy, Ináng.*

MAN, n. a human being, *tao;* adult male, *lalaki.*

MANAGE, v. to administer, *mangasiwà, pangasiwaan;* control or conduct, *mamahalà, pamahalaan;* guide, *mamatnubay, patnubayan;* direct, *mamatnugot, patnugutan;* superintend, supervise, *manihalà, panihalaan.*

MANAGER, n. *tagapangasiwà.*

MANDATE, n. *kautusán, mandato*, Sp.

MANDATORY, adj. *pautós;* obligatory, *sápilitán.*

MANDIBLE, n. (Anat.) jawbone, *sihang.*

MANE, n. (of horse) *kilíng.*

MANGER, n. *labangán, sabsaban.*

MANGO, n. (Bot.) *manggá.*

MANHOOD, n. *pagkalalaki.*

MANIFEST, adj. obvious, *halatâ;* clear, *malinaw;* plain, *kita.*

MANKIND, n. *sangkatauhan.*

MANNER, n. habit, *ugalì, gawì;* behavior, *kilos, pangingilos —* Good manners, *mabuting paguugalì, mabuting-asal.*

MANTLE, n. *manta*, Sp.; *kapa,* Sp.

MANUFACTURE, v. to make, *yumarì, gumawâ.*

MANURE, n. fertilizer, *abono*, Sp.; *patabâ*.

MANUSCRIPT, n. *orihinál*, Sp.

MANY, adj. *marami*.

MAP, n. *mapa*, Sp.

MARBLE, n. *marmol*, Sp.

MARCH, n. (month) *Marso*, Sp.; regular, measured step, *lakad*, *martsa*, Sp.—v. to move with regular steps, *lumakad*, *magmartsa*, Sp.

MARE, n. young female of the horse, *putrangká*, *Sp.*; female horse, *kabayong babae;* m. with young, *inahíng kabayo.*

MARGIN, n. edge, *gilid;* a border, *tabihán.*

MARINE, adj. *pandagat;* having to do with navigation, *pampagdaragát.*—n. *marino*, Sp.; *magdaragát.*

MARINER, n. *marino, marinero*, Sp.; *magdaragát.*

MARK, n. *tandâ, palátandaan;* brand, *markâ* Sp.; a visible imprint, *markâ,* Sp.; stain, *mansâ*, Sp.; *dungis; dumí.*

MARKET, n. *pámilihan; palengke, baraka*, Sp.

MARRIAGE, n. *pag-aasawa;* wedding ceremony, *kasál*, Sp.; *pag-iisáng dibdib.*

MARROW, n. (of bones) *utak ng butó; utak-butó.*

MARRY, v. to perform the ceremony of marriage, *magkasál*, Sp.; take in marriage, *pakasál, pakasalán;* be married, *ikasál, mákasál; mápakasál.*

MARSH, n. *latì, latian; labón.*

MARSHY, adj. *malatì, malabón.*

MARTIAL, adj. of or pertaining to war, *pandigmâ;* military, *panghukbó; militar,* Sp.

MARTYR, n. *martir*, Sp.

MARVEL, n. *kababalaghán.*—v. *magtaká; mámanghâ; manggilalás.*

MARVELOUS, adj. causing wonder, *kataká-taká; kamanghámanghâ.*

MASCULINE, adj. (Gram.) *panlalaki.*

MASK, n. *takíp sa mukhâ; máskará,* Sp.; disguise, *balátkayó.*

MASQUERADE, n. *pagbabalátkayó.*

MASS, n. Holy Mass, *Misa,* Sp.

MASS, n. aggregation of things into one body, *pamumuô;* bulk, size, *laki, bulto,* Sp.; the masses, *ang karamihang tao.*

MASSACRE, n. *pátayan.*

MASSAGE, n. *masahe*, Sp.; *hilot, paghilot.*—v. *masahihin; hilutin.*

MASSEUR, n. *masahista*, Sp.

MAST, n. *palo,* Sp.; *albór*, Sp.

MASTER, n. *amo*, Sp.; *panginoón;* chief, *punò;* expert, *dalubsà.*—M. of Arts, *Dalubsining,* nc.

MASTICATE, v. to grind with the teeth, *ngumuyâ, nguyaín;* chew (as gum or buyo), *ngumatâ, ngataín.*

MAT, n. flat piece of woven straw, *banig.*

MATCH, n. igniting stick, *púsporó,* Sp.; an equal, *kapantáy, katumbás.*

MATCHLESS, adj. cannot be equalled, *di-mapápantayán, dimatútularan;* peerless, *walangkatulad, waláng-kapantáy.*

MATE, n. companion, *kasama;* helper, *katulong;* spouse, *asawa.*

MATERIAL, adj. physical (not spiritual) *panlupà;* consisting of, or pertaining to, substance, *pangkalamnán; materyál,* Sp.;

—n. the substance of which a thing is made, *kayarián;* things u s e d, *kagamitán, sangkáp;* things for further elaboration, *sangkáp, panangkáp.*

MATHEMATICS, n. *palátuusan.*

MATRICULATE, v. *magmatrikulá,* Sp.; to enroll, *magpatalâ.*

MATRIMONY, n. marriage, *matrimonyo,* Sp.; *pag-aasawa;* the rite of marriage, *kasál, pagkakasál,* Sp.

MATTER, n. thing, *bagay;* substance, *lamán, kalamnán; sustánsiyá,* Sp.; material of which a thing is composed, *ṣangkáp, panangkáp; materya,* Sp.

MATTRESS, n. *kutsón,* Sp.

MATURE, adj. ripe, *hinóg;* full-grown, completely developed, *magulang na; ganáp na.*

MAXIM, n. precept, *kawikaán:* p r o v e r b, *saláwikaín;* adage, common saying, *kasabihán.*

MAXIMUM, n. *ang pinaka +* (number, quantity) *maramɪ;* (value) *mataás;* (importance) *mahalagá, (pinakamarami pinakamataás, pinakamahalagá).*

MAY, n. (month) *Mayo,* Sp.;—v. *maâari.* — May happen, *maaaring mangyari.*

MAYBE, adv. perhaps, *marahil;* possibly, *kaipalà.*

MAYONNAISE, n. *mayunesa.* Sp.

MAYOR, n. *alkalde,* Sp.; *punò ng bayan;* (of a city) *punò ng lunsód.*

ME, pron. to (for, with, in, on. at) me, *sa akin.*

MEADOW, n. *parang;* pastureland, *pastulan,* Sp.; *pánginainan,* nc.

MEAL, n. a repast, *pagkain; kumida,* Sp.; ground flour, *ginilɪng.*

MEAN, v. to signify, denote, *ɪpakahulugán;* intend, *sadyaɪn, tangkaín.* — adj. low, ignoble, *imbî;* low, humble, *hamak.*

MEANING, n. *kahulugán;* denotation, *pakahulugán; ang ibig sabihin.*

MEANTIME, adv. in the m., *samantala;* meanwhile, *habang.*

MEASLES, n. (Med.) *tigdás.*

MEASURE, n. *sukat.*—v. *sukatin, sumukat.*

MEAT, n. animal flesh used as food, *karné,* Sp.; *lamán;* victuals (not including bread or rice) *ulam.*

MECHANIC, n. *mekánikó,* Sp.

MEDAL, n. *medalya,* Sp.

MEDDLE, v. to interfere, *makialam; manghimasok, panghimasukan.*

MEDDLESOME, adj. *pakialám; mapanghimasok.*

MEDICINE, n. art or science of, *panggagamót, palágamutan; medisina,* Sp.; drug, *gamót, droga,* Sp.; remedy, *panlunas.*

MEDITATE, v. to cogitate, *magniláy-nilay;* muse upon, *magwarí-warì.*

MEDITATION, n. cogitation, *pagniniláy-nilay;* musing, *pagwawarí-warì.*

MEEK, adj. *mababang-loób;* gentle, *mayumì, maamò;* modest, *mahinhín.*

MEET, v. to come together in one place, *magtagpô;* see each other, *magkita;* come up to or approach from a different direct i o n, *sumalubong;* assemble, *magtipon;* hold a meeting, as a society, *magpulong.*

MEETING, n. a coming together of persons, *pagtatagpô; pagkikita;* an assembly, *pagpupulong, pulong.*

MELANCHOLY, n. dejection, *kahapisan*, despondence, *kalumbayan.*

MELODIOUS, adj. *mahimig, mataginting.*

MELODY, n. *himig; melodiya,* Sp.

MELON, n. *milón,* Sp.

MELT, v. *tunawin;* be melted. *matunaw.*

MEMBER, n. *kasapì, kaanib.*

MEMBRANE, n. *balok; balambán.*

MEMENTO, n. *alaala;* a reminder, *pagunitâ.*

MEMORANDUM, n. *memorandum,* Lat.; *pánandaan.*

MEMORIAL, n. *alaala, pang-alaala.*

MEMORIZE, v. to commit to memory, *magsaulo, sauluhin, isaulo;* Sl. *magkabisa,* Sp.; *kabisahin.*

MEMORY, n. remembrance, *alaala;* recollection, reminiscence, *gunitâ.*

MEND, v. to repair, *kumpunihín,* Sp.; *gawín,* reform, *baguhin, pagbutihin;* reform (self), *magpakabuti.*

MENTAL, adj. pertaining to the m i n d, *pandiwà;* intellectual, *pangkatalinuhan.*

MENTION, v. to refer to by name, *tukuyin;* tell, *sabihin:* speak briefly of, *banggitín.*

MENU, n. *menú,* Sp.; *taláulaman,* nc.

MERCHANDISE, n. *kalakal.*

MERCHANT, n. *mángangalakál; komersiyante,* Sp.; *negosyante.* Sp.

MERCIFUL, adj. compassionate, *mahábagin;* full of pity, *maawaín.*

MERCILESS, adj. *waláng-habág; waláng-awà.*

MERCURY, n. *asoge,* Sp.

MERCY, n. compassion, *habág;* pity, *awà.*

MERELY, adv. *lamang.*

MERIT, v. to deserve, *magindapat.*—n. excellence, *kagalingán;* due reward, *gantimpalà.*

MERITORIOUS, adj. worthy, *karapat-dapat.*

MERRY, adj. cheerful, *masayá;* happy, *maligaya;* jolly, animated, *masiglá;* amusing, *nakalilibáng.*

MESSAGE, n. *pahatíd;* communication, *patalastás.*

MESSENGER, n. *mensahero,* Sp.; errand runner, *utusán;* bringer of news, *tagapagbalità.*

METAL, n. *metál,* Sp.

METER, n. *metro,* Sp.

METHOD, n. *paraán, pamamaraán, kaparaanán;* procedure, *palakad;* orderly arrangement, *kaayusan;* system, *sistema,* Sp.

MEW, n. the cry of a cat, *ngiyáw; ingáw.*

MICROBE, n. *mikrobyo,* Sp.

MICROSCOPE, n. *mikroskopyo,* Sp.

MIDDAY, n. noon, *tanghalì; katanghalian.*

MIDDLE, n.-adj. *gitnâ, panggitnâ;* intervening, *pagitan.*

MIDNIGHT, n.-adj. *hating-gabí.*

MIDWIFE, n. *hilot.*

MIGHT, n. force, strength, *lakás;* power, *kapangyarihan.*

MIGHTY, adj. strong, *malakás;* powerful, *makapangyarihan.*

MIGRATE, v. *mangibáng-poók.*

MILE, n. *milya,* Sp.

MILITANT, adj. *manlalabán.*

MILITARY, adj. pertaining to soldiers, *pangkawal, pansundalo;* pertaining to arms, *pansandata;* to warfare, *pandigmâ;* to the army, *panghukbó; pangmi-litár*, Sp.

MILK, n. *gatas.*

MILL, n. grinding machine or apparatus, *gilingán.*—v. to grind, *gumiling, maggiling, gilingin.*

MILLION, n. *angaw.* — One m., *sang-angaw.*

MILLIONAIRE, n.-adj. *milyonaryo*, Sp.; *may-angaw*, nc.

MIMEOGRAPH, n. duplicator machine, *pánalinan*, nc.; *mímyográp*, Eng.

MIMICRY, n. *panggagaya; panggagagád.*

MIMOSA, n. (Bot.) *makahiyâ.*

MIND, n. *diwà.*

MINDFUL, adj. careful, *maingat, maalagà;* attentive, *maasikaso*, Sp.

MINE, pron. (prepositive) *akin*, (postpositive) *ko.*

MINE, n. excavation for minerals, *mina*, Sp.

MINERAL, n. *minerál*, Sp.

MINGLE, v. to associate with, *makisama, makihalò;* intermingle, *makihalubilo.*

MINIMUM, n.-adj. *pinakamaliít; pinakakákauntî;* lowest, *pinakamababà.*

MINISTER, n. *ministro*, Sp.; (of the nation) *kagawad-bansá.*

MINISTRY, n. *ministeryo*, Sp.; (in the government) *kágawaráng-bansá.*

MINOR, adj. not yet of age, *minór*, Sp.; *batà pa.*

MINORITY, n. *mınoriya*, Sp.; state or being not yet of age, *pagka-batà pa.*

MINUTE, n. 60 seconds, *minuto*, Sp.; a short time, *sandalí;* a moment, *saglít.*

MINUTE, adj. very small, *nápakaliít; katitíng;* Sl. *kapurát.*

MIRACLE, n. *himalá.*

MIRACULOUS, adj. *mapaghimalâ;* supernatural, *talulikás*, nc.

MIRE, n. *lusak;* mud, *putik;* slush, *burak; pusalì.*

MIRROR, n. *salamín.*

MIRTH, n. *pagkatuwâ;* laughter, *pagtatawá.*

MISADVENTURE, n. disaster, *kapahamakán.*

MISCHIEF, n. prank, *kalikután.*

MISCHIEVOUS, n. full of pranks, *malikót.*

MISERABLE, adj. mean, *imbí, hamak, abâ;* unhappy, *nalúlumbáy, naháhapis;* wretched, *kulang-palad.*

MISFORTUNE, n. *kasamaángpalad;* adversity, *kasáwian;* calamity, *sakunâ.*

MISLEAD, v. *iligáw.*

MISS, n. address to a young woman, unmarried, *binibini* (Bb.); (honorific) *gining.*

MISS, v. to fail to hit, *salahan, di-tamaan;* feel the loss of, *damdamín ang pagkawalâ.*

MISSAL, n. *misál*, Sp.; *dásalangpangmisa*, Sp.

MISSING, adj. lost, *nawáwalâ, nawalâ.*

MISSION, n. *pakay; misyón*, Sp.

MIST, n. *ulap.*

MISTAKE, n. error, *malî, kamálian.*

MISTAKEN, adj. *malì.*—You are m., *Malî ka.*

MISTER (Mr.), n. *ginoó* (Abbr. G.)

MISTY, adj. *maulap;* dim, *malabò.*

MIX, v. to blend together, *paghaluin;* mingle, *makihalò.*

MIXED, adj. *magkahalò, magkalahók.*

MIXER, n. (apparatus) *panghalò.*

MOAN, v. (from pain) *humaluyhóy;* (from sorrow) *tumaghóy.*

MOB, n. crowd, *libumbón.*

MOCK, v. to ridicule, *libakín, manlibák;* jeer, *tuydín, manuyâ.*

MOCKERY, n. *panlilibák; panunuyâ.*

MODE, n. m e t h o d, *paraán;* (Gram.) mood, *panagano.*

MODEL, n. pattern, *tularán; húwaran; ulirán.*

MODERATE, adj. not extreme or excessive, *kainaman, katamtaman.*

MODERATOR, n. adviser, *tagapayo.*

MODERN, adj. recent, *bago;* pertaining to the present time, *pangkasalukuyan.*

MODERNISM, n. *pagka-makabago.*

MODERNIST, adj.-n. *makabago.*

MODEST, adj. *mahinhín; mabini.*

MODESTY, n. *kahinhinán; kabinian.*

MODIFIER, n. (Gram.) *panturing, panuring.*

MODIFY, v. to change, alter, *baguhin;* (Gram.) *turingan.*

MOIST, adj. *halumigmíg;* slightly wet, *basá-basâ.*

MOISTURE, n. *halumigmíg; kahalumigmigan.*

MOLECULE, n. *titíng,* nc.

MOMENT, n. *saglít;* an instant, *sandali.*

MONARCHY, n. *pámahalaáng makaharì.*

MONDAY, n. *Lunes,* Sp.

MONEY, n. *kuwarta, kuwalta,* Sp.; *salapî; pera,* Sp.; *pilak.*

MONK, n. *monghe,* Sp.

MONSTER, n. *halimaw;* fig. *dambuhalà* (whale); *damulag* (big carabao).

MONSTROSITY, n. *kahalimawan;* unnatural hugeness, *kalakhán.*

MONTH, n. *buwán.*

MONTHLY, adj. *búwanan.*

MONUMENT, n. *bantayog; monumento,* Sp.

MOOD, n. temper of mind, *lagáy ng loób;* (Gram.) mode, *panagano.*

MOON, n. *buwán.*

MORAL, adj. *morál,* Sp.; government by virtuous conduct, *masanling,* nc.; (of women, specially) *matimtiman.*

MORE, adj. *lalò, lalò na.*—adv. *pa.*

MOREOVER, adv. besides, *sakâ;* also, *at gayundín;* further, *at higít pa.*

MORNING, n. *umaga.*

MOSQUITO, n. *lamók.*

MOSS, n. *lumot.*

MOST, adj. *pinaka-* plus positive adjective, as, *pinakamagandá,* most beautiful.

MOTHER, n. *iná.*

MOTION, n. *galáw; kilos, kibô;* formal proposal in a meeting, *mungkahì.* — m. pictures, *sine,* Sp.; *aninong gumágalaw.*

MOTIVATION, n. *panggaganyák.*

MOTIVE, n. *sanhî.*

MOTOR, n. *motór,* Sp.; *mákiná,* Sp.

MOTORCYCLE, n. *motorsiklo,* Sp.

MOTTO, n. *moto,* Eng.; *banság.*

MOUNT, v. to ascend, *umakyát;* get up, as on a horse, *sumakáy;* assemble, as machinery, *italatág, imuntár,* Sp.

MOUNTAIN, n. *bundók.*

MOUNTAINEER, n. *mámumundók.*

MOUNTAINOUS, adj. *bulubundukin; mabundók.*

MOURN, v. to grieve, *magdalamhatì, mamighatî;* wear clothes of mourning, *magluksâ.*

MOURNING, n. *pagluluksâ.*

MOUSE, n. *dagâ.*

MOUSTACHE, n. *bigote,* Sp.; *misay.*

MOUTH, n. *bibíg.*

MOUTHFUL, n. *sansubò. sansamuol.*

MOUTHPIECE, n. of musical instrument, *bokilya,* Sp.

MOVE, v. *gumaláw, kumilos.*

MOVEMENT, n. *galáw, paggaláw; kilos, pagkiloṣ.*

MOW, v. *gumapas, gapasin: taṇpasin.*

MUCH, adj.-adv. *marami: maraming-marami.*

MUD, n. *putik.*

MUDDY, adj. *maputik.*

MULE, n. *mula,* Sp.

MULTIFARIOUS, adj. *sarisari; diverse, ibá't ibá; ibá-ibá.*

MULTIPLY, v. to cause to increase in number, *paramihin, magparami.*

MULTITUDE, n. *karamihangtao;* crowd, *libumbón.*

MUMPS, n. (Med.) *baikî, bikî.*

MUNITION, n. arms, *sandata;* pl. war material, *kasangkapang pandigmâ.*

MURDER, n. *pagpatáy· ng tao.—*v. *pumatáy ng tao;* to kill, *patayin, kitilín.*

MURDERER, n. *mámamatay-tao.*

MURMUR, v. *bumulúng-bulóng.*

—n. *bulóng, ungol;* (of running streams) *aliw-iw.*

MUSCLE, n. *kalamnán.*

MUSCULAR, adj. *malamán; matipunò.*

MUSE, n. *paraluman; musa,* Sp.; *diwatà.—*v. to meditate in silence, *magniláy-nilay.*

MUSEUM, n. *museo,* Sp.; exhibition hall, *tanghalan.*

MUSHROOM, n. (edible) *kabuté;* (not edible) *mamarang.*

MUSIC, n. *músiká,* Sp.; musical composition, *tugtugin.*

MUSICAL, adj. having ear for music, *may-uwido,* Sp.; *músikál,* Sp.

MUSICIAN, n. *músikó,* Sp.; *mṻnunugtóg.*

MUST, v. *dapat, nárarapat, mṻrapat.*

MUSTARD, n. *mustasa,* Sp.

MUSTY, adj. moldy, *maamag, ámagin;* stale, *laón, panís;* soured, *kulasím.*

MUTE, adj. speechless, *umíd;* dumb, *pipi.*

MUTUAL, adj. *túgunan, pálitan; damayán.*

MUZZLE, n. *busál; sangkál.—*v. *busalán; sangkalán.*

MY, pron. (prepositive) *akin;* (postpositive) *ko.*

MYRRH, n. *mira,* Sp.

MYSTERIOUS, adj. *mahiwagà.*

MYSTERY, n. *hiwagà; misteryo,* Sp.

MYSTIC, n.-adj. *místikó,* Sp.

MYTH, n. ᴪlegend, *alamát.*

MYTHOLOGY, n. *paláalamatan.*

N

NAIL, n. *pakò.—*v. *ipakò, pakuan.*

NAKED, adj. (completely) *hubu't-hubád;* (from trunk upward) *hubád;* (from trunk downward) *hubô.*

NAME, n. *ngalan;* given n., *pangalan;* designation, *tawag;* reknown, *kabantugan.*

NAMELY, adv. *álalaóng bagá'y.*

NAP, v. *umidlíp;* doze, *mápaidlíp.*

NAPE, n. *batok.*

NAPKIN, n. *serbilyeta,* Sp.; *pámahirán.*

NARRATE, v. to relate a story, *magbuhay, ibuhay; magbida,* Sp.; *ibida.*

NARRATION, n. *pagbubuhay; pagbibida,* Sp.; short-story, *maiklíng-kathá.*

NARROW, adj. *makipot; makitid.*

NASAL, adj. (of sound) *pahumál;* pertaining to the nose, *pang-ilóng.*

NATION, n. *bansá (bansâ); nasyón,* Sp.

NATIONAL, adj. *pambansá, (pambansâ); nasyonál,* Sp.

NATIONALITY, n. *kabansahán, (kabansaán); lahì, lipì.*

NATIVE, adj. inborn, inherent, *katutubò;* born or produced in, *taál,* Sp.; or use. *tagá-* or *tubò sa...* + the place of birth.

NATIVITY, n. *kapangánakan.*

NATURAL, adj. *likás; naturál,* Sp.; inborn, innate, *katutubò.*

NATURE, n. *kalikasán.*

NAUGHT, n. nothing, *walâ.*

NAUGHTY, adj. *pilyo,* Sp.; mischievous, *malikót;* wayward, *makarás.*

NAUTILUS, n. *karakól,* Sp.

NAVY, n. *hukbóng-dagat.*

NEAR, adv. *malapit.*—prep. *malapit sa.*

NEARLY, adv. *halos.*

NECESSARY, adj. *kailangan.*

NECESSITY, n. *pangangailangan.*

NECK, n. *leég; liíg.*

NECKLACE, n. *kuwintás,* Sp.

NECKTIE, n. *kurbata,* Sp.

NEED, v. to stand in want, *mangailangan, kailanganin.*

NEEDLE, n. *karayom.*

NEEDY, n. *dahóp; hikahós.*

NEGATION, n. act of denying, *pagtanggí;* contradiction, *pananalansáng.*

NEGATIVE, adj. *patanggí; pasalansáng;* opposing, *laban, tutol.*

NEGLECT, v. *magpabayà, pabayaan;* to fail to pay attention to, *mákalingatán.*

NEGLECTFUL, adj. *pabayà; mapagpabayà.*

NEGOTIABLE, adj. for sale, *ipinagbíbilí;* can be bought, *mabíbilí.*

NEIGH, n. *halinghíng.*—v. *humalinghíng.*

NEIGHBOR, n. *kapitbahay.*

NEITHER, pron. not either, *alinmá'y hindí.*—conj. n. .... nor, *ni.... ni.*

NEPHEW, n. *pamangkíng lalaki.*

NERVOUS, adj. *ninénerbyos,* Sp.

NEST, n. *pugad.*

NEUROLOGY, n. *neurolohiya,* Sp.

NEUTER, adj. (Gram.) n. gender, *waláng kasarian.*

NEVER, adv. *kailanmá'y hindí.*

NEVERTHELESS, adv.-conj. *gayunmán.*

NEW, adj. *bago.*

NEWLY, adv. *bábago.*

NEWS, n. *balità.*

NEWSPAPER, n. *páhayagán.*

NEWSY, adj. *mabalità.*

NEXT, adj. *kasunód.*

NICE, adj. *mainam;* pleasant, *nakalúlugód.*

NICKEL, n. *nikel,* Sp.

NICKNACK, n. *alganás*, Sp.; *ka-gíkagí.*

NICKNAME, n. *palayaw; tagurî.*

NIECE, n. *pamangkíng babae.*

NIGHT, n. *gabí.*

NIGHTFALL, n. twilight, *takíp-silim.*

NIGHTLY, adj.-adv. *gabí-gabí.*

NIGHTMARE, n. *bangungot.*

NIMBLE, adj. quick, *maliksí.*

NINE, n.-adj. *siyám.*

NINETEEN, n.-adj. *labinsiyám.*

NINETEENTH, n.-adj. *ikalabin-siyám, ika-19.*

NINETIETH, n.-adj. *ikasiyamna-pû, ika-90.*

NINTY, n.-adj. *siyámnapû.*

NINTH, n.-adj. *ikasiyám, ika-9.*

NIPPLE, n. *utóng.*

NO, adv. *hindî;* don't, *huwàg.*

NOBLE, adj. *maharlikà;* high in rank, *mataás, matayog, mahál.*

NOBODY, pron. no one, *waláng sinumán;* of no value, *waláng-kabuluhan.*

NOCTURNAL, adj. *panggabí.*

NOD, v. *tumangô.*

NODE, n. *bukó.*

NOISE, n. *ingay;* clamor, *linggál*, outcry, *sigáw, hiyáw.*

NOISY, adj. *maingay;* clamorous, uproarious, *malinggál;* turbulent, *maguló.*

NOMINATE, v. to appoint, *hira-ngin;* propose or name (someone) for an office, *imungkahì.*

NOMINATIVE, adj. (Gram.) *palagyô.*

NONCHALANT, adj. *waláng-tigatig.*

NONE, pron. *walâ;* no one, *wa-láng sinumán.*

NONSENSE, n. *kahunghangán:* absurdity, *kabalighuán;* silliness, *kaululán.*

NOODLE, n. *miki*, Ch.

NOOK, n. *sulok, panulukan.*

NOON, n. *tanghalì.*

NOONTIME, n. *katanghalian.*

NOOSE, n. *silò.*

NORMAL, adj. *normál*, Sp.

NORTH, n.-adj. *hilagà.*

NORTHEAST, n-adj. *hilagang-silangan.*

NORTHWARD, adj.-adv. *pahila-gâ.*

NORTHWEST, n.-adj. *hilagang-kanluran.*

NOSE, n. *ilóng.*

NOSTRIL, n. *butas ng ilóng.*

NOT, adv. *hindî; walâ.*

NOTABLE, adj. worthy of attention, *kalimi-limì;* remarkable. *kapuná-puná;* distinguished, *li-táw, tanyág.*

NOTARY, n. *notaryo*, Sp.

NOTE, n. memorandum, *talâ, pa-gunitâ;* a letter, *liham, sulat;* mark or feature, *tandâ;* (Mus.) *nota*, Sp.—v. to observe, *pansi-nín;* pay attention to, *limiin.*

NOTEBOOK, n. *kuwaderno*, Sp.; *aklát-talaán.*

NOTED, adj. *litáw, tanyág.*

NOTEWORTHY, adj. *kapansín-pansín, kalimi-limì.*

NOTHING, n. *walâ.*

NOTICE. n. notification, *paunawà, pabatíd;* warning, *babalâ.*—v. to see, *mákita;* observe, *mápan-sín, pansinín.*

NOTICEABLE, adj. can be seen, *kita;* conspicuous, *lantád, ha-yág;* exposed to view, *litáw, kita.*

NOTIFY, v. to inform by notice, *magpaunawà, paunawaan;* have (it) told to, *magpasabi, pasabi-han.*

NOTION, n. *hakà;* idea, *akalà, isip.*

NOTWITHSTANDING, prep. *ka-hit...man* (as, n. the need, *ka-hit kailangan man*).—conj. *ga-yunmán.*—adv. *kahit na.*

NOUN, n. (Gram.) *pangngalan.*

NOURISH, v. to feed, *pakanin, magpakain;* foster, *kandilihin, kumandili.*

NOURISHMENT, n. food, *pagkain;* sustenance, *pang-agawbuhay;* nutriment, *pamawinggutom.*

NOVEL, n. *nobela,* Sp.; *kathambuhay.*—adv. of recent introduction, *bago; bagong labás, bagong litáw.*

NOVEMBER, n. *Nobyembre,* Sp.

NOVENA, n. *nubena,* Sp.; *pagsisiyám.*

NOVICE, n. *baguhan; nobisyo,* Sp.

NOW, adv. *ngayón.*

NOWADAYS, adv. *sa panahóng itó; sa kasalukuyan.*

NUCLEUS, n. *kabuurán,* nc.

NUMB, adj. *manhíd, namámanhíd.*

NUMBER, n. *bilang;* (Gram.) *kailanán;* a numeral, *pamilang.*

NUMERAL, n.-adj. *pamilang.*

NUMEROUS, adj. *maraming-marami.*

NURSE, n. *nars,* Eng.

NYMPH, n. *nimpa,* Sp.

O

OAR, n. *gaod, sagwán.*

OARSMAN, n. *manggagoad, mánanagwán.*

OATH, n. *sumpâ, panunumpâ.*

OBEDIENCE, n. *pagsunód, pagtalima.*

OBEDIENT, adj. *masúnurin.*

OBEY, v. *sumunód, sundín;* tumalima, talimahin.

OBJECT, n. aim, *pakay, adhíkain, layon;* (Gram.) *kagánapan, layon;* anything perceivable, *bagay.*

OBJECTION, n. *pagtutol; pagsalungát.*

OBJECTIONABLE, adj. undesirable, *di-kanais-nais.*

OBJECTIVE, adj. *láyunin, puntahin; nilálayon.*

OBLIGATION, n. duty, *tungkulin, katungkulan;* responsibility, *ságutin, kapanágutan.*

OBLIGATORY, adj. *sápilitán.*

OBLIGE, v. to compel by force, *pilitin; puwérsahín,* Sp.; gratify, *pagbigyán, pairugan.*

OBLIGING, adj. *mapagpairog.*

OBLIQUE, adj. *pahiwíd, pahirís.*

OBLITERATE, v. to erase, *pawiin, payiin.*

OBLIVION, n. *limot.*

OBLIVIOUS, adj. abstracted, *lingát, libáng;* forgetful, *malimutín.*

OBSCENE, adj. indecent, *mahalay.*

OBSCURE, adj. not clear, *malabò.*

OBSERVANCE, n. *pagtupád, pagganáp.*

OBSERVATION, n. *pagmamasíd, pagpansín;* remark, *pahayag, pansín; puná.*

OBSERVE, v. to see and note, *pansinín, limiin;* watch closely, *bantayán;* celebrate, *magdiwang, ipagdiwang.*

OBSERVER, n. *tagamasíd; tagapansín.*

OBSESSED, adj. *nahúhumaling.*

OBSESSION, n. act of being obsessed, *pagkahumaling;* (object) *kinahúhumalingan.*

OBSOLETE, adj. *lipás.*

OBSTACLE, n. *sagabal; balaksilà.*

OBSTINACY, n. *katigasán ng ulo.*

OBSTINATE, adj. *matigás ang ulo.*

OBSTRUCTION, n. *hadláng.*

OBVIOUS, adj. *halatâ;* easily seen, *kita;* evident, *malinaw.*

OCCASION, n. chance, opportunity, *pagkakátaón;* celebration, *pagdiriwang;* event, occurrence, *pangyayari.*

OCCASIONAL, adj. *paminsanminsan; manaká-nakâ.*

OCCULT, adj. concealed from observation, *tagô;* secret, *lihim;* hidden, *lingíd.*

OCCUPATION, n. act or state of possession, *pag-aarì; pamumusesyón,* Sp.; regular business or calling, *tungkulin, gáwain; trabaho,* Sp.

OCCUPY, v. to take possession, *kunin, pamusesyunán,* Sp.; dwell in, *tumirá, tirahán.*

OCCUR, v. to take place, *mangyari;* happen to come into one's mind, *máisip (sumaglì sa isip).*

OCCURRENCE, n. *pangyayari.*

OCEAN, n. *karagatan; dagat.*

OCTOBER, n. *Oktubre,* Sp.

ODD, adj. not even, *may-gansál;* peculiar, *kakatwâ.*

ODIOUS, adj. hateful, *kapoótpoót, nakapópoót.*

ODOR, n. *amóy;* scent, fragrance, *bangó, halimuyak.*

ODORIFEROUS, adj. scented, fragrant, *mabangó, mahalimuyak.*

OF, prep. in, on, *sa;* belonging to, *ng;* from, *galing sa, mulâ sa.*

OFF, adv.—The lid is off, *waláng takíp.*—My shoes are off. *Hubád ang aking sapatos.*—The trip is off. *Ang paglalakbáy ay di na mátutulóy.* — To take off

(something), *alisín, bakbakín.*— Two per cent off. *May-bawas na dalawáng bahagdán.*—Two miles of. *May-layong dalawáng milya.*—Off and on. *Manakánakâ.*—prep. Off the track. *Nápapalayô. Nápapalinsád.*—adj. — An òff day. *Araw na waláng gáwain. Araw na waláng pasok.* —The off side. *Kanan.*

OFFENCE, OFFENSE, n. act of angering, *panggagalit;* of vexing or annoying, *pangyayamót;* of affronting, *pandurustâ, paniniphayò.*

OFFEND, v. to make angry, *manggalit, galitin;* vex, annoy, *mangyamót, yamutin;* offer an affront, *mandustâ, dustain; maniphayò, siphayuin.*

OFFER, n, act of putting forward for acceptance. *alók;* proffer, *handóg;* act of setting down, *hayin, hain;* act of giving as memorial, *alay.*—v. *mag-alók, alukín;* to proffer, dedicate, *maghandóg, ihandóg, handugán;* set down, *maghayin, maghain; ihayin, ihain; hayinan, hainan;* give as memorial, *mag-alay, ialay, pag-alayan.*

OFFHAND, adj. extemporaneous, *biglaan.*—adv. *sa-biglaan.*

OFFICER, n. person who holds an office, *mánunungkulan; a* person of authority in the army or navy, *opisyál,* Sp.; *pinunò.*

OFFICIAL, adj. having to do with an office or officers, *pampámunuán;* approved by the proper authority, *opisyál,* Sp.; *pabatás,* nc.

OFFICIATE, v. *manúparan.*

OFFSPRING, n. *suplıng; anák.*

OFTEN, adv. *malimít frequent-*

OFTEN, adv. *malimít;* frequently, *madalás.*

OIL, n. *langís.*

OILER, n. *lángisan; aseytera.* Sp.

OILY, adj. *malangís; mamantikà,* Sp.

OLD, adj. *matandâ;* out of date, *lipás;* ancient, *laón;* of long experience, former, *dati, datihan.*

OLIVE, n. *oliba,* Sp.

OMELET, n. *torta,* Sp.; *tortilya,* Sp.

OMEN, n. *pángitaín.*

OMENTUM, n. (Anat.) *binubong.*

OMINOUS, adj. *nagbábalà; nagbábantâ.*

OMISSION, n. *paglaktáw; pagligtâ.*

OMIT, v. to leave out, *laktawán, iwan, bayaan; ligtaán.*

ON, prep. *sa;* above and touching, *nasà-ibabaw ng.*—adv. Go on. *Magpatuloy ka. Itulóy mo.*

ONCE, adv. *minsan.*—o. again, *minsan pa.*—o. in a while, *maminsan-minsan, paminsan-minsan.*

ONE, n.-adj. *isá.*—pron. anybody, *ang sínumán.*

ONENESS, n. *kaisahán; pagkaisá.*

ONEROUS, adj. burdensome, *mabigát.*

ONION, n. *sibuyas,* Sp.; *lasuná,* Ilok.

ONLOOKER, n. *mánonoód; mirón,* Sp.

ONLY, adj. sole, *tangì;* one and no more, *bugtóng, kaisá-isá.*—adv. merely, *lamang;* exclusively, *bukód-tangì.*

ONWARD, adv.-adj. forward, *pasulóng, patuloy.*

OPEN, adj. *bukás.* — v. *buksán, ibukás.*

OPENER, n. *pambukás.*

OPENING, n. hole, *butas;* beginning or manner of beginning,

pagsisimulâ; pag-uumpisá, Sp.; opportunity or chance, *pagkakátaón.*

OPERA, n. *óperá,* Sp.

OPERATE, v. to set in action or motion (as an engine or machine), *paandarín, magpaandár,* Sp.; *palakarin, magpalakad; patakbuhín, magpatakbó;* manage or direct, *mamahalà, pamahalaan; mangasiwà, pangasiwaan.*

OPERATION, n. (Surg.) *paninistís;* a surgical o. done, *pagkakátistís;* act of setting in action or motion, *pagpapaandar,* Sp.; *pagpapalakad, pagpapatakbó.*

OPINION, n. *palagáy;* belief, *paniwalà;* what one things about a subject, *pagpapalagáy, kurukurò.*

OPIUM, n. (Med.) *apyan,* Ch.

OPPONENT, n. *kalaban;* antagonist, *katunggalì;* enemy, *kaaway.*

OPPORTUNE, adj. timely, *nápapanahón, nasa-panahón.*

OPPORTUNIST, n. *taong mapagsamantalá.*

OPPORTUNITY, n. chance, *pagkakátaón;* convenient time, *kapanáhunan.*

OPPOSE, v. *lumaban, labanan;* to be or go against, *sumalungát, salungatín.*

OPPOSED, adj. *laban; salungát; tutol.*

OPPOSITE, adj. contrary, *salungát, kasalungát;* antagonistic, *kalaban;* placed or standing in front of, *katapát.*

OPPRESS, v. to crush by harsh or cruel rule, *siilín, maniíl;* treat with cruelty, *paglupitán, magmalupít.*

OPPRESSION, n. *paniníl;* cruel treatment, *pagmamalupít.*

OPPRESSOR, n. *máninííl.*

OPTICAL, adj. *pangmatá; ukol sa matá.*

OPTIMISM, n. *pagka-paláasá; pagka-maasahín.*

OPTIMIST, n.-adj. *paláasá; maasahín.*

OPTION, n. (Com.) *opsiyón,* Sp; *patalagá.*

OPULENCE, n. *kariwasaán.*

OPULENT, adj. *mariwasá.*

OR, conj. *o,* Sp.; *o kayá'y.*

ORACLE, n. *orákuló,* Sp.

ORAL, adj. using speech, *sa salitá; oral,* Eng.

ORANGE, n. *dalanghita,* Sp.; *sintunis, sinturis.*

ORATION, n. *talumpatì; patì.*

ORATOR, n. *mánanalumpatì; oradór,* Sp.

ORB, n. a circle, *bilog;* globe, *globo,* Sp.; sphere, *bilo.*

ORBIT, n. path of a star, *daángtalà.*

ORCHARD, n. *looban; hálamanán.*

ORCHESTRA, n. *orkesta,* Sp.

ORCHID, n. *sanggumay.*

ORDEAL, n. severe test, *mahigpít na pagtitikím;* terrible experience, *kahilá-hilakbót na karanasan.*

ORDER, n. sequence, *pagkakásunúd-sunód;* regular method of action, *ayos, kaayusan;* established custom, *kalakarán; kaugalián;* command, *utos;* rule, *tuntunin;* law, *batás;* regulation, *álituntunin;* public quiet, *katahimikan;* a direction to purchase, *pabilí; bilin, pabilin.*—v. to command, *mag-utos, utusan, pag-utusan;* arrange systematically, *mag-ayos, iayos, ayusin.*

ORDERLINESS, n. *kaayusan; pagka-maayos.*

ORDERLY, adj. in order, *maayos;* well-arranged, *mahusay; areglado,* Sp.; neat, *maimis;* peaceable, quiet, *tahimik.* — n. attendant, *katulong;* o. officer, *tagaganáp.*

ORDINANCE, n. statute, *kautusán; kabatasán.*

ORDINARY, adj. usual, *karaniwan;* commonplace, *pangkaraniwan.*

ORE, n. *inambató.*

ORGAN, n. *órganó,* Sp.; functional part (of an animal or plant) *bahagi, sangkáp;* means of expression, *tagabanság, tagapamanság.*

ORGANIZATION, n. act or process of putting together, *pagbubuô;*, of arranging, *pag-aayos, pagsasaayos;* association, society, *kapisanan, samahán.*

ORGANIZE, v. *magtatag, itatag.*

ORIENT, adj. rising (like the sun) *ninikat, ninilang;* pertaining to the east, *pansilangan.*— n. the east, *silangan.*

ORIENTAL, adj. eastern, *pansilangan, silanganín.*

ORIGIN, n. the beginning, *simulâ;* source, *pinagmulán, pinanggalingan;* cause, *dahil, sanhî;* derivation, *pinaghanguan.*

ORIGINAL, adj. first, *una;* primitive, *pángunahín;* not copied, *sariling-kathâ.*

ORNAMENT, n. decoration, *palamuti;* adornment, *gayák, parinoal.*

ORNITHOLOGY, n. *paláibunan.*

ORPHAN, n.-adj. *ulila.*

ORPHANAGE, n. *ampunan ng mga ulila.*

ORPHANED, adj. *naulila.*

OSCILLATE, v. to swing backward and forward, *tumayuntayon.*

OSMOSIS, n. *pagtayas.*

OSTENTATIOUS, adj. fond of show, *mapagparangyâ;* intended for vain display, *pamparangyâ.*

OSTRACIZE, v. *itakwíl.*

OTHER, adj.-pron. *ibá.*

OTHERWISE, adv. in a different way, *sa ibáng paraán.*—conj. *dili kayá'y, o kayá'y.*

OUGHT, v. aux. *dapat, nárarapat.*

OUNCE, n. *onsa,* Sp.

OUR, pron. (prepositive) *atin;* (postpositive) *natin.*

OUT, adv. outside, *sa labás.*—adj. not in, absent, *walâ.*

OUTBREAK, n. *pagsilakbó; silakbó.*

OUTCOME, n. consequence, *kinálabsán;* fruit, *bunga.*

OUTDO, v. to surpass, *malaluan; madaíg, daigín; mahigtán.*

OUTDOORS, n.-adv. *sa labás.*

OUTER, adj. *panlabás; labás.*

OUTFIT, n. equipment, *kagamitán.*

OUTGOING, adj. leaving, departing, *paalís.*

OUTGROWTH, n. *tubò, siból, suloy.*

OUTING, n. excursion, *eskursiyón,* Sp.; a pleasure trip, *pagliliwalíw.*

OUTLOOK, n. a place from which a person watches or observes, *bantayan, tánawan;* the view, *tánawin;* prospect for the future, hope, *pag-asa;* a way of looking at a thing, *pagtingín, tingín; palagáy.*

OUTLAW, n. *tulisán; bandido,* Sp.

OUTLET, n. *lábasan; pálabasán.*

OUTLINE, n. *banghây; balangkás.*

OUTNUMBER, v. to exceed in number, *malaluan sa bilang.*

OUTRAGE, n. a going beyond bounds, *kalampasán; kabalba-*

lán; unlawful violence, *karahasán; kapalibhasaan.*

OUTRIGGER, n. *katig; batangan.*

OUTSIDE, n. *labás;* outer surface, *pangibabaw.*—adj.-adv. *sa labás ng.*

OUTSTANDING, adj. prominent, *litáw, tanyág;* (Com.) uncollected, *síngilin;* (Com.) unpaid, *báyarin.*

OVAL, adj. *bilóg-habâ;* egg-shaped, *hugis-itlóg; tabas-itlóg.*

OVEN, n. *hurnó,* Sp.

OVER, prep. *sa ibabaw ng; sa itaás ng;* beyond the top or edge, *sa kabilâ ng, sa ibayo ng.*—adv. across, *sa kabilâ, sa ibayo;* turning top down, *pabaligtád.*

OVERALLS, n. *oberols,* Eng.

OVERCOME, v. to get the better of, *madaíg, daigín; makapanaíg;* conquer, *malupig, lupigin; matalo, talunin.*

OVERDUE, adj. *lampás sa taning.*

OVEREAT, v. *magpakabulták.*

OVERFLOW, v. to flood over, *bumahâ, bahaán;* (slight) *magsanaw, masanawan.*

OVERHEAR, v. *máulinigan.*

OVERLAP, v. *isanib, pagsanibin.*

OVERLAPPING, adj. *magkasanib; nagkakásanib.*

OVERRUN, v. *mangalat, pangalatan.*

OVERSIGHT, n. *pagkalingát.*

OVERTAKE, v. *abutan, maabutan.*

OVERTIME, n. *obertaim,* Eng.; (at night) *lamay.*

OVERTURN, v. to upset, *matiwás, tiwasín.*

OVERWHELM, v. to cover over completely, *mátabunan, tabunan;* bear down upon from all sides so as to crush or destroy, *pagtalikupan;* drown, *lunurin.*

OVERWORK, v. *magpakalabis sa paggawá.*

OWE, v. to be in debt, *magkautang.*—I owe you ten pesos. *May utang akóng sampúng piso sa iyó.*

OWL, n. *kuwago,* Sp.; *baháw.*

OWN, adj. *sarili, panarili.*—v. I own this, *Akin itó.*

OWNERSHIP, n. *pagka-may-arì.*

OYSTER, n. *talabá.*

P

PACE, n. step, *hakbáng;* gait, *bilís (tulin) ng lakad (takbó).*

PACIFIC, adj. peaceable, *mapanahimik.*—P. O c e a n, *Karagatang Pasípikó.*

PACIFY, v. to make quiet, *papanahimikin;* appease (as a baby), *patahanin, aluin.*

PACK, n. bundle, *balutan; bastá; binalot; pakete,* Sp.—v. to arrange securely and closely in a container, *mag-empake,* Sp.; *empakihin,* Sp.; crowd together, *siksikín;* fill, *punuin.*

PACKAGE, n. *pakete,* Sp.; *binalot, balutan.*

PACT, n. *kásunduan.*—Blood p., *sandúguan.*

PAD, n. cushion to lessen pressure, *sapín;* a block of sheets of paper. *pad,* Eng.

PADDING, n. *pading,* Eng.; *pampakapál.*

PADDLE, n. oar, *gaod, sagwán.*

PADLOCK, n. *kandado,* Sp.—v. *kandaduhan,* Sp.

PAGAN, n. *di-binyagan; pagano,* Sp.

PAGE, n. *páhiná,* Sp.; *panig, dahon.*

PAGEANT, n. *palabás, pakita;* exhibition, *tanghál.*

PAID, adj. *bayád na;* hired, *upahan.*

PAIL, n. *timbá; baldé,* Sp.

PAIN, n. *sakít; hapdi; kirót.*

PAINFUL, adj. *masakít; mahapdi; makirót.*

PAINT, n. coloring pigment, *pintura,* Sp.; *pampintá,* Sp.—v. to portray with paint, *magpintá, ipintá;* decorate by use of p., *pintahán.*

PAINTING, n. *pintura,* Sp.; *pintá,* Sp.

PAIR, n. *paris;* the two, *ang dalawá;* partners (in dancing), *magkapareha.*

PAJAMAS, n. *padyamas,* Eng.

PAL, n. *katoto.*

PALACE, n. *palasyo,* Sp.; *bahayharì; bahay-makaharì.*

PALATABLE, adj. *malinamnám;* savorous, *malasa.*

PALATE, n. (Anat.) roof of mouth, *ngaláŋgalá;* sense of taste, *panlasa.*

PALE, adj. *maputlá;* pallid, *barák.*

PALL, v. to become wearisome, *makainíp; makasuyà.* — (Ecc.) covering of a chalice or hearse, *palyo,* Sp.

PALLET, n. small, rough bed, *papag.*

PALLOR, n. lack of color, *kaputlaán;* (of the face) *kabarakán, pamamarák.*

PALM, n. (of hand) *palad.*

PALPABLE, adj. *nádaramá; nádadamá;* obvious, clear, *malinaw.*

PALPITANT, adj. throbbing, *tumítibók;* quivering, *sumísikdó.*

PALPITATE, v. to beat or throb, *tumibók;* flutter, *sumikdó, kumutób.*

PALSIED, adj. *nangángatál; pasmado,* Sp.

PALTRY, adj. small, *muntî;* very little, *katitíng.*

PAMPER, v. *palayawin; papamisanhín.*

PAMPHLET, n. *pamplet,* Eng.; *polyeto,* Sp.; *muntaklát,* cw.

PAN, n. tray, *bandeha,* Sp.— frying p., *kawalî.*—wash p., *batyá.*

PANIC, n. *giklá, gulilat;* fear, *takot.*

PANICKY, adj. *gulilát; takót.*

PANORAMA, n. *tánawin.*

PANT, v. *humingal.*—n. *hingal.*

PANTRY, n. *páminggalan.*

PAPA, n. father, *amá;* daddy, *tatay, tatang, itáy.*

PAPER, n. *papél,* Sp..—toilet p., *pang-iwang, pamandewang.*

PARABLE, n. *katháng may aral.*

PARACHUTE, n. *payong-bitinán,* nc.; *parakaida,* Sp.

PARADE, n. *parada,* Sp.

PARADISE, n. *paraiso,* Sp.

PARADOX, n. *kabalintunaan.*

PARAGRAPH, n. *talatà, puktô.*

PARALLEL, adj. (Geom.) *magkabalalay, kabalalay.*

PARALYSIS, n. (Med.) *parálisís,* Sp.; *pagkalumpó.*

PARAMOUNT, adj. *higít sa lahát.*

PARAPHERNALIA, n. accessories, *kagamitán; sangkáp, kasangkapan.*

PARASITE, n. *dapò.*

PARASITIC, adj. *dapò; máninipsip.*

PARASOL, n. *payong.*

PARCEL, n. *balutan; pakete,* Sp.

PARCHMENT, n. *pergamino,* Sp.

PARDON, n. *kapatawarán.* — v. *patawarin.*

PARDONABLE, adj. *mapatátawad.*

PARE, v. *talupan; akbahín.*

PARENT, n. *magulang;* source, *pinagmulán, pinanggalingan.*

PARENTAGE, n. birth, descent, *kaangkanan. angkán.*

PARENTHESIS, n. *panaklóng, pangulóng.*

PARISH, n. *parokya,* Sp.

PARK, n. *parke,* Sp.; *liwasan.*

PARLIAMENT, n. *parlamento,* Sp.; *bátasan.*

PARLOR, n. *salas,* Sp.

PARODY, n. *parodya,* Sp.; *patawá.*

PAROXYSM, n. *sasál; silakbó.*

PARROT, n. *loro,* Sp.; *papagayo,* Sp.

PARRY, v. *manalág, sumalág, salagín.*

PARSE, v. *suriin;* to analyze grammatically, *balarilain.*

PARSIMONIOUS, adj. stingy, *maramot;* close, *maimot, maigot.*

PARSIMONY, n. stinginess, *karamutan;* closeness, *kaimutan, kaigutan.*

PARSON, n. *klérigo,* Sp.; *kura,* Sp.; *parè* (*parì*), Sp.; *pastór,* Sp.

PART, n. *bahagi;* piece, *piraso,* Sp.; section, *pangkát;* element, *sangkáp.*—v. to divide, *hatiin;* separate, *maghiwaláy;* leave, *umalís.*

PARTAKE, v. to take some part in, *makisama;* partaking in any action is expressed by *maki-* plus the root denoting the action as, *makikain,* to eat together with others; *makikuha,* to join others in getting (something), etc.

PARTICIPANT, n. one who takes part, *kasali.*

PARTICIPLE, n. (Gram.) *pandiwarì.*

PARTICLE, n. a very small piece, *katitíng;* a bit, *sambutil;* (Gram.) *katagá.*

PARTICULAR, adj. distinct from others, *ibá, tangì, bukód;* fastidious, *maselang; palápili.*

PARTING, n. separation, *paghihiwaláy.*—adj. given when taking leave, *pahimakás.*

PARTITION, n. act of dividing, *paghahatì, pagbabahagi;* a wall dividing rooms in a building, *dindíng.*

PARTITIVE, adj. (Gram.) *pamahagi; panghatì.*

PARTLY, adv. not wholly, *dilahát.*

PARTNER, n. *kasama, kasamá;* (in dancing) *kasayáw;* (in business) *kasosyo,* Sp., *kabakas.*

PARTNERSHIP, n. (Com.) *bákasan.*

PARTURITION, n. *panganganák.*

PARTY, n. social gathering, *pagtitipon; parti,* Eng.; political group, *lápian; partido,* Sp.

PASS, v. *dumaán, magdaán.*—n. way, *daán, landás;* permit, *pases;* Sp.; *pahintulot.*

PASSENGER, n. *sakáy; pasahero,* Sp.

PASSERS-BY, n. *ang mga dumaraán.*

PASSION, n. suffering (as of Christ), *pagdurusa, sakit;* outburst of feeling, *damdaming masilakbó;* anger, *galit;* love, *pagibig, pagsintá;* intense desire, *pagkahumaling.*

PASSIONATE, adj. *madamdamin;* amorous, *masintahin.*

PASSIVE, adj. enduring without resistance, *waláng-tutol;* (Gram.) p. voice, *tinig balintiyák.*

PASSPORT, n. *pasaporte,* Sp.; *raw, nc.*

PASSWORD, n. *hudyát; kontrasenyas,* Sp.

PAST, adj. *nakaraán, nagdaán, nakalipas.*—n. the p., *ang nagdaán, ang nakalipas; ang kahapon.*

PASTE, n. glue, *kola,* Sp.; *pandigkít.*

PASTEBOARD, n *kartón,* Sp.

PASTIME, n. sport, *laró;* recreation, *áliwan;* diversion, *dibersiyón,* Sp.; *libangan.*

PASTURE, n. grass, *damó;* livestock feed, *kumpáy;* grassland, *pastulan,* Sp.; *damuhán.*

PAT, v. *tapikín.*—n. *tapík.*

PATCH, n. *tagpî.*

PATELLA, n. *bayugo ng tuhod.*

PATENT, adj. open to public view, *lantád, hayág.*—n. a right or privilege (as to manufacture an invention), *patente,* Sp.

PATH, n. footway, *landás;* track, *bagnós;* road *daán.*

PATHETIC, adj. *nakalúlunos; kalunus-lunos.*

PATHOLOGIST, n. *patólogó,* Sp.

PATHOLOGY, n. *patolohiya,* Sp.

PATHOS, n. *lunos, kalunusan.*

PATIENCE, n. *pagtitiis; pagtitiyagà, katiyagaán.*

PATIENT, adj. *mapagtiís, matíisin; matiyagâ, mapagtiyagâ.*

PATIENT, n. sick person, *ang maysakít.*

PATRIARCH, n. *apò.*

PATRIMONY, n. *mana, minana.*

PATRIOT, n. *makabayan; taong magiting.*

PATRIOTIC, n. *makabayan; magiting.*

PATROL, n. *patrolya,* Sp.; *ronda,* Sp.; *bantáy, tanod.*

PATRON, n. *tagataguyod; taga-pag-adya; patrón,* Sp.

PATTERN, n. *tularán, parisán, húwaran.*

PAUSE, v. *tumigíl sandalî.*

PAVEMENT, n. *latag na bató;* sidewalk, *banketa,* Sp.

PAWN, v. *magsanglâ, isanglâ.*

PAWNSHOP, n. *bahay-sanglaan.*

PAY, v. to make payment, *magbayad, bayaran;* (n. recompense for service) *umupa, upahan.*

PAYMASTER, n. *peymaster,* Eng.; *pagador,* Sp.; *tagabayad.*

PAYMENT, n. *bayad;* recompense, *upa.*

PEA, n. *gisantes,* Sp.; *kagyús.*

PEACE, n. *kapayapaán.*

PEACEFUL, adj. *payápà; mapayapà.*

PEACH, n. *milokotón,* Sp.

PEACOCK, n. *pábureál,* Sp.

PEAK, n. *taluktók; tugatog.*

PEAL, n. *kagungkóng;* echoing noise, *alingawngáw.*

PEANUT, n. *maní,* Cub.

PEAR, n. *peras,* Sp.

PEARL, n. *mutyâ; perlas,* Sp.

PEASANT, n. *taong-bukid, tagabukid.*

PECK, v. *tumukâ, manukâ, tukaín.*

PECULIAR, adj. *kaibá;* queer, *kakatwâ.*

PEDANTIC, adj. *mápagdunúng-dunungan.*

PEDDLER, n. *maglalakò; tagapaglakò.*

PEDESTAL, n. *patungán; pedestál,* Sp.; *pátuntungan.*

PEEK, v. to peep, *sumilip, silipin.*

PEEL, v. *talupan.*

PEERLESS, adj. without equal, *waláng-kapantáy.*

PEG, n. *kalabiha,* Sp.

PEN, n. instrument for writing with ink, *pluma,* Sp.; *panulat;* coop, *kulungín* (pigpen, *ulbó, banlát*).

PENALTY, n. *parusa;* fine or forfeit, *multa,* Sp.

PENANCE, n. *pagpapakasakit.*

PENCIL, n. *lapis,* Sp.

PENDING, adj. *nábibitin;* pending, Eng.; *tápusin, lútasin.*

PENDULUM, n. *palawít, patangô; péndulô,* Sp.

PENETRATE, v. *tumagós, tagusán; tumaláb, talbán;* to enter, *pumasok, sumuót; pasukin, suutin.*

PENINSULA, n. *halos-pulô,* nc.

PENITENCE, n. repentance, *pagsisisi.*

PENITENT, adj. *nagsísisi.*

PENITENTIARY, n. state prison, *bilibid;* jail, *píitan, bilangguan;* house of correction, *bahay-páwastuan.*

PENKNIFE, n. *lanseta, laseta,* Sp.

PENNANT, n. *bandirola,* Sp.

PENNILESS, n. *salát; hikahós; waláng-kuwarta.*

PENSION, n. *pensiyón,* Sp.

PENSIVE, adj. *nag-iisíp;* reflective, *mapanimdim;* musing, *mapagniláy-nilay.*

PENT-UP, adj. *tinimpî.*

PENULTIMATE, adj. (of stress of pronunciation) *malumay;* before the last, *una sa hulí.*

PEOPLE, n. *mga tao;* the public, *ang madlâ, ang públikó,* Sp.

PEP, n. *siglá, buhay; brio,* Sp.

PEPPER, n. (plant) *sili;* (powdered) *pamintá.*

PEPPERY, adj. (in taste) *maanghảng.*

PER, prep. through, *sa pamamagitan ng;* for each, *sa bawa't.*

PERCEIVE, v. to become aware of, *mápansín; mádamá.*

PER CENT, n. *bahagdán*, nc.

PERCENTAGE, n. *bahagdán*, nc.

PERCH, v. to roost, *humapon.*—n. roosting place, *hapunán.*

PERCHANCE, adv. *kaypalà;* perhaps, *marahil.*

PEREMPTORY, adj. decisive, *waláng-badlíng;* final, *tápusan.*

PERFECT, adj. complete, *ganáp;* utter, *labós;* finished, *tapós, yarì.*

PERFECTION, n. supreme excellence, *kágalíng-galingan;* completeness, *kálubús-lubusan.*

PERFIDIOUS, adj. *taksíl, lilo.*

PERFIDY, n. *kataksilán, kaliluhan.*

PERFORCE, adv. *sápilitán.*

PERFORM, v. to do, *gawín;* carry out, *isagawâ.*

PERFUME, n. *pabangó.*

PERGOLA, n. *balag.*

PERHAPS, adv. *marahil.*

PERIL, n. danger, *panganib.*

PERILOUS, adj. dangerous, *mapanganib.* .

PERIOD, n. a portion of time, *panahón;* a dot, *tuldók.*

PERISH, v. to be destroyed, *mapuksâ;* come to nothing, *malipol.*

PERISHABLE, adj. *masiraín.*

PERMANENT, adj. *pánatilihan; pámalagian.*

PERMISSION, n. *pahintulot, kapahintulután.*

PERMIT, v. *magpahintulot, pahintulutan.*

PERNICIOUS, adj. *paminsalà.*

PERPENDICULAR, adj. *patirík, tirík.*

PERPETUAL, adj. everlasting, *panghabang-panahón.*

PERPETUATE, v. to preserve, *pagyamanin.*

PERPLEX, v. to be confused, *ma-*

gulumihanan; bewilder, *lingmingin.*

PERSECUTION, n. *pag-uusig.*

PERSEVERANCE, n. *tiyagâ, pagtitiyagâ, katiyagaán, pagkamatiyagâ;* constant effort, *sigasig; sigsá.*

PERSEVERE, v. *magtiyagâ;* continue steadfastly, *magmasigasig, pagsigasigan;* continue industriously, *magsigsá, pagsigsahán.*

PERSIST, v. *magpilit, pagpilitan; magpakapilit; magpumilit, pagpumilitan.*

PERSON, n. man, *tao;* one'ş self, *sarili;* personality, *katauhan, pagkatao;* (Gram.) *panauhan.*

PERSONABLE, adj. attractive, *kaakit-akit.*

PERSONAL, adj. *panarili, pansarili;* (Gram.) *panao.*

PERSONALITY, n. *katauhan, pagkatao;* individuality, *kasarilihan.*

PERSONNEL, n. *tauhan.*

PERSPIRATION, n. sweat, *pawis.*

PERSPIRE, v. *pawisan.*

PERSUADE, v. *manghikayat, hikayatin.*

PERSUASION, n. *paghikayat, panghihikayat.*

PERSUASIVE, adj. *mapanghikayat.*

PERTURB, v. to produce mental disquiet, *tigatigin.*

PERTURBATION, n. disquiet of the mind, *pagkatigatig.*

PERTUSSIS, n. (Med.) *ubóngdalahit.*

PERVERSE, adj. *balakyót.*

PESSIMISTIC, adj. *may-lumangpag-asa; patáy-pag-asa.*

PEST, n. *peste,* Sp.; plague,. *salot.*

PETAL, n. (Bot.) *talulot.*

PERSECUTE, v. *usigin, pag-usigin.*

PETITION, n. *hiling, kahilingán.*

PETROLEUM, n. *gas,* Sp.; *petrolyo,* Sp.

PHANTASY, n. hallucination, *talimuwáng;* illusion, *kinikitá.*

PHARMACY, n. *parmasya,* Sp.

PHILOSOPHER, n. *pilósopó,* Sp.; *talisik,* nc.

PHILOSOPHY, n. *pilosopyá,* Sp.; *tálisikan,* nc.

PHLEGM, n. *plema,* Sp.; *kanighalá, kalaghalá.*

PHONETICS, PHONICS, n. *palátinigan.*

PHONOGRAPH, n. *ponógrapó,* Sp.

PHOTOGRAPH, n. *larawan;* retrato, Sp.

PHOTOGRAPHER, n. *retratista,* Sp.

PHRASE, n. (Gram.) *parirala.*

PHYSICIAN, n. *manggagamot; médikó,* Sp.

PHYSICS, n. *písiká,* Sp.

PHYSIOGNOMY, n. *pagmumukhá.*

PIANIST, n. *piyanista,* Sp.

PIANO, n. *piyano,* Sp.

PICK, v. to choose, select, *pumili, piliin, mamili.*

PICKET, n. pointed stake, *tulos, urang.*

PICKLE, n. *atsara,* Sp.

PICNIC, n. *piknik,* Eng.; *kurà.*

PICKPOCKET, n. *mandurukot.*

PICTURE, n. *larawan.*

PIECE, n. a part of anything. *kuputol; kapiraso,* Sp.

PIER, n. *piyér,* Eng.; *doongán, dáungan.*

PIERCE, v. to punch with a hole, *butasin.*

PIETY, n. *kabánalan.*

PIG. n. *baboy.*

PIGEON, n. wild dove, *batubató;* dove, *kalapati.*

PIGMENT, n. coloring matter, *pangulay; pangulór,* Sp.

PIGTAIL, n. queue, *tirintás.*

PILE, n. heap, *buntón.*—v. to heap up, *ibuntón, magbuntón.*

PILFER, v. *mang-umít, umitín.*

PILGRIM, n. *maypakay.*

PILGRIMAGE, n. *pamamakay.*

PILL, n. *pildurás,* Sp.; *butil.*

PILLAR, n. post, *haligi.*

PILLOW, n. *unan.*

PILOT, n. *piloto,* Sp.; *tagaugit.*

PIMIENTO, n. *pamintón,* Sp.

PIMPLE, n. *tagihawat.*

PIMPLY, adj. *matagihawat, tágihawatín.*

PIN, n. (for clothes) *aspilí,* Sp.—safety p., *emperdible,* Sp.—hair p., *aguhilya,* Sp.; *talsók.*—bowling p., *bulilyo,* Sp.

PINCERS, n. *sipit, pansipit.*

PINCH, v. to squeeze between finger and thumb, *mangurót, kurutín.*

PINEAPPLE, n. *pinyá,* Sp.

PINK, n.-adj. *rosas,* Sp.

PINNACLE, n. *karurukan;* summit, *taluktók.*

PIOUS, adj. *banál.*

PIPE, n. tube, *tubo,* Sp.; smoking p., *kuwako, pipa,* Sp.; (musical) *pito,* Sp.

PISTOL, n. *rebolber,* Sp.

PISTON, n. *pistón,* Sp.

PIT, n. hole in the ground, *hukay;* hollow, *lugóng.*

PITCH, n. asphalt, *aspalto;* high tone, *tinís, katinisán.* — v. to erect, *itayô, itindíg;* throw, hurl, *ihagis.*

PITCHER, n. (in baseball) *pitser,* Eng.; container for liquids, *pitsél,* Sp.

PITFALL, n. *pábuslutan; kahúhulugan, ikahúhulog;* trap, *patibóng.*

PITH, n. *ubod.*

PITIABLE, adj. arousing pity, *nakaháhabag, kahabág - habág;* arousing sympathy, *nakalúlunos, kalunus-lunos.*

PITILESS, adj. *waláng-habág;* merciless, *waláng-awà.*

PITY, n. *habág;* compassion, *pagkaawà.*

PIVOT, n. *páikután; pinagpápaikutan.*

PLACARD, n. *kartelón,* Sp.

PLACE, n. *poók; lugál, lugár,* Sp.; (Gram.) *lunán.*

PLAGIARISM, n. *pláhiyó,* Sp.; *panunulad.*

PLAGIARIST, n. *plahiyadór,* Sp.; *mánunulad.*

PLAGUE, n. scourge, *salot.*

PLAIN, adj. level, *patag;* clear (as, p. view) *kita, lantád;* without decoration, not luxurious or rich, *lisdíng.*

PLAINS, n. broad stretches of level country, *kapatagan.*

PLAINTIFF, n. (Law) *maysakdál.*

PLAINTIVE, adj. *malumbáy;* sad, *malungkót.*

PLAN, n. *bangháy;* diagram, *balangkás;* a way proposed, *panukalà.*

PLANE, adj. flat, *lapád;* tool for smoothing wood, *katám.*

PLANET, n. *planeta,* Sp.; *talà.* (Star, *bituin*).

PLANK, n. *tablá.*

PLANT, n. *taním, pananim;* machinery, apparatus, etc., *planta,* Sp.

PLANTATION, n. hacienda, *asyenda,* Sp.; *pátaniman.*

PLANTER, n. *magtatanim.*

PLASMA, n. (Med.) *pinakatubig; plasma,* Lat.

PLATE, n. metal in sheets, *ohas,* Sp.; *dahon;* dish, *pinggán; plato,* Sp.

PLATEAU, n. *talampás.*

PLATFORM, n. *plataporma.* Sp.

PLATING, n. *kalupkóp.*

PLAY, n. game, *larô;* jest, *birò.*— v. to engage in sport, *maglaró;* toy with, *paglaruán.*

PLAYER, n. *manlalarò.*

PLAYFUL, adj. *malaró; mapaglarô.*

PLAYGROUND, n. *pálaruan.*

PLAYING CARDS, n. *baraha,* Sp.

PLAYMATE, n. *kalarô.*

PLAYTHING, n. toy, *laruán.*

PLAYWRIGHT, n. *mandudulà.*

PLEA, n. entreaty, *pamanhík, pakiusap;* appeal, *panawagan.*

PLEAD, v. *mamanhík, makiusap:* make an appeal, *manawagan.*

PLEASANT, adj. pleasing, *nakalúlugód, kalugúd-lugód.*

PLEASE, v. to give pleasure, *magbigáy-lugód;* gratify, *pairugan;* be pleased, *malugód.* — adv. expressed by *ngâ* or by *paki-* and *ipaki-,* as, to please get, *pakikunin;* to request that something be taken, *ipakikuha,* etc.

PLEASURE, n. *lugód;* enjoyment, *pagtatamasa;* joy, *galák.*

PLEBISCITE, n. *plebisito,* Sp.

PLEDGE, n. *sanglâ;* guaranty, *akò;* promise, *pangakò.*

PLENTIFUL, adj. abundant, *saganà;* in seasonal plenty, *saksâ.*

PLENTY, n. abundance, *kasaganaán.*

PLIERS, n. *plais,* Eng.

PLOT, n. a small area of ground. *isáng lagáy ng lupà;* a conspiracv, *sábuwatan, sápakatan.*

PLOW, n. *araro,* Sp.—v. *magararo, araruhin.*

PLOWSHARE, n. *sudsód.*

PLUCK, v. to pull off or out, *bunutin;* pick (flowers), *mamitás, pitasín;* pull off (feathers of fowl or bird), *himulmulán;* twang (a stringed musical instrument), *kalbitín, tugtugín.*

PLUCKY, adj. *may malakás na loób; malakás ana loób·* brave, *matapang.*

PLUG, n. anything used to stop a hole, *pasak.*

PLUMBER, n. *plumero,* Sp.: *tubero,* Sp.

PLUNDER, v. *mandambóng;* to steal, *magnakaw.*

PLURAL, adj. (Gram.) *máramihan.*

POCKET, n *bulsá,* Sp.; bag, pouch, *supot.*

POEM, n. *tulâ.*

POET, n. *makatà.*

POETIC, adj. *patulâ; túlain.*

POINT, n. sharp end, *tulis;* tip of sharp end, *tilos;* tip, *dulo;* period, dot, *tuldók.*—v. to indicate something by the finger or some stick, *iturò.*

POINTED, adj. *tulís, matulis, patulis.*

POINTER, n. *puntero,* Sp.: *panturò.*

POINTLESS, adj. senseless, *waláng-tinútungo.*

POISE, n. steadiness, *pagka-matatág;* personal carriage, *tindíg, kiyà.*

POISON, n. *lason.*

POISONOUS, adj. *maylason.*

POLE, n. post, *poste,* Sp.; (made of bamboo) *tikín.*

POLICE, n. *pulís,* Eng.

POLICY, n. a fixed course or method, *pasunód, palakad;* insurance agreement, *pólisá,* Sp.

POLISH, v. to make smooth and glossy, *bulihin, pakintabín.*—n. smooth and glossy surface, *buli,*

kintáb; social good manners, *kabutihang-asal.*

POLITE, adj. courteous, *magalang, mapitagan.*

POLITICAL, adj. *pampolítiká,* Sp.

POLITICIAN, n. *polítikó,* Sp.

POLITICS, n. *polítiká,* Sp.

POLL, n. casting of votes, *pagboto,* Sp., *paghahalál;* recording of votes *pagtatalâ ng mga boto;* the place where votes are cast, *presinto,* Sp.

POMADE, n. *pumada,* Sp.

POMP, n. *karingalan.*

POND, n. *dagatan: munting dagatan.*

PONDER, v. *magniláy-nilay, pagniláy-nilayin; pagkurú-kuruin.*

PONIARD, n. *punyál,* Sp.; *daga, balarâw.*

POOL, n. amount contributed in a venture, *bákasan;* small body of standing liquid, *sanaw;* small body of fresh water, *dayatan.*—swimming p., *pálanguyan.*

POOR, adj. *dukhâ, mahirap;* needy, *salát, dahóp.*

POPCORN, n. *binusáng mais; busá.*

POPE, n. *Papa,* Sp.

POPLIN, n. *paplín,* Eng.

POPULAR, adj. approved by many people, *populár,* Sp.; widespread, *laganap, palasak;* of the common people, *pangmadlâ;* easy to understand, *magaán, maalwán.*

POPULATION, n. *mámamayán;* the people, *ang mga tao.*

POPULOUS, adj. *matao.*

PORK, n. *karning-baboy,* (*karné,* Sp.)

PORRIDGE, n. (of rice) *nilugaw;* (of beans, peas, etc.) *sinigáng.*

PORT, n. harbor, *sadsaran, doongán, dáungan.*

PORTABLE, adj. *dálahin, bitbitin; portatíl,* Sp.

PORTER, n. doorkeeper, *portero,* Sp.; *bantáy-pintô;* attendant, *tcqapaglingkód.*

PORTFORLIO, n. *lukbutan; portpolyo,* Eng.

PORTION, n. share, *bahagi.*

POSITION, n. *lagáy, kalágayan; tayô, katáyuan;* employment, *tungkulin, empleo,* Sp.; job, work, *trabajo,* Sp.

POSITIVE, adj. definite, certain, *tiyák;* f a vo r a b l e, *paayón,* (Gram.) *lantáy.*

POSSESS, v. *magtagláy;* to own, *mag-arì.*

POSSESSION, n. property, *pagaarì;* act of holding as one's own, *pamumusesyón,* Sp.

POSSESSIVE, adj. *mapang-arì;* (Gram.) *paarî.*

POSSIBLE, adj. *maáarì.*—p. to happen, *maáaring mangyari.*

POST, n. *poste,* Sp.; *haligi,* (used as support) *tukod;* mail, *koreó.* —p. of duty, *tungkulin.*

POSTAGE, n. *halagá ng selyo.*

POSTAL, adj. *pangkoreo,* Sp.

POSTERIOR, adj. *hulí, hulihán, panghulí.*

POSTERITY, n. *angkáng-sunód.*

POSTMARK, n. *taták-koreo,* Sp.

POSTMASTER, n. *posmaster,* Eng.

POSTPONE, v. *ipagpalíban; ipagpaibáng-araw.*

POSTSCRIPT, n. *habol, pahabol;* addition, *dagdág.*

POT, n. (earthen) *palayók;* (metallic) *kaldero,* Sp.; (for flowering plants) *masetera,* Sp; *pasô.*

POTATO, n. *patatas,* Sp.

POTENT, adj. effective, *mabisà;* powerful, *makapangyarihan.*

POULTRY n. chicken, *manók;* turkey, *pabo,* Sp.; duck, *itik; pato,* Sp.; geese, *gansâ,* etc.—p. yard, *mánukan.*

POUND, n. (weight) *libra,* Sp.; enclosure, *kulungán.*

POUR, v. *isalin, ibuhos.*

POVERTY, n. *korukhaán;* want, lack, *kasalatán;* neediness, *kadahupán.*

POWDER, n. *pulbós,* Sp.

POWER, n. *kapangyarihan,.* ability, *kakayahán;* influence, *lakás.*

POWERFUL, adj. *makapangyarihan;* mighty, *malakás.*

PRACTICAL, adj. *magágawâ; sa gawâ;* useful, *mapakíkinabangan;* inclined to do rather than just plan, *masikháy.*

PRACTICE, v. to do repeated exercises in, *magsanay;* train, *sanayin.*—n. exercise, *pagsasanay;* application of a theory, *pagsasagawâ.*

PRAISE, n. *papuri.*—v. *purihin.*

PRAISEWORTHY, adj. *kapuripuri.*

PRAY, v. *manalangin, dumalangin; magdasál,* Sp.

PRAYER, n. *dalangin; dasál,* Sp.

PREACH, v. *mangaral.*

PREACHER, n. *mángangarál, tagapangaral.*

PREAMBLE, n. *punong-sabi; páunáng-salitâ.*

PRECARIOUS, adj. *waláng-katiyakán.*

PRECAUTION, n. care, *pagtingat;* caution, *pangangalagà.*

PRECEDE, v. *manguna.*

PRECEPT, n. *pátuntunan.*

PRECIOUS, adj. of value, *maha-*

lagá; cherished, *tangì, itinatangì.*

PRECIPICE, n. *tangwá; labíng.*

PRECISION, n. definiteness, *katiyakán.*

PREDECESSOR, n. *ang hinalinhán, ang sinundán.*

PREDICAMENT, n. *masamáng kalágayan.*

PREDICATE, n. (Gram.) *panagurì; panabi.*

PREDICT, v. to foretell, *manghulà, hulaan.*

PREDOMINANT, adj. superior in strength, *nakapanánaíg;* (in number) *nakarárami;* (in authority) *nakapangingibabaw.*

PREFACE, n. *punong-salitâ.*

PREFERABLE, adj. *lalong kanais-nais.*

PREFIX, n. (Gram.) *unlapì.*

PREGNANT, adj. *buntís, nagdúdaláng tao.*

PREJUDICE, adj. bias, *hilig, kiling.*

PRELUDE, n. *pambungad, pasimulâ.*

PREMATURE, adj. *maaga; yapsáw.*

PREMISES, n. *bakuran; lupaín.*

PREPARATION, n. *paghahandâ.*

PREPARE, v. *maghandâ, ihandâ.*

PREPARED, adj. *handâ, náhahandâ, nakahandâ.*

PREPOSITION, n. (Gram.) *pang-ukol.*

PREREQUISITE, n.-adj. *unang kailangan.*

PRESCRIBE, v. to order, *iutos;* lay down as a rule of action, *ipasunód, ibatás;* order the use of a remedy for sickness, *ireseta,* Sp.

PRESCRIPTION, n. (of a physician) *reseta,* Sp.; *patimplá.*

PRESENT, adj. (here) *náriritó;* (t h e r e) *náririyán, nároroón;*

current, *kasalukuyan;* (Gram.) *pangkasalukuyan.*—n. gift, *bigáy; regalo,* Sp.; *alaala.*

PRESENTIMENT, n. *kutób; sagimsim.*

PRESERVE, v. to keep from injury or destruction, *pangalagaan, ingatan;* protect, *ipagsanggaláng;* treasure, *pagyamanin.*— n. *imbák, inimbák.*

PRESIDE, v. *mangulo.*

PRESIDENT, n. *pangulo; presidente,* Sp.

PRESS, v. to bear down upon, *idiín. diínán;* squeeze, *pisilín, pisaín;* smooth out by ironing, *plánsahín.* Sp.

PRESTIGE, n. *kabantugan.*

PRESUME, v. to suppose to be true without proof, *akalain, sapantahain;* venture; *pangahasán.*

PRETEND, v. *magkunwâ, magkunwarì.*

PRETTY, adj. good-looking, *magandá;* fine, *mainam.*

PREVAIL, v. to triumph, *magtagumpáy;* become widespread, *mangalat.*

PREVENT, v. *hadlangán, pigilan; sawatain.*

PREVENTION, n. *pagpigil; pagsawatâ.*

PREVIOUS, adj. *dati; una.*

PRICE, n. *halagá.*

PRIDE, n. *kapurihán;* a high opinion of self, *pagmamataás.*

PRIEST, n. *parì,* Sp.

PRIMARY, adj. first, *una;* principal, *punò;* basic, *batayán;* fundamental, *panimulâ, pábatayán.*

PRINCE, n. *prinsipé,* Sp.

PRINCIPAL, n. *punò;* basic sum of money, *puhunan.*

PRINCIPLE, n. *simulain.*

PRINT, n. *limbág, taták.*—v. *maglimbág, ilimbág, limbagín.*

PRINTER, n. *tagalimbág, manlilimbág.*

PRINTERY, n. *pálimbagan.*

PRISON, n. *piitán, bilangguan.*—state p., *bilibid.*

PRISONER, n. *bilanggo.*

PRIVATE. adj. *panarili, pansarili.*

PRIVILEGE, n. *pribiléñiyó,* Sp.; right, *tanging karapatán.*

PRIZE, n. *gatimpalà.*

PROBABLE, adj. *maáaring magkátotoó.*

PROBLEM, n. (immediate) *súliranín;* (in general) *súliranin.*

PROCEED, v. *magpatuloy, ipagpatuloy.*

PROCESSION, n. *prusisyón.* Sp.

PROCLAIM, v. to announce publicly, *ihayág, ilathalà.*

PROCLAMATION, n. *pamahayag.*

PROCURE, v. *kumuha, kunin.*

PROFESSOR, n. *propesór,* Sp.; *gurò.*

PROFIT, n. *tubò;* benefit, *pakinabang.*

PROFITEER, n. *manghuhuthót.*

PROGRAM, n. *palátuntunan.*

PROGRESS, n. *kaunlaran.*

PROGRESSIVE, adj. *maunlád.*

PROGRESSIVENESS, n. *kaunlarán; pagka-maunlád.*

PROMINENT, adj. distinguished, *tanyág, litáw;* conspicuous, *kita, halatá.*

PROLONG, v. *pahabain,* (in time) *patagalán.*

PROHIBIT, v. *ipagbawal.*

PROMISE, n. *pangakò.* — v. *mangakò.*

PROMOTE, v. to help the growth, success, etc., *itaguyod, magtaguyod;* advance in position, *itaás, pataasín;* (at school) *ipasá, papasahín,* Sp.

PROMOTER, n. *tagataguyod.*

PROMPT, adj. *maagap;* quick, *maliksí.*

PRONOUN, n. (Gram.) *panghalíp.*

PRONOUNCE, v. *bumigkás, bigkasín.*

PRONUNCIATION, n. *bigkás.*

PROOF, n. *patunay, patibay.*

PROPAGATE, v. *magpalaganav, palaganapin.*

PROPER, adj. appropriate, *nárarapat, marapat;* suitable, *bagay.* —(Gram) p. noun, *pangngalang pantañgì.*

PROPERTY, n. *pag-aarì, aríarian.*

PROPHET, n. *propeta,* Sp.; *manghuhulà.*

PROPOSE, v. to suggest, *imungkahì;* present as plan, *panukalain, ipanukalà.*

PROPOSAL, n. suggestion, *mungkahì,* plan, *panukalà.*

PROPOSITION, n. subject, theme, *paksâ;* subject in argumentation, *súliranín.*

PROPRIETOR, n. *may-arì.*

PROPRIETY, n. ·suitability, *kabagayán;* correctness, *kawastuán.*

PROSE, n.-adj. (Lit.) *túluyan.*

PROSECUTOR, n. *tagausig.*

PROSPECT, n. anticipation, *pagasám;* expectation, *pag-asa.*

PROSPER, v. to flourish, *lumagô, yumabong;* progress, *umunlád.*

PROSPERITY, n. *kariwasaán; kasaganaan.*

PROTECT, v. *ipagsanggaláng.*

PROTEST, v. *tumutol, tutulan.*

PROTESTANT, n.-adj. *protestante,* Sp.; *maytutol, mayprotesta,* Sp.

PROTRUDE, v. to stick out, *umuslî.*

PROUD, adj. haughty, *mapagmataás;* arrogant, *mayabang, hambóg;* conceited, *makaakó.*

PROVE, v. *magpatunay, patunayan;* to convince of the truth of, *patotóhanan, magpatotoó;* make a trial of, *tikmán.*

PROVIDE, v. *paghandaán;* to supply, *bigyán;* stipulate, *itakdá, itadhanà.*

PROVIDENCE, n. *awa't tulong ng Maykapál; kalooban ng Diyós; talagá ng Diyós.*

PROVINCE, n. *lalawigan; probínsiyá,* Sp.

PROVINCIAL, adj. of, for a province, *panlalawigan;* from a, *taga-lalawigan, probinsiyano,* Sp.

PROVISIONAL, adj. *pansamantalá.*

PROVOCATIVE, adj. serving to cause anger, *nakagágalit, kagalit-galit.*

PROVOKE, v. to arouse, *pukawin;* stir up, *bulyawán;* bring about, *ibunsód;* cause to be angry, *galitin.*

PROVOST, n. chief, *punò.*

PROW, n. *proa,* Sp.; *unahán, ulo.*

PRUDENT, adj. *may-baít.*

PRUNE, v. to cut off (as branches, twigs, etc.) *putulan, pulakin.*

PSEUDONYM, n. *sagisag; panagisag.*

PUBERTY, n. (for boys) *pagbibinatâ;* (for girls) *pagdadalagá.*

PUBLIC, adj. having to do with the people as a whole, *pangmadlá;* open or common to all, *panlahát;* generally known, *hayág, kalát;* (Govt.) having to do with activities for the people, *pambayan.*

PUBLICATION, n. act of publishing, *paglalathalà;* a thing published, *lathalà, palathalà;*

palimbág; periodical, *páhayagán.*

PUBLISH, v. *ilathalà, ipalathalà, maglathalà.*

PUDDING, n. *puding,* Eng.

PUDDLE, n. *sanaw.*

PUERILE, adj. *parang batà; pahát.*

PUFF, n. pant, *hingal;* short, sudden discharge of air, steam, etc., *sirit, singáw; bugá.*

PUG, adj. as in p. nose, *sarát, dapâ, sungadngád.*

PULL, n. *hila, batak.*—v. *hilahin, humila; batakin, bumatak.*

PULLET, n. *dumalaga (dumalagang manók).*

PULLEY, n. *kalô.*

PULP, n. *kalamnán.*

PULPIT, n̄. *púlpitó,* Sp.; *sermunan,* Sp.

PULSATE, v. to throb, *tumibók;* quiver, *mangatál.*

PULSE n. *pulsó,* Sp.; *tibók.*

PULVERIZE, v. *pulbusín,* Sp.; *durugin.*

PUMP, n. *bomba,* Sp.

PUMPKIN, n. *kalabasa,* Sp.

PUNCH, n. a blow with the fist, *sumbî, suntók;* a tool for perforating, *pambutas, pamutas.*

PUNCTILIOUS, adj. *maselang.*

PUNCTUAL, adj. *maagap.*

PUNCTUATION, n. *bantás.*

PUNISH, v. *parusahan; papagdusahin.*

PUNISHMENT, n. *parusa.*

PUNY, adj. stunted, *puríl;* weak, *mahinà.*

PUP, n. a puppy, *tutà, bilót.*

PUPIL, n. (at school) *nag-áaral;* (of the eye) *balintataó, balintatáw.*

PUPPET, n. person who does blindly what another wishes done, *uldóg.*

PURCHASABLE, adj. *mabíbilí; mábíbili.*

PURCHASE, v. *bumilí, bilhín.*

PURCHASER, n. *mámimili;* assigned buyer, *tagapamilí.*

PURE, adj. *dalisay, wagás.*

PURELY, adv. *panáy; pulós.*

PURGATIVE, adj.-n. *purgá, pamurgá,* Sp.

PURGATORY, n. *purgatoryo,* Sp.

PURGE, v. to cleanse, *linisin;* purify, *dalisayin;* cleanse or clear the bowels by means of medicine, *magpurgá; purgahín.*

PURIFY, v. *dalisayin, magdalisay.*

PURIST, n. *maka-dalɪsay.*

PURITY, n. *kadalisayan.*

PURPLE, n. *murado,* Sp.; *kulayubi.*

PURPOSE, n. end in view, *túnguhin.* *puntahin;* intention, *hangád, hángarin; tangkâ; panukalà;* object, *layon; pakay.*

PURPOSELY, adv. *sinadyâ; tinikís.*

PURSE, n. *pitakà,* Sp.

PURSUE, v. to chase, *pagatin;* run after, *habulin, hagarin;* follow with an end in view (as, p. a course) *itaguyod, magtaguyod.*

PUS, n. *nanà.*

PUSH. v. *itulak.*

PUSSY, n. *pusà.*

PUT, v. *ilagáy, maglagáy;* (into a small container) *isilíd, magsilíd.*

PUTRID, adj. *bulók;* (fish) *halpók, hampók, bilasâ.*

PUTTY, n. *masilya,* Sp.

PUZZLE, n. riddle, *bugtóng;* problem for testing mental cleverness, *paláisipán.*—v. to perplex, *papagkuruin, papag-isipín;* bewilder, *lingmingín, tuliruhín;* confuse, *guluhin, ligaligin.*

PYGMY, n. *unano,* Sp.

PYJAMAS, n. *padyamas,* Eng.

PYRAMID, n. *tagiló.*

PYRE, n. *sigâ; siláb.*

Q

QUADRILATERAL, adj. *ápatang gilid.*

QUAFF, v. *tunggaín, tumunggâ.*

QUAGMIRE, n. *kuminóy; lumbák.*

QUAIL, n. small game bird, *pugò.*
—v. to lose spirit and power of resistance, *manghilakbót;* lose heart, *mawalán ng loób;* shrink as from fear, *mahintakutan.*

QUAKE, v. to quiver, *mangatóg;* shudder, *mangatál;* tremble, *manginíg.*

QUALIFICATION, n. *katángian;* fitness, *pagka-marapat; pagkabagay.*

QUALIFIED, adj. fitted, *karapatdapat, marapat; bagay.*

QUALITY, n. excellence, *kagáling-ngan;* kind, *urì.*

QUANTITY, n. *dami.*

QUARANTINE, n. *kuwarentenas,* Sp.; *walayô,* nc.

QUARREL, n. *away;* disagreement, *pagkakasirâ;* alteration, *basag-ulo;* petty fight, *bangayán.*

QUARRELSOME, adj. *paláaway.*

QUARRY, n. open digging (for building stone, etc.) *tíbagan.*

QUARTER, n.-adj. a fourth part, *sangkapat, ikaapat na bahagi.*

QUARTERLY, n.-adj. *tatluhangbuwán.*

QUARTERMASTER, n. *tagatustós, pánustusan.*

QUEEN, n. *reyna*, Sp.

QUEENLY, adj. *malareyna*, Sp.

QUEER, adj. *kakaibá;* odd, *kakatwá.*

QUELL, v. *supilin; sugpuín.*

QUENCH, v. to put out (as fire), *patayín.*—to q. the thirst, *patirin ang uhaw.*

QUERULOUS, adj. *madáingin; takaw-usap.*

QUERY, n. *tanóng;* inquiry, *usisà.*

QUEST, n. *pakay; pithayà.*

QUESTION, n. *tanóng*, (act of) *pagtatanóng.*

QUESTIONNAIRE, n. *palátanungan.*

QUICK, adj. *madalî; maliksí.*

QUICKLY, adv. in a quick manner, *múdalian;* at once, *agád;* hastily, *daglian.*

QUICKSILVER, n. *asoge*, Sp.

QUICKSAND, n. *kuminóy.*

QUIESCENT, adj. motionless, *waláng-galáw, waláng-kilos.*

QUIET, adj. *tahimik;* free from noise, *waláng-ingay;* free from disturbance, *waláng-guló.*

QUIETNESS, QUIETUDE, n. *katahimikan.*

QUILL, n. feather, *pakpák.*

QUININE, n. *kinina*, Sp.; cinchona, *ditâ.*

QUINSY, n. (Med.) *anghiña*, Sp.

QUINTESSENCE, n. *kákanggatâ; kauburan.*

QUIRE, n. a measure of 24 sheets of paper, *sangmano* (Sp. *mano*).

QUIT, v. to cease, *tumigil;* stop going to school, *umawás.*

QUITE, adv. completely, *ganáp*, wholly, *buô;* really, *tunay.*—It's q. true, *tunay ngâ; totoó ngâ.*

QUIVER, v. to tremble, *manginíg.*

QUIZ, n. *pagsubok;* examination, *iksamen*, Sp.

QUIZZICAL, adj. bantering, *pabiró;* teasing, *patuksó; patudyó.*

QUOTATION, n. (G r a m.) q. marks, *panipì;* words repeated, *sipì, sinipì.*

QUOTE, v. to repeat a passage, *ulitin; sipiin.*

R

RABBIT n. *kuneho*, Sp.

RABID, adj. *mapusók;* extremely violent, *mabugasók.*

RACE, n. contest in speed, *pátulinán;* (in running) *takbuhan; unahán*, Sp.; a division of mankind, *lahì.*

RACK, n. a framework for holding articles, *bastagan.*

RACKET, n. a confused noise. *linggál;* (for tennis) *raketa*, Sp.

RADIANCE, n. *ningning.*

RADIANT, adj. *maningning.*

RADIATE, v. *magningníng.*

RADIO, n. *radyo*, Lat.

RADIUM, n. *radyum*, Lat.

RAFFLE, n. *ripa*, Sp.

RAFT, n. *balsá*, Sp.; *lamò.*

RAFTER, n. *tahilan.*

RAG, n. *basahan.*

RAGE, n. uncontrolled anger, *pagiinit; pagkagalit, galit.*

RAID, n. *pagsalakay.*—v. *sumalakay, manalakay.*

RAIL, n. railroad track, *riles*, Sp.; *daang-bakál.*

RAILING, n. *barandilya*, Sp.

RAILROAD, n. *tren, pérokaríl*, Sp.

RAIMENT, n. *damít;* garments, *pananamit;* wearing apparel, *kasúutan.*

RAIN, n. *ulán.*—v. *umulán.*

RAINBOW, n. *bahagharì, balangáw.*

RAINCOAT, n. *kapote,* Sp.; *pangulán; kalapyáw.*

RAINY, adj. *maulán.*

RAISE, v. to lift from the ground, *buhatin;* to cause to be in a higher position, *itaás;* construct, *magtayô, itayô;* grow, *magtanim.*

RAISIN, n. *pasas,* Sp.

RAJAH, n. *rahá,* Hnd.

RAKE, n. *kalaykáy.*

RALLY,. v. *magpamuling-siglá.*— n. *pagmumuling-siglá.*

RAMBLE, v. *magpagala--galà, magpalibut-libot.* — n. *pagpapagalá-galà, pagpapalibút-libot.*

RAMIFY, v. *magsangá; magsangá-sangá.*

RAMPANT, adj. unrestrained, *waláng-pigil.*

RANCID, adj. *maantá.*

RANCOR, n. grudge, *pagtataním;* resentment, *samâ ng loób.*

RANDOM, adj. *pasumalá.*

RANGE, n. row, *hanay;* line of direction, *dako, bandá;* scope, *sakláw,* reach, *abót.*

RANK, n. row, *hanay;* orderly formation, *ayos, kaayusan;* high station, *taás, kataasán; tayog, katayugan.*

RANSOM, n. *tubós.*—v. *tubusín.*

RAP, v. to knock, *tumuktók, kumatók.*—n. *tuktók.*

RAPACIOUS, adj. given to plunder, *mapandambóng;* greedy, *matakaw, masibà;* grasping, *mapangamkám.*

RAPE, v. *manggahasà, mandahás.*—n. *panggagahasà, pandarahás.*

RAPID, adj. very swift, *matulin; mabilís;* done quickly, *madalì, maliksí.*

RAPINE, n. *pandaragit, pangangagaw.*

RAPTURE, n. *malabis na pagkalugód.*

RARE, adj. unusual, *di-pangkaraniwan;* scarce, *bihirà.*

RASCAL, n.-adj. scoundrel, *tampalasan.*

RASH, adj. *padalús-dalos; pabiglá-biglâ.*

RASP, v. to scrape, *kayurin.*

RAT, n. *dagâ.*

RATE, n. amount, *halagá;* number, *bilang;* condition, *lagáy;* speed, *bilís, tulin.*

RATIFY, v. *pagtibayin, magpatibay.*

RATING, n. *kaurian.*

RATIO, n. *katumbasán.*

RATION, n. *rasyón,* Sp.; fixed share, *takdáng kabahagi.*

RATIONAL, adj. *may-talino;* pertaining to reason, *pangkatwiran;* in accord with reason, *may-katwiran, makatwiran.*

RATIONALIZE, v. *isakatwiran.*

RATTAN, n. *yantók, uwáy; palasan.*

RATTLE, n. *kalantóg.*

RAVAGE, v. to lay waste, *mamuksâ.*

RAVE, v. to utter wildly, *magngangawâ.*

RAVENOUS, adj. furiously hungry, *dayukdók;* extremely greedy, *nápakasibà.*

RAVINE, n. *talabís.*

RAW, adj. uncooked, *hiláw;* unskinned, *bakbák ang balát;* novice, *baguhan;* painful, *mahapdi.*

RAY, n. *sinag.*

RAZOR, n. *pang-ahit; labaha, labasa,* Sp.

REACH, v. to touch or grasp with the extended hand, *abutín;* arrive at, come to, *sumapit, ma-*

karatɪng; extend as far as, *makaabót, makasapit.*

REACT, v. *tumaulî.*

REACTION, n. *taulî, pagtaulî, pagtataulî.*

READ, v. *bumasa, basahin; magbasá.*

READABLE, adj. *mabábasa, nabábasa.*

READILY, adv. *agád, kaagád; karakáraka.*

READER, n. one who reads, *mambabasa;* a reading book, *aklát na babasahín.*

READY, adj. *handâ;* prompt, *maagap.*

READY-MADE, adj. *yarì na.*

REAGENT, n. *pantaulî.*

REAL, adj. *tunay;* true, *totoó.*

REALITY, n. *katunayan;* truth, *katotóhanan.*

REALIZATION, n. act of feeling fully and vividly, *pagkatantô.*

REALIZE, v. to accomplish, *gawín;* feel fully and vividly, *mapagtantô.*

REALLY, adv. *tunay ngâ, totoó ngâ.*—It's really true. *Talagá ngang totoó.*

REAM, n. *resma,* Sp.

REAP, v. to harvest, *mag-ani, anihín;* cut down (as with a scythe, etc.); *gapasin, gumapas;* receive as a reward, *matamó.*

REAR, n. back, *likurán, likód;* hinder part, *hulihán, hulî.*—adj. pertaining to the back part, *panlikurán, panghulihán.*—v. bring up, *magpalakí, palakihin.*

REASON, n. faculty of reasoning, *katwiran;* common sense, *baít;* the cause for an opinion or act, *dahilán, sanhî.*

REASONABLE, adj. *may-katwiran;* just, *makataruŋgan;* sensible, *mabaít.*

REBEL, n. *manghihimaksík.*—v. *manghimagsík.*

REBELLION, n. *panghihimagsík.*

REBELLIOUS, adj. *mapanghimagsík.*

REBOUND, v. *tumalbóg.*

REBUKE, n. *sisi;* chiding, *suwát.*—v. *sisihin;* to chide, *suwatán.*

REBUTTAL, n. *pagsalansang.*

RECALL, v. to summon back, *pabalikín, pauwiín;* remember, *máalaala, mágunitâ;* take back, *bawiin.*

RECEDE, v. *umurong.*

RECEIPT, n. written acknowledgment of something received, *resibo,* Sp.; act of receiving, *pagtanggap.*

RECEIVE, v. *tumanggáp, tanggapín.*

RECENT, adj. new, *bago;* modern, *makabago;* fresh, *sariwà;* only today, *ngángayón.*

RECEPTACLE, n. *sisidlán; lalagyán.*

RECEPTION, n. acceptance, *pagtanggáp;* social occasion for greeting guests, *resepsiyón,* Sp.

RECESS, n. intermission between work, *pahingá;* (at school), *risés,* Eng.

RECITATION, n. rendering of something committed to memory, *pagbigkás;* the repeating of a lesson to a teacher, *ulit-aral,* nc.

RECITE, v. to repeat aloud from memory, *bigkasín;* repeat a lesson to a teacher, *ulit-sabihin.* nc.; *ulit-aralin.*

RECKLESS, adj. heedless of consequences, *waláng-tarós;* careless, *waláng-ingat;* thoughtless, *waláng-bahalà.*

RECLINE, v. *humilig, sumandál;* to lie down, *humigâ.*

RECOGNITION, n. *pagkilala.*

RECOGNIZE, v. *mákilala, kilala-nin (kilanlín).*

RECOLLECT, v. *mágunitá, máalaala.*

RECOMMEND, v. to offer to the favor, attention, or use of another, *ipagtagubilin;* advise, *ipayo;* suggest, *imungkahì.*

RECOMMENDATION, n. *tagubilin;* advice, *payo;* suggestion, *mungkahì.*

RECOMPENSE, n. *gantí;* reward, *gantimpalà;* compensation, *gantimpagál, bayad-pagál.*

RECONCILE, v. to restore peace or friendship between, *papagkásunduín.*

RECONCILIATION, n. *pagkakásundô.*

RECONSTRUCT, v. *magmulíngtatag.*

RECONSTRUCTION, n. *pagmumulíng-tatag.*

RECORD, n. *talâ;* a register, *aklát-tálaan;* phonograph disk, *plaka.*—v. to set down or jot down, *italâ.*

RECOURSE, n. an appeal for aid or protection, *pagdulóg;* a person to whom one turns for aid, *dúlugan, takbuhan.*

RECOVER, v. *mabawì.*

RECOVERY, n. act of regaining, *pagkabawì;* r e s t o r a t i o n to health, *paggalíng.*

RECREATION, n. *pag-aalíw, paglilibáng.*

RECRUIT, n. one who has just joined any cause, *bagong-anib.*

RECTIFY, v. to set right, *iwastô.*

RECTITUDE, n. uprightness, *kawastuán;* honesty, *pagkamarangál.*

RECTUM, n. (Anat.) *tumbóng.*

RECUPERATE, v. to r e g a i n health, *lumakás; gumalíng.*

RECUR, v. to come back, *bumalík, magbalík;* happen again, *umulit.*

RECURRENT, adj. *pabalik-balík; paulit-ulit.*

RED, n. *pulá.*—adj. *mapulá.*

REDDEN, v. to make red, *papulahín;* become red, blush, *mamulá.*

REDDISH, adj. *mapulá-pulá.*

REDEEM, v. *tubusín.*

REDEEMER, n. *mánunubos.*

REDEMPTION, n. *katúbusan.*

REDOLENT, adj. *mahalimuyak;* fragrant, *mabangó.*

REDOUBLE, v. *pag-ibayuhin.*

REDUCE, v. to lessen, *bawasan.*

REDUCTION, n. *bawas;* (act of) *pagbabawas.*

REDUNDANT, adj. unnecessary to the sense, *maligoy;* too wordy, *madiwarà; kalabisán.*

REDUPLICATE, v. to make double, *pagdalawahín;* repeat, *ulitin.*

REECHO, v. *umalingawngáw.*

REED, n. *tambô.*

REEK, v. to send out disagreeable odor, *umalingasaw.*

REEL, v. to stagger or sway, *sumuray-suray, gumiray-giray.*

REFER, v. to submit to another person or authority, *iharáp;* allude, *banggitín; tukuyin.*

REFEREE, n. *tagahatol; réperi,* Eng.

REFINE, v. to make pure, *dalisayin;* clear from dross or worthless matter, *pakinisin.*

REFINED, adj. without coarseness, *mabinì, makinis;* cultivated, *nilináng.*

REFINEMENT, n. *kabinihan, kakinisan.*

REFLECT, v. to give or throw back as light, *manganinag;* consider carefully in the mind. *dilídilihin, bulaybulayin.*

REFLECTION, n. act of throwing back (light), *pangangani-nag, panginginnáng;* attentive consideration, *pagdidilidili, pagbubulaybulay.*

REFLEXIVE, adj. (Gram.) *pasarilí.*

REFORM, n. change for the better, *pagbabago; pagbuti; pagpapabuti.*—v. *magbago, baguhin.*

REFORMATION, n. *pagbabago.*

REFORMATORY, n. *páwastuan; repormatoryo,* Sp.

REFORMED, adj. *nagbago;' binago; nabago.*

REFRAIN, v. to hold oneself back, *magpigil, magtimpî.*

REFRESH, v. *s a r i w a i n;* to strengthen, *palakasín;* enliven, *pasiglahín.*

REFRESHMENT, n. (food, drink, etc., which restores or revives) *pampalamíg.*

REFRIGERATOR, n. *pálamigan.*

REFUGE, n. *kanlungan, kublihan.*

REFUND, v. *isaulî.*

REFUSAL, n. *pagtanggí; pagayáw.*

REFUSE, v. *tumanggí; umayaw.*

REFUTATION, n. *pagpapasinungaling.*

REFUTE, v. *magpasinungaling, pasinungalingan.*

REGAIN, v. *mabawî.*

REGAL, adj. *makaharî.*

REGARD, n. affection, *paggiliw;* respect, *paggalang;* esteem, *pagtingín, patatangî.*—v. to observe closely, *pagmasdán;* heed, *pansinín;* esteem, *itangî.*

REGARDING, prep. concerning. *tungkól sa;* about, *hinggil sa;* with respect, to, *tungód sa.*

REGIMENT, n. *rehimyento,* Sp.

REGION, n. *lupaín;* district, *purók.* (Expressed by *ka...an* or *ka...han* with the name of a region as root-word, as, *kabikulan,* Bicol region; *kailukuhan,* Ilocos region; *katagalugan,* Tagalog region; *kamorohan,* the Moro region, etc.)

REGISTER, n. (book) *aklát-tálaan.*

REGISTRAR, n. *tagatalâ.*

REGISTRATION, n. *pagtatalâ; pagpapatalâ.*

REGRET, n. feeling of loss, *panghihinayang;* mild remorse, *pagsisisi;* moral distress, *panimdím.*

REGRETTABLE, adj. *nakapanghihinayang;* fit to cause sorrow, *nakalúlungkót, nakalúlumbáy.*

REGULAR, adj. *karaniwan, pangkaraniwan;* permanent, *pánatilihan.*

REGULATE, v. *isaayos; ialituntón,* nc.

REGULATION, n. *álituntunin;* rule, *tuntunin;* law, *batás.*

REHABILITATE, v. *papanumbalikin.*

REHEARSAL, n. *insayo,* Sp.; exercise, *pagsasanay.*

REHEARSE, v. *mag-insayo,* Sp.; to exercise, *magsanay.*

REIGN, v. *magharì;* to prevail, *makapangyari, mangibabaw.*

REIN, n. *riyenda,* Sp.

REINFORCE, v. to give new strength to, *palakasín;* support, *itaguyod, katigan.*

REITERATE, v. *ulit-ulitin.*

REJECT, v. to decline, *tanggihán. tumanggí.*

REJOICE, v. *magsayá; matuwâ;* to gladden, *pasayahín.*

REJOICING, n. *sayá; túwâ; galák.*

REJOINDER, n. *paklí.*

REJUVENATE, v. *pabatain.*

RELAPSE, n. the return of a disease after partial recovery, *pag kabinat, pagkabaynát.*

RELATE, v. to narrate, *magsalaysáy, isalaysáy;* to show a connection between, *iugnáy.*

RELATION, n. act of narrating, *pagsasalaysáy;* connection, *kaugnayan;* a relative, *kamaganak.*

RELATIVE, adj. (Gram.) *pamanggít.*

RELAX, v. to make less tight or firm, *paluwagán, luwagán;* relieve from stress, *palubayán;* cause one's body to be at ease, *magpaalwán;* rest, *magpahingá.*

RELAXATION, n. act of resting, *pagpapahingá;* of loosening, *pagpapaluwág;* of easing bodily tension, *pagpapaalwán;* of removing strain, *pagpapalubáy.*

RELEASE, n. act of setting free, *pagpapalayà;* deliverance, *paglayà.*—v. *magpalayà, palayain.*

RELENT, v. *maglubag ang loób;* to yield, *maghunusdilì.*

RELIABLE, adj. *maáasahan; mapagkakátiwalaan.*

RELIANCE, n. *pag-asa; tiwalà, pagtitiwalà; pagkakátiwalà.*

RELIC, n. *relikya,* Sp.

RELIEF, n. *ginhawa;* help given in time of danger or difficulty, *paginhawa, tulong, abuloy.*

RELIEVE, v. *magpaginhawa, paginhawahin.*

RELIGION, n. *relihiyón,* Sp.

RELIGIOUS, adj. *relihiyoso,* Sp.; pious, *banál;* pertaining to religion, *panrelihiyón,* Sp.

RELINQUISH, v. to retire from, *tumiwalág;* give up using or having, *talikdán.*

RELISH, n. taste or preference, *pangnamnám;* flavor, *lasa, linamnám.*

RELUCTANT, adj. indisposed, *matamláy;* disinclined, *walánggustó; urung-sulong, atubilì.*

RELY, v. to trust, *umasa, asahan; manghawak;* have confidence, *magkátiwalà, pagkátiwalaan.*

REMAIN, v. to stay behind when others go, *paiwan;* be left, *maiwan, mátirá;* endure, *magtagál, manatilì.*

REMAINS, n. a dead body, *bangkáy;* portion left, *labí, mga nálabí.*

REMAINDER, n. what is left, *nátirá; naiwan;* surplus, *labis.*

REMARK, n. act of noticing, *pansín, puná;* observation, *pagmamasíd.*—v. to take note of, *pansinín, punahín;* observe, *pagmasdán.*

REMARKABLE, adj. noteworthy, *kapansín-pansín;* unusual. *dipangkaraniwan.*

REMEDY, n. *lunas;* a helpful medicine, *kagámutan, gamót;* remedyo,* Sp.

REMEMBER, v. *máalaala;* to think of anew, *gunitaín;* keep in mind carefully, *tandaán.*

REMEMBRANCE, n. *alaala;* recollection, *gunitâ.*

REMIND, v. *magpaalaala, ipaalaala.*

REMINISCENCE, n. *gunitâ.*

REMIT, v. *magpadalá, ipadalá.*

REMNANT, n. *labí;* surplus, *labis;* what is left, *tirá; nátirá; sobra,* Sp.; short length of fabric left, *retaso,* Sp.

REMODEL, v. *baguhin, magbago.*

REMONSTRANCE, n. *tutol; salansáng.*

REMONSTRATE, v. *tumutol; sumalansáng.*

REMORSE, n. keen reproach of oneself, *pagdadaláng-sisi.*

REMOTE, adj. *malayò.*

REMOVABLE, adj. *naáalís; náipagpápalipat-lipat; náililipat.*

REMOVAL, n. *paglilipat;* dismissal, (as from office) *pagtitiwalág.*

REMOVE, v. to take out of the way, *alisín, ialís;* transfer from one place to another, *lumipat maglipat, ilipat;* (r. from office), *itiwalág.*

REMUNERATE, v. to pay (someone), *bayaran;* compensate, *gumantí, gantihín; gantihán.*

REMUNERATION, n. *bayad;* compensation, *gantimpagál.*

RENAISSANCE, n. *bagong pagsilang; mulíng pagsilang.*

RENDEZVOUS, n. *poók na tagpuan; típanan.*

RENEW, v. *magpanibago.*

RENEWAL, n. *pagpapanibago.*

RENOUNCE, v. to disown, *itakwíl;* give up, *talikdán, tumalikód;* cast off, *iwaksí.*

RENOWN, n. *kabunyián;* fame, *kabantugán.*

RENOWNED, adj. *bunyî, mabunyî;* famous, *bantóg, balità.*

RENT, n. *upa, bayad.*—v. to lease, *umupa;* hire, *mangupahan.*

RENUNCIATION, n. act of disowning, *pagtatakwíl;* act of giving up, *pagtalikód.*

REORGANIZATION, n. *pagmumulíng-ayos; pagbabaguntatág.*

REORGANIZE, v. *magmulíngayos; magbaguntatág.*

REPAIR, v. to mend, *magkumpuní, kumpunihín,* Sp.—n. *pagkukumpuní.*

REPAST, n. *pagkaín.*

REPAY, v. *pagbayaran.*

REPEAL, v. *iurong;* to annul, *pawaláng-bisà.*

REPEAT, v. *ulitin;* to do again, *umulit.*

REPEATEDLY, adv. *paulit-ulit.*

REPENT, v. *magsisi, pagsisihan.*

REPENTANCE, n. *pagsisisi.*

REPENTANT, adj. *nagsísisi*

REPERCUSSION, n. reverberation, *alingawngáw.*

REPETITION, n. *pag-ulit, paguulit.*

REPLACE, v. to put back in place, *isaulî;* take or fill the place of, *palitán, halinhán.*

REPLY, n. *tugón.*—v. *tumugón.*

REPORT, n. *ulat.*—v. *magbigáyulat.*

REPORTER, n. *tagapagbalità;* reporter, Eng.

REPOSE, n. act of resting, *pagpapahingá.*

REPOSEFUL, adj. restful, *maginhawa.*

REPRESENT, v. to portray, *ilarawan, maglarawan;* stand for, *kumatawán, katawanin.*

REPRESENTATION, n. portrayal, *paglalarawan;* act of standing for, *pagkatawán.*

REPRESENTATIVE, n. *kinatawán.*

REPRESS, v. to keep under control, *magpigil, pigilin;* subdue, *sumupil, supilin.*

REPRESSION, n. act of keeping under control, *pagpipigil;* act of subduing, *pagsupil.*

REPREHENSIBLE, adj. *kasisisisi; masísisi.*

REPRIEVE, n. *palugit.*

REPRIMAND, v. *pangusapan; suwatán.*

REPRINT, n. *mulíng-limbág, mu-*

líng-paglilimbág. — v. *limbagin ulî.*

REPRISAL, n. *higantí.*

REPROACH, n. rebuke, *sisi.*—v. *sisihin.*

REPROACHFUL, adj. *mapanisi; naninisi.*

REPROBATE, n. sinful person, *makasalanan;* perfidious person, *sukáb, palamara;* cunning person, *kuhilâ.*

REPRODUCE, v. to repeat, *ulitin;* bear, *manganák; umanák;* yield, *magbunga, bumunga;* bring forth, *magsupang, sumupang;* copy, *tularan.*

REPROOF, n. *pananalampák; pagsuwát.*

REPTILE, n. *ahas.*

REPUBLIC, n. *repúbliká,* Sp.

REPUDIATE, v. *itakwíl, magtakwíl;* to refuse to admit, *itatwâ, magtatwâ.*

REPUGNANCE, n. *pagkasuklám.*

REPUGNANT, adj. *nakasúsuklám.*

REPULSE, v. to drive back, *pabalikín, mapabalík; mapaurong;* beat off, *máitabóy, máiabóy; iwaksí, máiwaksí.*

REPULSION, n. a feeling of aversion, *panganganí, pagkarimarim.*

REPULSIVE, adj. *nakákanganí, nangánganí, kanganí-nganí.*

REPUTATION, n. good name, *mabuting pangalan;* honor, *dangál; puri, kapurihán.*

REPUTED, adj. considered as being, *ipinalálagáy.*

REQUEST, n. *pakiusap, pamanhík.*—v. *makiusap, mamanhík.*

REQUIEM, n. *Rekyém,* Lat.

REQUIRE, v. to demand or insist upon, *hingín, hilingín;* have need of, *mangailangan, kailanganin.*

REQUIREMENT, n. demand, *hingî, hiling;* need, *pangangailangan.* (pl.) conditions, *mga kailangan, mga káilanganin.*

REQUISITE, n. *kinákailangan.* -- adj. *kailangan.*

REQUISITION, n. *hingî, hiling.* —v. *humingî, humiling.*

RESCRIPT, n. *kautusán.*

RESCUE, v. *sagipín;* to save, *iligtás, magligtás;* liberate, set free, *palayain, magpalayà.*

RESEARCH, n. *saliksík, pananaliksík.*—v. *magsaliksík, manaliksík.*

RESEMBLANCE, n. *pagká-kawangis.*

RESEMBLE, v. *magkátulad; magkáwangis.*

RESENT, v. *ikagalit; ipagdamdám.*

RESENTFUL, adj. *nagágalit.*

RESENTMENT, n. *galit.*

RESERVATION, n. a h o l d i n g back, *pagtitimpî;* a keeping back of a right or interest, *pagtataán, paglalaán.*

RESERVE, v. to set aside for future use, *itaán, ilaán.*

RESERVED, adj. showing little feeling, *matimpî, matimpiín;* kept back for future use, *nakataán.*

RESERVOIR, n. (of water) *tubigan; imbakang-tubig.*

RESIDE, v. *tumirá; manirá, manirahan.*

RESIDENCE, n. *tinítirahán, kinatítirahán;* state of living in a place, *paninirahan.*

RESIDENT, n. *ang nakatirá; ang naninirahan.*

RESIDENTIAL, adj. *pámbahayán, pantáhanan.*

RESIDUE, n. *ang nátirá; latak.*

RESIGN, v. to withdraw from a position or office, *magbitíw; tumiwalág.*

RESIGNATION, n. withdrawal from a position, *pagbibitíw; pagtiwalág.*

RESIGNED, adj. yielding, *waláng-tutol.*

RESIST, v. to oppose, s t r i v e against, *lumaban;* refuse to obey or agree, *tumutol, di-sumunód.*

RESISTANCE, n. *paglaban; pagtutol.*

RESOLUTION, n *pasiyá, kapasiyahán.*

RESOLVE, v. to decide, *magpasıyá, ipasiyá.*

RESONANCE, n. *tagintíng.*

RESONANT, adj. *matagintíng.*

RESORT, n. a place much visitea, *dáyuhan;* that to which, or person to whom, one applies for aid, *dúlugan, takbuhan.*—v. to apply for assistance, *dumulóg, dulugán.*

RESOUND, v. *umalingawngáw.*

RESOURCE, n. that on which one depends for supply, *kukunán;* an expedience, *paraán;* knowledge of what to do in an emergency or difficuity, *kapamaraanán;* (pl.) means usable or convertible into money, *mapangíngilakan; mapagkúkunan.*

RESOURCEFUL, adj. *mapamaraán.*

RESPECT, n. *paggalang, pamimitagan.*—v. *gumalang, igalang; magpitagan, mamitagan, pamitaganan.*

RESPECTABILITY, n. *pagka-kinaáalang-alanganan.*

RESPECTABLE, adj. *kaalang-alang; kinaálang-alanganan.*

RESPECTFUL, adj. *magalang, mapitagan.*

RESPECTIVE, adj. *kaní-kaniyá; ukul-ukol.*

RESPIRATION, n. *paghingá; hingá;* breath, *hiningá.*

RESPIRE, v. to breathe, *humingá.*

RESPITE, n. *sandalíng ginhawa;* reprieve, *palugit.*

RESPLENDENCE, n. *luningning.*

RESPLENDENT, adj. *maluningning.*

RESPOND, v. *tumugón;* to answer, *sumagót.*

RESPONDENT, n. *katugón.*

RESPONSE, n. *tugón; sagót.*

RESPONSIBILITY, n. *kapanágutan; ságutin.*

RESPONSIBLE, adj. *may-kapanágutan; nanánagót.*

RESPONSIVE, adj. inclined, *mahilig.*

REST, n. repose, *pahingá;* (act of) *pagpapahingá, pamamahingá;* the others, *ang ibá pa.*

RESTAURANT, n. *restaurán,* Fr.; (native) *kárihan.*

RESTFUL, adj. *maginhawa.*

RESTITUTION, n. *pagsasaulí.*

RESTIVE, adj. fidgety, *di-mápalagáy.*

RESTLESS, adj. without repose, *waláng-pahingá;* unsettled, *di-mápakalí, di-matalí.*

RESTORATION, n. *pagpapanaguli.*

RESTORATIVE, adj. *pambawì; pampasaulí.*

RESTORE, v. *papanag-ulíin, ibalík, isaulí.*

RESTRAIN, v. *magpıgil, pigilin.*

RESTRAINT, n., *pagpipigil.*

RESTRICT, v. *maghigpit, paghigpitán.*

RESULT, n. consequence, *kináhangganán, ang pinangyarihan;* effect, *kálalabsán; kinálabsán.*

RESUME, v. *magpasimulâ ulí;* to

take up again after interruption, *ipagpatuloy, magpatuloy, itulóy.*

RESURRECT, v. to become risen from the dead, *muling mabuhay;* raise from the dead, *muling buhayin.*

RESURRECTION, n. *muling pagkabuhay.*

RETAIL, n. *tingî, tíngian; pagtitingî.*—v. *magtingî, ipagtíngian.*

RETAIN, v. to hold, *taglayín;* keep in possession, *papanatilihin.*

RETALIATE, v. *gumantí.*

RETALIATION, n. *gantí, pagganti.*

RETARD, v. to cause to move slowly, *parahanin;* delay, *balamin;* cause to take a longer time, *tagalán, patagalán.*

RETARDATION, n. (See RE-TARD) *pagpaparahan; pagbalam; pagpapatagál.*

RETIRE, v. *umurong; iurong;* to go to bed, *matulog.*

RETIRED, adj. having given up business or active life, *tigil na; pahingá na.*

RETIRING, adj. *mabinî;* giving-up a post, *umáalís, paalís.*

RETORT, n. *pakli.*

RETRACT, v. *umurong, iurong;* to withdraw something said or written, *tumalikwás, talikwasán.*

RETRACTION, n. *pag-urong; pagtalikwás.*

RETREAT, v. *umurong.*

RETRIBUTION, n. *gantí.*

RETRIEVE, v. *mabawì.*

RETROGRADE, adj. *pauróng.*—v. to go from better to worse, *sumamâ.*

RETROSPECT, n. *salamisim.*

RETURN, v. to come or go back, *magbalik;* begin or appear again, *bumalik;* restore, *isauli, magsauli.*—n. act of coming back, *pagbabalik;* restoration, *pagsasauli.*

REUNION, n. *muling pagtitipon.*

REVEAL, v. to make known, *ihayág.*

REVEL, n. *pagkakalinggál.*—v. *magkalinggál.*

REVELATION, n. *paghahayág.*

REVENGE, n. *higantí.*—v. to avenge, *maghiganti, ipaghigantí.*

REVENGEFUL, adj. *mapaghigantí.*

REVENUE, n. income from any property, *kita;* tax, *buwís.*

REVERBERATE, v. *umalingawngáw.*

REVERE, v. *pagpitaganan.*

REVERENCE, n. *pagpipitagan.*

REVEREND, adj. *kapitá-pitagan.*

REVERENT, adj. *mapitagan.*

REVERIE, n. *gunamgunam.*

REVERSAL, n. *pagtutumbalík, pagpapatumbalík.*

REVERSE, n. *ang kabaligtarán;* the back, *likód;* the other side, *kabilá.*

REVERSED, adj. *baligtád.*

REVERSIBLE, adj. *báligtarin; nabábaligtád.*

REVERY, n. See REVERIE.

REVIEW, n. *repaso,* Sp.; *pagbabalik-aral,* nc. — v. *'magrepaso, repasuhin,* Sp.; *magbalik-aral, pagbalík-aralan.*

REVILE, v. to vilify, *laitin, manlait;* treat with abuse, *upasalain, mang-upasalà.*

REVISE, v. to change and correct, *iwastô;* improve, *pagbutihin.*

REVISION, n. *pagwawastô.*

REVIVAL, n. *pagbabagong-buhay, muling pagkabuhay.*

REVIVE, v. to come back to life,

mulíng mabuhay, mulíng buha-
yin.

REVOCATION, n. *pagpapawa-*
lang-bisà; repeal, *pag-uurong.*

REVOKE, v. *pawaláng-bisà;* to repeal, *iurong.*

REVOLT, n. rebellion, *panghihi-*
magsík.—v. manghimagsík.

REVOLTING, adj. disgusting, *na-*
kangángani; loathsome, *nakarí-*
rimarim.

REVOLUTION, n. rebellion, *parg-*
hihimagsík; the round-and-round
motion of a body, *pag-inog, pag-*
ikot.

REVOLUTIONIST, n. *manghihi-*
magsík.

REVOLUTIONIZE. v. *baguhin*
nang lúbusan.

REVOLVE, v. to rotate, *uminog,*
umikot.

REVOLVER, n. *rebolber,* Sp.

REVULSION, n. *igtád;* change,
pagbabago; transfer, *lipat.*

REWARD, n. *gantí, gantimpalà.*
—v. gantihán, gantimpalaan.

RHAPSODY, n. *pagtatalík, kata-*
likán, nc.

RHETORIC, n. *retóriká,* Sp.; *sa-*
yusay, nc.; *palapatian,* nc.

RHETORICAL, adj. *.panretóriká,*
Sp.; *panayusay,* nc.

RHETORICIAN, n. *retórikó,* Sp.;
mánanayusáy, nc.

RHEUMATIC, adj. *reumátikó,*
reumahin, Sp.

RHEUMATISM, n. *reuma, reuma-*
tismo, Sp.

RHYME, n. *rima,* Sp.; *tugmâ.—*
v. *itugmâ, paatugmaín.*

RHYTHM, n. *ritmo,* Sp.: *indayog.*

RHYTHMIC, RHYTHMICAL,
adj. *maindayog.*

RIB, n. *tadyáng.*

RIBBON, n. *laso,* Sp.; *sintás,* Sp.

RICE, n. cereal grain, *palay;*
(hulled) *bigás;* (cooked) *kanin.*

RICH, adj. *mayaman.*

RIDDLE, n. *bugtóng;* puzzle, *pa-*
láisipán.

RIDE. v. *sumakáy, sakyán.*

RIDER, n. (on horseback) *mánga-*
ngabayó; (on a vehicle) *sakáy.*

RIDGE, n. (of roof) *palupo;*
range of mountains, *tagaytáy.*

RIDICULE, n. *paglibák, pagtuyâ.*

RIDICULOUS, adj. *kalibák-libák,*
kakutyá-kutyâ.

RIFLE, n. *riple,* Sp.; gun, *baríl.*

RIFT, n. cleft, *siwang.*

RIGHT, adj. straight, *matuwíd;*
correct, *wastô;* opp. of left, *ka-*
nan.

RIGHTEOUS, adj. *makatwiran;*
just, *makatárungan.*

RIGID, adj. *mahigpít;* stiff, *ma-*
tigás.

RIM, n. border, *gilid.*

RING, n. *singsíng.*

RING, v. to sound, *tugtugín.*

RINGLEADER, n. *pasimunò.*

RINGLET, n. small ring, *munting*
singsíng; a curl of hair, *ringlet,*
Eng.

RINSE, v. *huwhawán.*

RIOT, n. *balasaw;* *guló, kaguló.*

RIOTOUS, adj. *mabalasaw, magu-*
ló.

RIP, v. *punitin;* to undo the seam
of, by cutting the stitches, *mag-*
tastás, tastasin.

RIPE, adj. *hinóg.*

RIPEN, v. *mahinóg;* to cause to
r., *pahinugín, magpahinóg.*

RIPPLE, n. (of water or hair)
alún-alón; (sound) *aliw-iw, sa-*
luysóy.

RISE, v. (from a sitting position)
tumindíg, tumayô; (from a lying
position) *bumangon.*

RISK, n. peril, *panganib.—v. ma-*
nganib; iharáp sa panganib.

RISKY, adj. *mapanganib.*
RITE, n. *rito,* Sp.
RIVAL, n. *kaagáw; kapangagáw.*
RIVALRY, n. *pagpapangagáw.*
RIVET, n. *rematse,* Sp.; *silsíl.*
RIVULET, n. *ilug-ilugan; sapà.*
ROAD, n. *daán.*
ROAM, v. *gumalà, magpagalagalà.*
ROAN, n.-adj. *rosilyo,* Sp.
ROAR, *ungal.—v. umungal.*
ROAST v. *mag-ihaw; magsangág; r.* pig, *litsón,* Sp.
ROB, v. *magnakaw, nakawin, nakawan.*
ROBBER, n. *magnanakaw.*
ROBBERY, n. *nákawan; pagnanakaw.*
ROBUST, adj. *matipunò.*
ROCK, n. *bató, batóng-buháy.*
ROCKET, n. *kuwites,* Sp.
ROCKY, adj. *mabató.*
ROD, n. (metal or wood) *baras,* Sp.; whip, *pamalò.*
ROGUE, n. *taong tampalasan, buhóng.*
ROLL, v. to cause to move onward by turning over and over, *pagulungin;* wrap upon itself or some other object, *ilulón, maglulón.—*n. *paggulong; lulón.*
ROLLER, n. (of a printing machine) *rodilyo,* Sp.
ROMANCE, n. *romansa,* Sp.; (of love) *palásintahan.*
ROMANTIC, adj. *romántikó,* Sp.; (lovelorn) *masintahin.*
ROOF, n. *bubóng; bubungán.*
ROOM, n. *silíd; kuwarto,* Sp.
ROOMY, adj. spacious, *maluwáng.*
ROOST, n. *hapunán.—*v. *humapon.*
ROOSTER, n. *tandáng.*
ROOT, n. *ugát.—*v. *mag-ugát.*
ROPE, n. *lubid.*
ROSARY, n. *rosaryo,* Sp.

ROSE, n. (shrub) *rosas.*
ROSTER, n. *tálaan.*
ROTATE, v. *painugin, paikutin.*
ROTTEN, adj. decayed, *bulók, sirâ;* (eggs) *bugók;* (fish) *bilasâ, halpók, hampók.*
ROTUND, adj. *bilóg, bilugán.*
ROUGE, n. *papulá; pangulay.*
ROUGH, adj. *magaspáng.*
ROUGHEN, v. *pagaspangín.*
ROUND, adj. *bilóg.*
ROUSE, v. to awaken, *gisingin;* stir to thought or action, *pukawin.*
ROUTE, n. *daánan, pagdáraanan.*
ROUTINE, n. *karaniwang palakad; karaniwang gáwain.*
ROW, n. series in a line, *hanay; hilera,* Sp.
ROW, v. to propel (by oars), *sumagwán, managwán; gumaod.*
ROYAL, adj. *pangharì, makaharì.*
ROYALTY, n. *pagkaharì.*
RUB, v. *kuskusín; magkuskós.*
RUBBISH, n. trash, *yamutmót; kagikagi;* garbage, *basura,* Sp.
RUBY, n. *rubí,* Sp.
RUDDER, n. *ugit; timón,* Sp.
RUDDY, adj. *namúmulá-mulá.*
RUDE, adj. impolite, *bastós,* Sp.; impudent, *waláng-pakundangan.*
RUDIMENT, n. *simulâ, pasimulâ.*
RUE, v. to be sorry for, *ikalungkót;* wish undone, *ipagsisi, pagsisihan.*
RUEFUL, adj. sad, *malungkót.*
RUFFIAN, n. *tampalasan.*
RUG, n. *alpombra,* Sp.
RUGGED, adj. *bakú-bakó;* wrinkled, *kulubót.*
RUIN, n. *pagkagibá, pagkaguhô. pagkalugsô.—*v. *gibaín, iguhô, ilugsô.*
RUINOUS, adj. destructive, *nakagígibá;* hurtful, *nakasásamâ.*
RULE, n. *tuntunin;* regulation, *álituntunin.*

RULE, v. *maghari, magpunò;* to manage, *mamahalà.*

RULER, n. one who governs, *nagháhari, namúmunò;* wood or metal guide, *panuto; regladór,* Sp.

RUM, n. (wine) *ron,* Sp.

RUMBLE, n. *dagundóng; ugong.*

RUMOR, n. *bali-balità; sabi-sabi.*

RUMP, n. *puwitan.*

RUMPLE, v. *gusutín.*

RUMPUS, n. *guló.*

RUN, n. *tumakbó; magtatakbó.*

RUNG, n. (of ladder) *baitáng*

RUNNER, n. *mánanakbó.*

RUNWAY, n. *pátakbuhan.*

RUPTURE, n. break, *sirà;* hernia, *luslós.*

RURAL, adj. *pambukid, pangkabukiran.*

RUSE, n. *lalâng.*

RUSH, v. to hurry, *magmadali,* —adj. *mádalian.*

RUSSIAN, n.-adj. *Ruso,* Sp.

RUST, n. *kalawang.*

RUSTLE, v. *lumagitík.*

RUSTY, adj. *makalawang, kálawangin.*

RUT, n. groove, *ukà.*

RUTHLESS, adj. *waláng-awà.*

S

SABER, n. *sable,* Sp.

SABOTAGE, n. *pamiminsalà.*

SACK, n. large bag, *sako, kustál; supot;* (of reed) *bayong.*

SACK, v. to plunder, pillage, *mandambóng, dambungín; manupot.*

SACRAMENT, n. *sakramento.* Sp.

SACRED, adj. *sagrado,* Sp.; pertaining to religion, *panrelihiyón.*

SACRIFICE, n. offering, *alay, hain;* the losing or giving up of something for another's sake, *paypapukasakit, sákripisyo,* Sp. —v. to offer, *mag-alay, maghain;* destroy or give up something for another's sake, *maypukasakit, magsákripisyo,* Sp.

SACRILEGE, n. *kalapastanganan.*

SACRISTY, n. *sakristiya,* Sp.

SAD, adj. sorrowful, *malungkót;* mournful, *mapangláw.*

SADDEN, v. *papamanglawín.*

SADDLE, n. *siya,* (Sp. *silla*).

SAFE, adj. *ligtás;* trustworthy, *mapagkákatiwalaan.*

SAFE, n. iron or steel chest, *kaha de yero,* Sp.; *kabáng-bakal.*

SAFEGUARD, v. *ipag-adyá, adyahán; ipagsanggaláng.*

SAFETY, n. *kaligtasan.* — s. match. *pósporó,* Sp.—s. pin, *imperdible,* Sp.

SAG, v. to droop under pressure, *lumundô;* hang down or droop by one's own weight, *lumayláy.*

SAGACIOUS, adj. shrewd, *matalas;* intelligent, *matalino.*

SAGACITY, n. shrewdness, *katalasan;* intelligence, *katalinuhan.*

SAGE, adj. wise, *maalam;* indicating profound wisdom, *pantás.*

SAGE, n. (Bot.) *sambóng; sálbiyá,* Sp.

SAGO, n. (Bot.) *sagó.*

SAIL, n. *layag.*—v. *lumayag.*

SAILBOAT, n. (with outriggers) *paráw;* (smaller than *paráw*) *sibirán.*

SAILOR, n. *mandaragát; marinero,* Sp.

SAINT, n. *santó*, Sp.; *banál.*

SAINTLY, adj. pious, *banál.*

SAKE, n. regard, *alang-alang.*— For the s. of the argument, *alang-alang sa pagtatalo.*

SALAD, n. *ensalada*, Sp.; *salad*, Eng.

SALARY, n. *sahod; suweldo*, Sp.

SALE, n. *pagbibili.*

SALESMAN, n. *tagapagbili, tagapaglakò.*

SALINE, adj. *maalat.*

SALIVA, n. *laway.*

SALLOW, adj. of a pale, sickly yellow color, *barák.*

SALMON, n. *salmón*, Sp.

SALOON, n. hall, *bulwagan.*

SALT, n. *asín.*—v. *asnán.*

SALTPETER, n. *salitre*, Sp.

SALTY, adj. tasting of salt, *maalát;* somewhat salt, *parang asín.*

SALUTATION, n. *batì.*

SALUTATORIAN, n. (at a graduation) *pangalawáng dangál.*

SALUTE, n. greeting, *batì;* bow, *yukód;* taking off of hat, *pugay;* (military) *saludo*, Sp.—v. to greet, *bumatì, batíin;* bow, *yumukód;* take oif one's hat to, *magpugay, pagpugayan;* (among the military) *sumaludo*, saluduhan, Sp.

SALVAGE, n. *pagsagíp.*—v. *sumagíp, sagipín.*

SALVATION, n. *kaligtasa:..*

SALVO, n. *pasalbá*, Sp.

SAME, adj. identical, *iyundín;* alike, *magkatulad; magkagaya, magkaparis.*

SAMPLE, n. *muwestra*, Sp.; something shown, *pakita;* something given for tasting, *patikim.*

SANCTIFY, v. *idambanà, dambanaɪn.*

SANCTION, n. *pagpapatɪbay.*—v. *pagtibayin, magpatibay.*

SANCTITY, n. *kabánalan.*

SANCTUARY, n. *santuwaryo*, Sp.; altar, *dambanà.*

SAND, n. *buhangɪn.*

SANDAL, n. *sandalyás*, Sp.; *pangyapák.*

SANDPAPER, n. *pangaskas; papél de liha*, Sp.

SANDY, adj. *mabuhangin.*

SANE, adj. *matinó;* healthy, *malusóg.*

SANGUINE, adj. *may maalab na kaloobán.*

SANITARY, adj. clean, *malinɪs.*

SANITATION, n. cleanliness, *kalɪnɪsan.*

SANITY, n. *katinuán.*

SAP, n. juice, *katás.*

SAPLING, n. *supling.*

SAPPHIRE, n. *sápiró*, Sp.

SARCASM, n. *uyám, pag-uyám.*

SARCASTIC, adj. *nakaúuyám.*

SARDINE, n. *sardinas*, Sp.

SARSAPARILLA, n. *sarsaparilyá.*

SATIATE, v. *busugín;* to be satiated, *mabusóg.*

SATIETY, n. *kabusugán.*

SATIN, n.-adj. *satín*, Sp.

SATIRE, n. *tuyâ, uyam.*

SATIRIC, adj. *nakatútuyâ, mánunuyá; nakaúuyám, mang-uuyám.*

SATISFACTION, n. *ʋasiyahán.*

SATISFACTORY, adj. *nakasísiyá.*

SATISFY, v. *magbigáy-kasiyahán, bigyáng-kasiyahán.*

SATURATE, v. *tigmakín.*

SATURATION, n. *katigmakán.*

SATURDAY, n. *Sábadó*, Sp.

SAUCE, n. *sarsa*, Sp.; *sawsawan.*

SAUCER, n. *platito*, Sp.

SAUSAGE, n. *suriso.*

SAVAGE, adj. *ganid;* ferocious, *mabangis.*

SAVANT, n. *pantás; pahám.*

SAVE, v. *iligtás, magliqtáś;* to refrain from spending, *magtipíd, tipirín.*

SAVE, prep. except, *kundî, máliban.*

SAVIOR, n. *tagapagligtás.*

SAVOR, n. taste, *lasa;* flavor, *linamnám.*

SAVORY, adj. tasty, *malasa;* palatable, *malinamnám.*

SAW, n. (Carp.) *lagarì*—v. *maglagarì.*

SAWDUST, n. *pinaglaqarian; serín,* Sup.

SAWMILL, n. *pálagarian.*

SAXOPHONE, n. *saksopón,* Eng.

SAY, v. *magsabi, sabihin.*

SAYING, n. *kasabihán.*

SCAB, n. *langíb.*

SCABBARD, n. *kaluban.*

SCABBY, adj. *súgatin.*

SCABROUS, adj. *makaliskís.*

SCAFFOLD, n. execution platform, *bibitayán.*

SCALD, v. *magbanlî, banlián;* to be scalded, *mábanlián.*

SCALE, n. one pan of a balance, *panimbáng;* (pl.) *timbangan.*

SCALES, n. small horny plates covering fish, reptiles, etc., *kaliskís.*

SCALP, n. *balat-ulo; anit.*

SCALPEL, n. *panistís.*

SCALY, adj. *makaliskís.*

SCANDAL, n. *iskándaló,* Sp.; *alinagasngás;* gossip, *satsatan, daldalan;* slander, *paninirang-puri.*

SCANDALOUS, adj. *iskandaloso* (-a), Sp.; *maalingasngás.*

SCANTY, adj. *kákauntì; katiting.*

SCAPULA, n. (Anat.) shoulder blade, *paypáy.*

SCAPULAR, n. *eskapularyo, kalmén,* Sp.

SCAR, n. *piklát, pilat.*

SCARCE, adj. not common, *di-ka-* *raniwan;* not plentiful, *madalang, kákauntî;* not equal to the demand, *di-sapát.*

SCARE, v. *takutin, manakot;* to be scared, *matakot.*

SCARECROW, n. *pátakót, panakot.*

SCATHING, adj. *nakasásakít, nakapanánakít.*

SCATTER, v. *isabog, magsaoog; pasabugin;* to strew loosely about, *ikalat, magkalat; pakalatin.*

SCENE, n. *tagpô;* view, *pánoorín, tánawin.*

SCENERY, n. *tánawin.*

SCENT, n. sense of smell, *pangamóy;* odor, *amóy.*

SCEPTER, n. *setro,* Sp.

SCEPTIC, adp *di-mapaniwalaín.*

SCHEDULE, n. *palátuntunan.*

SCHEME, n. plan, *panukalà; balak;* device, *paraán, pamamaraán.*

SCHISM, n. division, *paghahatì;* separation, *paghihiwaláy.*

SCHOLAR, n. student, *nag-áaral, mag-aarál;* learned person, *pantás.*

SCHOOL, n. *páaralán; eskuwélahán,* Sp.

SCIENCE, n. knowledge, *karunungan; siyénsiyá,* Sp.

SCIENTIFIC, adj. *pangkarunungan; siyentípikó,* Sp.

SCIENTIST, n. *siyentípikó,* Sp.

SCINTILLATE, v. *kumisláp.*

SCINTILLATION, n, *pagkisláp.*

SCION, n. sprout or shoot, *supang;* descendant, *supling.*

SCISSORS, n. *gunting.*

SCOFF, v. *mang-aglahì, aglahiin.*

SCOLD, v. *magmurá, murahin.*

SCOOP, v. *sumalok, salukin; su* *mandók, sandukin.*

SCORCH v. to burn slightly, *pa-*

suin; be burned slightly, *mapasò;* cause to be parched, *idaráng.*

SCORE, n. number, *bilang;* twenty, *dalawampû.*—v. to keep a record, *magtalâ;* find fault with, *pintasán, mamintás;* be able to make a tally or advance a point, *makabilang.*

SCORN, v. *manlibák, libakín;* to despise as unworthy, *manghamak, hamakin.*

SCORNFUL, adj. *mapanlibák; mapanghamak.*

SCORPION, n. *alakdán*

SCOUNDREL, n.-adj. *walángdangál;* low, mean, *imbí.*

SCOUR, v. *isisín.*

SCOURGE, n. *pamalò, pambugbóg.*

SCOUT, n. *iskaut,* Eng.

SCOWL, v. *mangunot-noó, pagkunutáng-noó;* to look sullen, *magmukháng-galit.*

SCRAMBLE, v. to clamber on hands and feet, *mang-ukyabit, umukyabit, pag-ukyabitan;* struggle for something eagerly or rudely, *makipagpángagawán, magpángagawán.*

SCRAP, n. fragment, *kapıraso,* Sp.; junk metal, *iskráp,* Eng.

SCRAPBOOK, n. *aklát-sipián.*

SCRAPE, v. *magkayod, kayurin.*

SCRAPER, n. *pangayod;* (for coconuts) *kudkuran.*

SCRATCH, v. *kumamot, kamutin.*

SCREAM, v. to utter in a loud, piercing voice, *humiyáw;* s. at, *hiyawán;* utter a sharp, shrill cry, *tumilî.*

SCREEN, n. *tabing.*

SCREW, n. *turnilyo,* Sp.—s. driver, *pamihit-turnilyo; desturnilyadór,* Sp.

SCRIBE, n. *mánunulat.*

SCRIPT, n. *sulat-kamáy;* manuscript, *oríhinál,* Sp.; cursive, *kursiba,* Sp., *hilíg.*

SCRIPTURE, n. (Holy) *Banál na Kasulatan.*

SCROLL, n. *balumbón.*

SCRUB, v. *magkuskós, kuskusín.*

SCRUPLE, n. hesitation, *pag-aalangán.*

SCRUPULOUS, adj. inclined to be conscientious, *mapangalagà; careful, maingat.*

SCUFFLE, v. to fight or struggle hand to hand, *magpanunggáb;* drag the feet in a slovenly manner, *dumagos, dumagusdós.*

SCULLERY, n. back kitchen, *batalan.*

SCULLION, n. *bataan.*

SCULPTOR, n. *manlililok, eskultór,* Sp.

SCULPTURE, n. *panlililok; eskultura,* Sp.

SCUM, n. *lináb; kapa,* Sp.

SCURF, n. dandruff, *balakubak.*

SCURRY, v. *magtatakbó; kumarimot ng takbó.*

SCYTHE, n. *lilik, karit.*

SEA, n. *dagat.*

SEAL, n. stamp or die, *selyo,* Sp.; *taták.*—v. to set or affix a seal to, *sélyuhán,* Sp.; *tatakán* (of envelopes) to paste the flap, *idikit;* fill up cracks or crevices, *pasakan, takpán.*

SEAM, n. *tahî; pinagtahián.*

SEAMAN, n. *mandaragát; taongdagat.*

SEAMLESS, adj. *waláng-tahî; di-tinahî.*

SEAPORT, n. *dáungang-dagat.*

SEARCH, v. to seek, *hanapin, paghanapin.*

SEARCHLIGHT, n. *sulóng panaliksík.*

SEASHORE, n. *baybayin, tabingdagat.*

SEASICKNESS, n. *pagkalulà, lulà; pagkahilo.*

SEASICK, adj. *nalúlulà, nahíhilo.*

SECRET, n.-adj. *lihim.*—adj. hidden, *nakatagò, tagô.*

SEASON, n. *panahón.*

SEASONABLE, adj. *nápapanahón.*

SEASONAL, adj. *paná-panahón.*

SEASONING, n. *pampalasa, pampalinamnám; rekado,* Sp.

SEAT, n. *úpuan.*

SEAWEED, n. *damóng-dagat.*

SECEDE, v. *tumiwalág.*

SECESSION, n. *pagtiwalág.*

SECLUDED, adj. remote, *malayò;* separated, *hiwaláy.*

SECOND, n.-adj. *ikaláwá, pangalawá.*—n. 60th part of a minute, *segundo,* Sp.; *saglít.*

SECONDHAND, adj. *lumà; gamít na; sigundamano,* Sp.

SECRETARY, n. *kalihim; sekretaryo* (-a), Sp.

SECRETIVE, adj. *mapaglihím.*

SECT, n. *sekta,* Sp.; *pangkát.*

SECTARIAN, adj. *may-pangkatin.* (Non-s., *waláng-pangkatin*).

SECTION, n. portion, *bahagi;* subdivision, *pangkát.*

SECTIONAL, adj. *bahá-bahagi; pangkát-pangkát.*

SECTIONALISM, n. *kapanarilihán; rehiyonalismo,* Sp.

SECULAR, adj. (Ecc.) *seglár,* Sp.

SECURE, adj. *tiwasáy.*—v. to gain possession of, *makuha, mátamó.*

SECURITY, n. *katiu·sayán.*

SEDATE, adj. calm, composed, *mahinahon.*

SEDIMENT, n. *latak.*

SEDITION, n. *sedisyón,* Sp.

SEDITIOUS, adj. *labág sa bayan.*

SEDUCE, v. *manghibò, hibuin; manlamuyot, lamuyutin.*

SEDUCTION, n. *panghihibò; panlalamuyot.*

SEDUCTIVE, adj. *mapanghibò; mapanlamuyot.*

SEDULOUS, adj. *masigasig.*

SEE, v. to behold, *mákita;* visit, *dumalaw, dalawin;* try to meet, *makipagkita;* comprehend, *maunawaan.*

SEED, n. *butó.*

SEEDLING, n. *binhî, punlâ.*

SEEDY, adj. *mabutó.*

SEEK, v. *maghanáp, paghanapin.*

SEEM, v. translated as adverb: *tila, warì.* The sky seems blue. *Ang langit ay tila bugháw.*— *Warì* uses the ligature. I seem to be floating. *Waring akó'y nakalutang.*

SEEP, v. *kumayat.*

SEEPAGE, n. *kayat.*

SEER, n. *manghuhulà.*

SEESAW, n. *palátimbangan.*

SEETHE, v. to boil, *kumulô, sumulák.*

SEGMENT, n. portion, *bahagi.*

SEGREGATE, v. *ibukód, ilayô, ihiwaláy.*

SEGREGATION, n. *pagbubukód, paglalayô, paghihiwaláy.*

SEIZE, v. to take possession of forcibly or suddenly, *kamkamín, mangamkám;* snatch, *agawin, umagaw, mang-agaw.*

SEIZURE, n. *pangangamkám, pag-agaw, pang-aagaw.*

SELDOM, adv. *bihirà.*

SELECT, adj. *pilì, pinilì.*—v. *pumilì, mamilì; humirang.*

SELECTION, n. *pagpilì, paghirang.*

SELF, n. *ang sarili.* (Myself, *ang aking sarili;* yourself, *ang iyóng sarili;* pl. *ang inyóng sarili;*

himself, herself, *ang kaniyáng sarili*, etc.)

SELF-CONCEIT, n. *pagka-maka-akó*.

SELF-CONFIDENCE, n. *tiwalà sa sarili*.

SELF-CONSCIOUS, adj. *mahiyain, mahinhín*.

SELF-CONTROL, n. *pagpipigil sa sarili*.

SELF-DEFENSE, n. *pagtatanggól sa sarili*.

SELF-DENYING, adj. *mapagtimpî*.

SELF-GOVERNMENT, n. *panariling-pámahalaán*.

SELFISH, adj. *maka-sarili;* avaricious, *sakím, masakím, maramot*.

SELFISHNESS, n. *pagkamakasarili; kasakimán*.

SELL, v. *magbilí, ipagbilí;* (to) *pagbilhán;* to tend a store, *magtindá*.

SEMBLANCE, n. *wangis;* image, *larawan*.

SEMESTER, n. 6 months, (half-year), *hating-taón;* a school s., *hatintaón*.

SEMICOLON, n. *tuldukuwít*.

SEMINAR, n. *pantás-aral*, nc.

SEMINARY, n. *seminaryo*, Sp.

SEMIVOWEL, n. *malapatinig*.

SENATE, n. *senado*, Sp.

SENATOR, n. *senadór*, Sp.

SEND, v. *magpadalá, ipadalá*.

SENIOR, adj.-n. elder, *nakatátandâ;* the last year in school or college course, also the student in such final year, *sinyor*, Eng.; *ang nagtátapós*.

SENSATION, n. *pakiramdám.—* He created a s., *Siyá'y nakapukaw ng damdamin*.

SENSATIONAL, adj. *makapukaw-damdamin; kasindál-sindál*.

SENSE, n. the power to see or feel, *pandamá; sentido*, Sp.; the

power to perceive, *pang-unawà;* sound, clear mind, *diwà;* meaning, *kahulugán;* that which expresses wisdom or sanity, *bait*.

SENSELESS, adj. without feeling, *waláng-damdamin:* nonsensical, *waláng-diwà, waláng-saysáy*.

SENSIBILITY, n. *pakiramdám;* mental discernment, *katalusán*.

SENSIBLE, adj. reasonable, *maykatwiran*.

SENSITIVE, adj. capable of feeling, *may-pakiramdám;* easily affected, *muramdamin; mapagdamdám, mahiyain*.

SENTENCE, n. (Gram.) *pangungusap;* (Law) judgment, *hatol*.

SENTIMENT, n. *damdamin, damdám*.

SENTIMENTAL, adj. emotional, *maramdamin;* affectedly tender, *malambíng*.

SENTINEL, SENTRY, n. *bantáy, tanod*.

SEPARATE, adj. *bukód, hiwaláy.—v.* to divide, *hatiin;* disunite, *paghiwalayín;* disconnect, *tanggalín;* set apart, *ibukód*.

SEPARATION, n. *paghihiwaláy*.

SEPARATOR, n. *panghiwaláy*.

SEPTEMBER, n. *Setyembre*, Sp.

SEPULCHER, n. *líbingan*.

SEPULTURE, n. *paglilibíng*.

SEQUEL, n. *karugtóng*.

SEQUENCE, n. *pagsusunúd-sunód, pagkakásunúd-sunód*.

SERENADE, n. *harana; serenata*, Sp.—v. *magharana, haranahin*.

SERENE, adj. *mahinahon; mabinì*.

SERENITY, n. *kahinahunan, kabinihan*.

SERF, n. slave, *alipin, busabos*.

SERGEANT, n. *sarhento*, Sp.

SERIAL, adj. *dugtúng-dugtóng*.

SERIES, n. *pánunuran; serye,* Sp.

SERIOUS, adj. formal, *pormál,* Sp.; sober, *matinô;* in a grave condition, *malubhâ, mabigát.*

SERMON, n. *pangaral; sermón,* Sp.

SERMONIZE, v. *mangaral; magsermón,* Sp.

SERPENT, n. *ahas; serpiyente,* Sp.

SERRATE, adj. *ngipín-ngipín.*

SERVANT, n. *alilà, bataan.*

SERVE, v. *maglingkód, paglingkurán; magsilbí, pagsilbihán;* to be of use to, *magamit.*

SERVICE, n. *paglilingkód; serbisyo,* Sp.—Civil s., *Serbisyo Sibíl.* — Public S., *Pálingkurang Pangmadlâ.*

SERVICEABLE, adj. *magágamit; mapakíkinabangan.*

SERVITOR, n. *tagapaglingkód.*

SERVITUDE, n. *kaalipinán, pagkaalipin.*

SESSION, n. (at school) *pagaaral, pagkaklase,* Sp.; the holding of meetings, *pagpupulong.*

SET, v. to put, *ilagáy, maglagáy;* sink, *lumubóg;* fix, *magtakdâ, itakdâ.*

SETBACK, n. *pag-urong.*

SETTLE, v. to establish self in a place, *tumahán, manahanan;* colonize, *maniruhan;* conclude, *wakasán;* decide, *pagpasiyahán;* set in order, *ayusin, mag-ayos;* pay (a bill) *magbayad, pagbayaran;* become clarified, as a liquid, *luminaw;* come to an agreement, *magkásundô.*

SEVEN, n. adj. *pitó.*

SEVENFOLD, n.-adj. *pitóng ibayo.*

SEVENTEEN, n.-adj. *labimpitó.*

SEVENTEENTH, n.-adj. *ikalabimpitó (ika-17).*

SEVENTH, n. adj. *ikapitó (ika-7).*

SEVENTY, n.-adj. *pitumpû.*

SEVER, v. to separate with violence, *tanggalín;* (the head) *pugutin, pugutan.*

SEVERAL, adj. *mga ilán;* various, *ibá-ibá.*

SEVERE, adj. strict, *mahigpít;* harsh, *mabagsík.*

SEVERITY, n. strictness, *kahigpitán;* harshness, *kabagsikán.*

SEW, v. *tahiin, maytahi, manahî.*

SEWER, n. *páagusan, pádaluyan.*

SEX, n. *tauhín;* (Gram.) gender, *kasarian.*

SEXTET, n. *ániman; sesteto,* Sp.

SHABBINESS, n. *panlilimahid.*

SHABBY, adj. *nanlilimahid.*

SHACKLE, n. (pl.) *pangáw: gapos.*

SHADE, n. *lilim; lilom.*

SHADOW, n. *anino.*

SHADOWY, adj. dim, *malabò.*

SHADY, adj. *malilim; malilom.*

SHAFT, n. stem (as of arrow). *tagdán;* the arrow itself, *panà, palasô;* plant stalk, *tangkáy;* handle, *hawakán, tatangnán.*

SHAGGY, adj. *mabuhók, mabalanibo;* rough with long hair, *malambâ.*

SHAKE, v. *ugaín; umugâ;* to cause to shiver, *paugaín;* tremble, *manginíg, mangatál.*—To s. hands with, *makipagkamáy.* — To s. a bottle, *alugín (kalugín) ang bote.*

SHAKY, adj. *umúugâ;* wavering, *mabuwáy.*

SHALL,—expressed in the future tense forms of verbs.

SHALLOW, adj. *mababaw.*

SHAM, adj. *paimbabáw.*

SHAME, n. *hiyâ.*—v. to cause to be ashamed, *hiyaín.*

SHAMEFUL, adj. *kahiyá-hiyá; nakahihiyâ.*

SHAMELESS, adj. *waláng-hiyâ.*

SHAMPOO, n. *panggugò.* — v. *maggugò, guguan.*

SHANK, n. *paá.*

SHAPE, n. form, *anyô;* contour, *tabas;* figure *hugis.*

SHAPER, n. *panghugis.*

SHARE, n. portion allotted, *kabahagi;* portion of capital stock, *aksiyón,* Sp.—v. to divide and distribute, *ipamahagi;* partake of, *makibahagi, makisama.*

SHARK, n. (Biol.) *pating.*

SHARP, adj. having fine, thin edge, as a knife, *matalím, matalas;* ending in a fine point, as a needle, *matulis.*

SHARPEN, v. *ihasà, maghasà.*

SHATTER, v. *durugin; basagin.*

SHAVE, v. (self) *mag-ahit;* (others) *umahit, mana-ahit; ahitin.*

SHAWL, n. *panyulón,* Sp.; *alamdúy.*

SHE, pron. *siyá.* See HE.

SHEAR, v. *gupitin.*

SHEARS, n. *panggupít; gunting.*

SHEATH, n. *kaluban.*

SHED, v. *tumulò; dumaloy;* to let fall, (as leaves) *malaglág.*

SHEEP, n. *tupa.*

SHEEPSKIN, n. *balát-tupa.*

SHEET, n. (of paper) *pilyego,* Sp.; *dahon;* (of cloth) *piraso,* Sp.

SHELF, n. *istante,* Sp.

SHELL, n. outer covering, *balát;* cartridge, *kartutso,* Sp.—v. to take out the outside covering or separate from the cob, *maghimáy, himayin.*

SHELLAC, n. *laka,* Sp.

SHELTER, n. *kublihan, kanlungan.*—v. to protect or shield from injury, *ipag-adyá;* take refuge, *magkublí, mangublí; kumanlóng, manganlóng.*

SHEPHERD, n. *pastól,* Sp.; *tagapag-alagà.*

SHIELD, n. *kalasag, pananggá; sanggaláng.*

SHIFT, n. substitution, *paghahalili;* a changing, *pagbabago, paglilipat.*

SHIMMER, v. *umandáp-andáp, kumuráp-kuráp.*

SHIN, n. (Anat.) *lulód.*

SHINE, v. to emit rays of light, *sumikat;* be bright, *magningning.*

SHINING, adj. radiant, *maningning;* giving light, *maliwanag.*

SHINY, adj. *makintáb;* polished, *makinis, binuli;* bright, *maningning.*

SHIP, n. *sasakyáng-dagat; bapor,* Sp.—v. *ilulan sa bapór.*

SHIPMENT, n. *palulan.*

SHIPWRECK, n. *pagkabagbág (ng bapór).*

SHIRT, n. *kamisadentro,* Sp.

SHIVER, v. to tremble, *manginíg;* (from cold) *mangaligkíg;* (from fright) *mangatál.*

SHOAL, adj. shallow, *mababaw.*

SHOCK, n. impact, *dagok;* sudden disturbance, *kabiglaanan, pagkabiglâ.*

SHOCKING, adj. causing to shake (as by a blow), *nakayáyanig;* causing disturbance of feelings, *nakapangíngilabot.*

SHOE, n. *sapatos,* Sp.

SHOEMAKER, n. *sapatero,* Sp.; *magsasapatós.*

SHOOT, v. to let fly, discharge with sudden force, *tumudlâ, tudlaín;* kill with a gun, *barilín,* Sp.; fire off or discharge a weapon, *magpaputók.*

SHOOT, n. a young branch or growth, *supang.*

SHOP, n. store, *tindahan;* factory, *págawaan;* a mechanic's place of work, *gáwaan.*

SHOPKEEPER, n. *magtitindá, tagapagtindá; tindero (a)*, Sp.

SHORE, n. (of sea or lake) *tabíng-dagat, baybayin;* (of river) *pampáng.*

SHORT, adj. not long, *maiklî, maigsî;* brief in time, *madalî.*

SHORTAGE, n. *kakulangán, kulang.*

SHORTEN, v. *paikliín, paigsiín.*

SHORTENING, n. that which makes pastry crisp and brittle, *pampalutóng.*

SHORTLY, adv. soon, *sandali na lamang.*

SHORT-WINDED, adj. *madalíng humingal.*

SHOULD, v. aux. *dapat, nararapat.*

SHOULDER, n. *balikat.*

SHOUT, n. *sigáw, hiyáw.*—v. *sumigáw, humiyáw;* to s. at, *sigawán, hiyawán.*

SHOVE, n. *tulak.*—v. *itulak.*

SHOVEL, n. *pala*, Sp.

SHOW, v. to present to view, *ipakita;* exhibit, *itanghál.*

SHOWER, n. a brief fall of rain, *ambón.*—v. *umambón.*

SHOWY, adj. attracting attention, *tánawin;* gorgeous, *marilág;* pretentious, *mapagparangyá.*

SHREWD, adj. keen, *matalas.*

SHRIEK, n. *tilî.*—v. *tumilî.*

SHRIMP, n. *hipon.*

SHRINE, n. altar, *dambanà.*

SHRINK, v. to contract, *umurong, mangikli.*

SHRIVEL, v. to be drawn into wrinkles, *mangulubót.*

SHROUD, n. *sapot.*—v. *saputan.*

SHRUG, v. *magkibít ng balikat.*

SHUDDER, v. *manginíg, mangatál.*

SHUFFLE, v. to rearrange playing cards, *bumalasa, magbalasa;* move with a dragging motion (as the feet in walking or dancing) *umingkáng-ingkáng.*

SHUN, v. to avoid, *ilagan, layuán.*

SHUT, v. to close, *sarhán, magsará*, Sp.; *ipinid.*

SHY, adj. timid, *kimî;* bashful, *mahiyain.*

SICK, adj. *may-sakít, may-karamdaman.*

SICKENING, adj. *nakapagkákasakít;* nauseating, *nakapangángasim ng sikmurà.*

SICKLE, n. *lilik, karit.*

SICKLY, adj. *masasaktín;* never well, *hímatlugin.*

SICKNESS, n. *pagkakasakít; pagkakaramdám.*

SIDE, n. edge, *tabí, tabihán;* surface or face of a solid, *panig.*—v. to take the part of one against another, *kumampí, kampihán; pumanig, panigan; kumatig, katigan.*

SIDEWALK, n. *bangketa*, Sp.

SIDEWAYS, adv. *patagilíd.*

SIEGE, n. *pagkubkób.*

SIFT, v. to pass through a sieve, *salain; bithayín.*

SIFTER, n. *salaán; bitháy.*

SIGH, n. *buntúnghiningá.*—v. *magbuntúnghiningá.*

SIGHT, n. *tingín, paningín;* spectacle, *pánoorín.*

SIGN, n. symbol, *tandâ;* omen, *pángitaín.*—v. to affix a signature, *lumagdâ, lagdaán; pumirmá, pirmahán*, Sp.

SIGNAL, n. sign agreed upon, *hudyát.*—adj memorable, *di-malílimutan.*—v. to communicate with by means of flags, signs, etc., *humudyát, hudyatán.*

SIGNATURE, n. *lagdâ; pirmá*, Sp.

SIGNBOARD, n. *karátulá*, Sp.

SIGNIFICANCE, n. *kahulugán.*

SIGNIFICANT, adj. *makahulugán.*

SIGNIFY, v. to mean, *ipakahulugán.*

SILENCE, n. *katahimikan.*

SILENT, adj. not given to speech, *waláng-imík;* quiet, *tahimik.*

SILK, n. *sutlá; seda,* Sp.

SILL, n. bottom piece in a window frame, *pasamano,* Sp.

SILLY, adj. weak in intellect, *hangál;* stupid, *utó.*

SILT, n. *banlík.*

SILVER, n. *pilak; platc* Sp.

SILVERY, adj. *pinilakan.*

SIMILAR, adj. *katulad, kawangis.*

SIMILE, n. *paghahalintulad.*

SIMMER, v. *bumulák.*

SIMPER, v. *ngumisi.*—n. *ngisi.*

SIMPLE, adj. single, *nag-íisá, íisá;* not mixed, *waláng-halò;* (Gram.) not compounded or affixed, *payák;* plain, unadorned, *lisdíng.*

SIMPLIFY, v. to make easier, *magpagaan, pagaanín; paalwanín.*

SIMULATE, v. to assume the character or semblance of, *magsa-* (plus what is being simulated).

SIMULTANEOUS, adj. *magkasabáy, magkakasabáy, sabáysabáy.*

SIN, n. *sala, kasalanan.*—v. *magkásala.*

SINCE, adv. from a certain past time until now, *mulâ noón.*—conj. *yáyamang.* — prep. *mulâ noón.*

SINCERE, adj. true, *tapát;* honorable, *marangál.*

SINFUL, adj. *makasalanan.*

SING, v. *umawit, awitin; kumantá, kantahín,* Sp.

SINGER, n. *mang-aawit; mángangantá,* Sp.

SINGLE, adj. alone, *rag-íisá;* one only, *íisá;* not married, *waláng-asawa;* (masc.) *binatà,* (fem.) *dalaga.*

SINGULAR, adj. (Gram.) *ísahan;* peculiar, *ka-kaiba;* unique, *tangì; bukód-tangì.*

SINK, v. *lumubóg.*

SINKER, n. *pabigát.*

SINNER, n. *taong makasalanan.*

SINUOUS, adj. crooked, *baluktót.*

SIP, v. *sumimsím, simsimín;* to taste, *tumikím, tikmán.*

SIR, n. *ginoó,* (Abb. G.)

SIREN, n. *sirena,* Sp.

SIRLOIN, n. *solomilyo,* Sp.

SIRUP, n. *harabe,* Sp.; *pulót; sirup,* Eng.

SISTER, n. *kapatíd na babae.*

SISTER-IN LAW, n. *hipag.*

SIT, v. *umupô, maupô.*—to s. on, *upuán.*—to cause to s. down, *paupuín.*

SITE, n. position, *tayô, katáyuan;* situation, *l a g á y, kalágayan;* place where built, *pinagtayuán;* place in which to be built, *pagtátayuan.*

SITUATED, adj. located, *nakatayô (sa).*

SITUATION, n. *kalágayan.*

SIX, n.-adj. *anim.*

SIXTEENTH, n.-adj. *ikalabíng-anim, ika-16.*

SIXTH, n.-adj. *ikaanim, ika-6.*

SIXTY, n.-adj. *animnapû.*

SIZE, n. *laki.*

SIZZLE, v. *sumirit.*

SKELETON, n. *kalansáy.*

SKID, v. to slip or slide, *mádulás.*

SKILFUL, SKILLFUL, adj. deft, *sanáy, bihasa;* expert, *dalubhasà.*

SKILL, n. *kasanayán;* expertness, *kadalubhasaan.*

SKIM, v. *hapawín, humapáw.*

SKIMPY, adj. narrow, *makipot.*

SKIN, n. *balát.*

SKINNY, adj. emaciated, *butó't-balát;* lean, *payát.*

SKIP, v. to leap over, *lumuksó, lumundág;* omit, *kaligtaán, ligtaán.*

SKIRMISH, n. *pánaklutan.* — v. *magpánaklutan.*

SKIRT, n. *saya.*

SKULK, v. *managò.*

SKULL, n. *bungò;* bony case inclosing brain, *bao ng ulo.*

SKY, n. *langit.*

SLANDER, n. *sirang-puri; paninirang-puri.*—v. *manirang-puri.*

SLANDEROUS, adj. *mapanirang-puri.*

SLANG, n. *balbál; salitáng-lansangan.*

SLANGY, adj. *balbál.*

SLAP, n. *tampál;* (on the cheek) *sampál.*—v. *tampalín;* (on the cheek) *sampalín.*

SLASH, n. cut, *hiwà, iwà;* a stroke of whip, *hagupít.*

SLAUGHTER, n. *pátayan, pagpapatáy.*

SLAVE, n. *alipin.*

SLAVERY, n. *kaalipinan; pangaalipin.*

SLAY, v. to kill, *patayín, kitilín.*

SLED, n. *paragos.*

SLEEP, n. *tulog.*—v. *matulog.*

SLEEPY, adj. *nag-áantók, ináantók;* (habitually) *antukin.*

SLEEVE, n. *manggás,* Sp.

SLENDER, adj. *balingkinitan;* narrow in proportion to the length or height, *habâ;* relatively small, *muntî.*

SLICE, n. *putol, hiwà.*

SLICK, adj. *makinis.*

SLIGHT, adj. *kcuntî, kákauntî.*

SLIM, adj. of small diameter, *patpatin;* small, *muntî, kauntî.*

SLIME, n. *lusak;* mud, *putik, burak.*

SLIMY, adj. *malusak;* muddy, *maputik, maburak.*

SLIP, v. to slide, *mádulás, mápadulás.*

SLIPPERS, n. *sinelas, tsinelas,* Sp.

SLOGAN, n. *pamanság.*

SLOPE, n. *dahilig; gulod.*

SLOVEN, adj. *burará; alisagâ.*

SLOW, adj. not rapid in motion, *marahan;* not prompt, *makupad;* occupying a long time, *mabagal;* behind time, *atrasado,* Sp.

SLUMBER, v. *matulog; humimláy.*

SLY, adj. underhand, *pailalím;* deceitful, *mapanlinláng, madayà; magdarayà.*

SMALL, adj. *maliít, muntî.*

SMALLPOX, n. *bulutong.*

SMART, adj. clever, *matalino;* shrewd, *matalas.*

SMASH, v. to break in pieces, *durugin;* (glass or pottery) *basagin;* to be thrown violently against, *mábanggâ.*

SMEAR, v. to spread with anything greasy, *pahiran;* soil in any way, *dumhán; dungisan; mansahán,* Sp.

SMELL, v. *amuyin, umamóy.*—n. *amóy.*

SMILE, n. *ngitî.*—v. *ngumitî.*—To s. at, *ngitián.*

SMITE, v. *hampasín; dagukan.*

SMITH, n. *pandáy.*

SMITHY, n. *pandayan.*

SMOKE, n. *asó, usok.*—v. *umasó, umusok.*—To s. cigarettes or cigars, *humitít;* (*manigarilyo, manabako.*)

SMOKEY, adj. *maasó, mausok.*

SMOOTH, adj. *makinis.*

SMOTHER, v. *inisín.* — To be smothered, *mainís.*

SNAIL, n. *susô.*

SNAKE, n. *ahas.*

SNAP, v. to break suddenly, *masapák,* snatch at something suddenly with the teeth, *sakmalín, sumakmál;* crackle, *lumagitik;* speak crossly, *manikmát, sikmatán.*

SNAPPY, adj. energetic, *madalî, maliksí;* brisk, *masiglá.*

SNARE, n. *bitag.*

SNARL, v. *umangil, angilan.*—n. *angil.*

SNATCH, v. to seize suddenly, *halbutín.*

SNEER, v. *manuyâ, tuyaín.*

SNEEZE, v. *bumahín; mápabahín.*

SNORE, v. *maghilík.*

SNOUT, n. *ngusò.*

SNUB, v. to slight intentionally, *magmalakí, pagmalakhán.*

SNUG, adj. *maginhawa.*

SO, adv. in such manner, *ngâ.*— conj. therefore, *kayâ.*

SOAP, n. *sabón,* Sp.

SOAPY, adj. *masabón,* Sp.

SOB, v. *humikbî.*—n. *hikbî.*

SOBER, a dj. n o t intoxicated (with liquor), *di-lasíng;* calm, *mahinahon.*

SOCIABLE, adj. companionable, *palásama; masamahín.*

SOCIAL, adj. relating to general conditions of human life, *panlípunan;* pertaining to men as living in association with one another, *pagsasamahán, pakikipagtúnguhan.*

SOCIALISM, n. *sosyalismo,* Sp.

SOCIALIST, n. - adj. *sosyalista,* Sp.

SOCIETY, n. people in general, *lípunan;* organized body of persons, *kapisanan, sámahan.*

SOCIOLOGY, n. *sosyolohiya,* Sp.; *karunungang panlípunan.*

SOCKS, n. *medyas,* Sp.

SOCKET, n. (Elec.) *saket,* Eng.

SOD, n. *damuhán.*

SODA, n. *soda,* Sp.

SOFT, adj. easily yielding to pressure, *malambót;* (of light) not glaring, *malamlám;* (of sound) *marahan, mababà;* gentle, *mabini.*

SOFTEN, v. *palambutín; pahinain.*

SOIL, n. *lupà.*

SOJOURN, v. *tumigil, tumahán.*

SOLDER, n. *panghinang.*—v. *hinangan, ihinang.*

SOLDIER, n. *kawal; sundalo.*

SOLE, n. the under side of the foot, *talampakan;* (of shoes) *suwelas,* Sp.

SOLE, alj. being alone, *nag-iisá;* single, *iisá, tangì;* only, *lamang.*

SOLEMN, adj. *solemne,* Sp.; inspiring awe or fear, *kagilá-gilalás;* attended with ceremonies, *maringal.*

SOLICIT, v. to ask for, *humilíng, humingî;* entreat, *makiusap, mamanhík.*

SOLICITOUS, adj. concerned, *maasikaso,* Sp.

SOLID, adj. compact, *pikpík, masinsín;* firm, *matibay;* not hollow, *buô.*

SOLIDIFY, v. *mamuô.*

SOLIDITY, n. hardness, *katigasán;* volume, *kabuuán.*

SOLITAIRE, n. *sulitaryo,* Sp.

SOLITARY, adj. living by oneself, *nag-iisá;* lonely, *nalúlumbáy.*

SOLITUDE, n. *pag-iisá.*

SOLUBLE, adj. *natútunaw.*

SOLUTION, n. process of causing to be absorbed into a liquid. *pagtunaw;* a solving, *tuos, katuusán.*

SOLVE, v. *magtuos, tuusín: kuwentahín.*

SOLVENT, n. *pantunaw, panunaw.*

SOME, pron. *ilán.*—adj. *ilán, kaunti.*

SOMEBODY, n. *tao.*

SOMEHOW, adv. *sa paánumán, sa papaánumán.*

SOMETHING, n. *anumán.*

SOMETIME, adv. formerly, *noóng una;* once, *minsan;* at a time in the future, *sa panahóng dárating, sa ibáng araw.*

SOMETIMES, adv. once in a while, *paminsan-minsan, kung minsan.*

SOMEWHAT, n. expressed by *ma-* plus the character or quality, as *maputí-putî,* somewhat white; or by *may-ka..an (han)* as, *may-kalayuan,* somewhat far.

SOMEWHERE, adv. *kung saán.*

SON, n. *anák na lalaki.*

SONATA, n. *sunata,* Sp.

SONG, n. *awit; kantá,* Sp.

SON-IN-LAW, n. *manugang na lalaki.*

SONNET, n. *soneto,* Sp.

SONOROUS, adj. *matagintíng.*

SOON, adv. *sandalî na lamang;* without delay, *agád.*

SOPHOMORE, n.-adj. *sópomór,* Eng.

SORCERER, n. *manggagaway, mangkukulam.*

SORDID, adj. without noble ideals, *hamak;* vile, *imbí;* greedy ot gain, *sakím, sakré.*

SORE, adj. tender or painful to the touch, *mahapdî;* afflicted, *may-sakít;* distressing, *kasakitsakit;* resentful, *galít.*

SORROW, n. *pighati;* distress, *sakit, dalamhatî;* sadness, *iungkót, kalungkutan.*

SORROWFUL, daj. *namimighatî; nagdádalamhati; malungkót.*

SORRY, adj. *nalúlungkót; nagdáramdám.*—I am s., *Ikinalúlungkót ko.*

SORT, n. kind, *urì.*—v to classify, *uriin; pagbukúd-bukurín.*

SOUL, n. *káluluwá.*

SOUND, adj. whole, *buô;* founded on truth, *tunay, totoó;* honorable, *marangál.*

SOUND, n. sensation perceived by the ear, *tunóg;* noise, *ingay.*—v. to cause to make a noise, *patunugín.*

SOUND, v. to fathom or measure the depth of, *arukín.*

SOUNDLESS, adj. *waláng-ingay.*

SOUP, n. *sopas,* Sp.

SOUR, adj. *maasim.*

SOURCE, n. *mulâ, pinagmulán; pinagbuhatan; pinanggalingan.*

SOUTH, n. *timog,* Bis.

SOUTHEAST, n.-adj. *timog-silangan.*

SOUTHWEST, n.-adj. *timog-kanluran.*

SOUVENIR, n. *alaala, paalaala; pagunitâ, súbenír,* Eng.-Fr.

SOVEREIGN, adj. *may-kapangyarihan.* — n. *maykapangyarihan.*

SOW, n. *inahíng baboy.*

SPACE, n. (atmospheric) *alangaang;* distance between, *pagitan, puwáng, agwát;* a length of time, *tagál.*

SPACIOUS, adj. *maluwáng.*

SPAN, n. distance from end of thumb to tip of middle finger, *dangkál* (in English, 9 in., in Tagalog, ordinarily 8 in.); length, *habà;* arch, *balantók.*

SPANIARD, SPANISH, n. *Kastilà.*

SPANK, v. *tapikín (sa puwít)*; *paluin.*—To be spanked, *mápalò.*

SPARE. v. to use frugally, *tipirín;* forgive, *patawarin;* give, *ibigáy.*

SPARK, n. *tilamsík;* sudden flash, *kisláp;* small particle, *butil.*—v. to emit sparks, *manilamsík;* produce an electric spark, *kumidláp, kumisláp.*

SPARROW, n. *maya.*

SPARSE, adj. *madalang;* thinly scattered, *kalát-kalát.*

SPASM, n. *pulikat; pasmá.*

SPEAK, v. *magsalitâ.*

SPEAKER, n. *mananalumpatî;* Eng.

SPEAKING, adj. *nagsásalitâ.*

SPEAR, n. *sibát.*

SPECIAL, adj. *tangì;* designed for, *sadyâ;* different, *ibá;* uncommon, *di-pangkaraniwan;* espesyál, Sp.

SPECIALIZE, v. *magdalubhasà, pagdadalubhasaan.*

SPECIFIC, adj. *tiyák.*

SPECIFY, v. to mention particularly, *tukuyin.*

SPECIMEN, n. *ulirán;* example, *halimbawa.*

SPECTACLE, n. *pánoorín.*

SPECTACLES, n. *salamín sa matá.*

SPECTRAL, adj. *parang multó.*

SPECTER, n. ghost, *multó,* Sp.

SPECULATION, n. mental theorizing, *haka-hakà;* (Comm.) purchase of stocks at a risk for future gain, *pagbabaká-sakalì.*

SPEECH, n. power of uttering words, *pagsasalitâ;* manner of speaking, *pananalitâ;* (Gram.) part of s., *bahagi ng panalitâ;* public discourse, *talumpatì.*

SPEED, n. *tulin, bilís.*

SPERM, n. a white, waxy solid, *isperma,* Sp.

SPHERE, n. *bilog.*

SPICE, n. *panrekado,* Sp.; relish, *linamnám.*

SPICY, adj. *malinamnám, malasa;* fragrant, *mabangó;* pointed in thought expression, *may-sinásabi.*

SPIDER, n. *gagambâ; álalawa.*

SPILL, v. to flow over, *máligwák;* cause to flow over, *paligwakín.*

SPIN, v. to draw out and twist into threads, *magsulid, sulirin;* cause to whirl rapidly, *paikutin, painugin.*

SPINAL, adj. *panggulugód.*—s. column, *gulugód.*

SPINDLE, n. *súliran, sudlán.*

SPINE, n. backbone (spinal column), *gulugód.*

SPINY, adj. *matinik, tinikán.*

SPIRAL, adj. *anyóng-susô; ikid, paikid.*

SPIRIT, n. life, *buhay;* principle of life, *hilagyô;* soul, *káluluwá;* real meaning, *diwà.*

SPIRITED, adj. animated, *buháy;* lively, *masiglá.*

SPIRITUAL, adj. of or pertaining to the mind, *pandiwà;* pertaining to the soul, *pangkáluluwá.*

SPIRITUALISM, n. *espiritwalismo,* Sp.

SPITE, n. *pagkagalit, pagkayamót.*—In s. of, *kahit. .man.*

SPLASH, v. to spatter liquid about in drops, *magwilíg, magwisík.*—n. noise of anything striking in or upon water, (or a liquid), *lagunsá.*

SPLEEN, n. *lapáy.*

SPLENDID, adj. gorgeous, *marilág, marikít;* brilliant, *maluningning;* glorious, *maluwalhatì.*

SPLICE, n. dugsóng.

SPLINTER, n. tatal; (bamboo) patpát.

SPOIL, v. to destroy, sirain; ruin, lansagin.

SPONGE, n. espongha, Sp.

SPONGY, adj. esponghado (-a), Sp.; buhaghág.

SPONSOR n. (masc.) padrino, Sp.; ináamá; (fem.) madrina Sp., iníiná.

SPONTANEOUS, adj. bukál; natural, katutubò, likás.

SPOOK, n. ghost, multó, Sp.

SPOOL, n. cylinder of wood, ridged at each end, karetes, Sp., ikirán; reel, ulák, ulakán.

SPOON, n. kutsara, Sp.

SPOONFUL, n. sangkutsara, Sp.

SPORADIC, a d j. kalát-kalát; putá-putaki.

SPORT, n. pastime, libangan; game, larô.

SPOT, n. a blot, batík; stain, mansá, Sp.; dungis; place, lugál; locality, poók.

SPOTLESS, adj. wuláng-batík; waláng-bahid; pure. dalisay.

SPOUSE, n. asawa.

SPOUT, n. nozzle, bukilya, Sp.: stream or jet of liquid, tulò. daloy.

SPRAIN, n. bali, pilay.—v. mabalian, mapilayan.

SPRAWL, v. tumimbuwáng; to spread in an irregular manner, as a plant, mangalat, gumapang.

SPRAY, n. (water) tilamsík. tibalsík.—v. magwilig, wiligán.

SPREAD, v. to scatter, kumalat, ikalat; propagate, magpalaganap, palaganapin.

SPRING, v. to leap, lumuksó; bound, lumundág; issue, luma-

bás.—n. season when plants begin to grow, tagsiból.

SPROUT, n. supang —v. sumupang.

SPUMOUS, adj. mabulâ.

SPURIOUS, adj. counterfeit, huwád; not genuine, palsó, Sp.

SPURT, n. bigláng buhos; silakbó.

SPY, n. tiktík; batyáw; espiyá, Sp.

SQUALL, n. unós.

SQUALOR, n. karumihán.

SQUANDER, v. mag-aksayá, aksayahín.

SQUARE, n.-adj. parisukát.

SQUASH, n. (Bot.) kalabasa, Mex.

SQUAT, v. to sit on ones heels, tumingkayád, maningkayád; crouch, lumupagî.

SQUEEZE, v. to press between two bodies, ipitin; draw forth by pressure, pigain; force into place by pressure, isiksík, sumiksík.

SQUINT-EYED, adj. duling; banlág.

SQUID, n. pusít.

SQUIRM, v. to writhe, mamilipit.

STAB, v. saksakín, manaksák.

STABILITY, n. katatagán, pagkamatatág.

STABILIZE, v. patatagin.

STABLE, adj. matatág.

STABLE, n. stall for horses, kabalyerisa, Sp.

STACK, n. (of hay) mandalá; orderly pile, salansán; chimney, páusukán.

STADIUM, n. istadyum, Lat.

STAGE, n. intablado, Sp.

STAGGER, v. to totter, reel, gumiray-giray.

STAGNANT, adj. timik.

STAGNATE, v. tumimik.

STAIN, n. bahid; mansá. Sp.;

taint, dungis; dye, dampól, ti-
nà.

STAIR, n. baitáng.

STAIRWAY, n. hagdanan, hagdán.

STAKE, n. urang, tulos.

STAKES, n. pustá, Sp.

STALE, adj. not fresh or new,
lumà; beginning to decay
(food), panís; (fish) halpók,
bilasá.

STALK, n. stem of plant, suwî;
stem of leaf, tangkáy.

STALK, v. to approach cautious-
ly and under cover, manubok,
subukan.

STALL, n. booth, tindahan; stable, kabalyerisa, Sp.

STALWART, adj. matipunò.

STAMMER, v. magpautál-utál.

STAMP, n. mark or design, taták; (postage) selyo, Sp.—v. to
mark, tatakán; attach a postage s. to, selyuhán.

STAMPEDE, n. pagkabulagog.—
v. mabulabog, bulabugin.

STAND, v. tumayô.

STANDARD, n. pámantayan, tularán.

STANDING, n. station, kalágayan, katáyuan; tayo.

STANDPOINT, n. pananaw.

STANDSTILL, n. a halt, pagtí-
gil, tigil; rest, pahingá.

STANZA, n. talatà; estropa, Sp.

STAPLE, n. pángunahing-kaila-
ngan.

STAR, n. bituin.

STARCH, n. arina, Sp.

STARE, v. titig.—v. tumitig, titigan.

STARK, adj. utter, complete. lubós.

START, v. to begin, magsimulà;
mag-umpisá, Sp.

STARTLE, v. gulatin, mágulat;
sindakin, masindák.

STARVATION, n. gutom.

STARVE, v. magutom; to distress or subdue by famine, gu-
tumin.

STATE, n. position, katáyuan,
condition, kalágayan; manner
or condition of being, kaanyuán.
—n. a political body, estado,
Sp.; government, pámahaladn.
—v. to tell, magsabi, sabihin.

STATELY, adj. majestic, makaharì; dignified, mabunyî.

STATEMENT, n. something stat-
ed, sabi, sinabi; report, ulat.

STATESMAN. n. estadista, Sp.

STATION, n. regular stopping
place on a railroad or bus line,
istasyón, Sp.; himpilan; location, kinalálagyán.

STATIONARY, waláng-galáw.

STATIONERY, n. istasyoneri,
Eng.; mga kagamitáng ukol sa
pagsulat.

STATUE, n. bantayog; istatwa,
Sp.

STATURE, n. tayog, tads.

STATUS, n. lagáy, kalágayan.

STATUTE, n. law, batás.

STAY, v. to stand still, tumigil;
remain, mátirá; reside or live
in, tumirá, manirahan; restrain, magpigil, pagilin.

STEADFAST, adj. (of women),
timtiman, matimtiman; un-
changing, waláng-bago.

STEALY, adj. firm, matibay;
calm, mahinahon; not nervous
or easily scared, waláng-tigatig.

STEAK, n. beefsteak, bisték,
Eng.

STEAL, v. magnakaw, nakawin.

STEALTH, n. lihim.

STEALTHY, adj. palihím; fur-
tive, pailalim.

STEAM, n. vapor, singáw.—s
roller, pisón, Sp.

STEAMSHIP; n. bapór, Sp.;
buke, Sp.; sasakyáng-dagat.

STEEL, n. *asero*, Sp.; *talím*.

STEEP, adj *matarík*.

STEER, v. (a boat or ship) *umu-git, mag-ugit;* to guide, *mamat-nubay, patnubayan*.

STEM, n. *tangkáy*.

STENCH, n. *bahò*.

STENCIL, n. *istensil*, Eng.

STENOGRAPHER, n. *takígrapó*, Sp.

STEP, n. a movement of the foot, *hakbáng;* (of stairs) *baitáng;* footstep, *yabág.*—v.—to move by rasing one foot and placing, it on another spot. *humakbáng;* walk, *lumakad*.

STERILE, adj. *baog*.

STERILIZE, v. *isterilisahín*, Sp.

STERN, adj. *mahigpít*.

STEW, v. *maglagà, ilagà.*—n. *ni-lagà*.

STICK, n. (of bamboo) *patpát.*-v. to adhere, *dumigkít;* cause to adhere, *idigkít;* fasten, *ika-bít*.

STICKY, adj. *malagkít*.

STIFF, adj. *matigás;* not flowing easily (thick and heavy), *malapot*.

STIFLE, v. to smother, *inisín*.

STILL, adj. motionless, *waláng-kilos, waláng-galáw;* quiet, *ta-himik;* silent, *waláng-ingay.*— adv. as yet, *pa;* up to this time, *hanggá ngayón.*—conj. however, *gayunmán*.

STILT, n. *tayakád*.

STING, n. *tusok; kagát*.

STINGY, adj. *maramot*.

STINK, n. *bahò.*—v. *bumahò, ma-mahò*.

STIR, v. to mix, dissolve, or make, by motion of a spoon, fork, etc., *haluin;* arouse, *pu-kawin, mamukaw*.

STIRRUP, n. *estribo*, Sp.; *tuntu-ngan*.

STITCH, v. *tahiín, manahí*.

STOCK, n. supply of goods for sale, *panindá*.

STOCKHOLDER, n. *aksiyonısta*, Sp.; *kasapi ng mámumuhunán*.

STOCKY, adj. *pandák; pandakin*.

STOMACH, n. (Anat.) *sikmurà;* (abdomen, *tiyán*).

STONE, n. *bató*.

STOOL, n. seat without back with three or four legs, *bangkô*, Sp.

STOOP, v. *yumukô*.

STOOPED, adj. *kurkubado*, Sp.; *uklô*.

STOP, v. to check the movement, progress, action, etc., *patigilin;* halt, *tumigil*.

STORE, n. *tindahan*, Sp.

STOREKEEPER, n. *magtitindá*, Sp.

STORM, n. *bagyó.*—v. *bumagyó*.

STORY, n. a floor, *sahíg;* (of a building) *saray, palapág;* a narrative, *kuwento*, Sp.; *salay-sáy*.

STOUT. adj. robust, *matipunò*.

STOVE, n. *kalán*.

STRADLE, v. (standing) *kuma-ang;* (sitting) *sumakláng*.

STRAIGHT, adj. *tuwíd*.

STRAIGHTEN, v. to make straight, *ituwíd, tuwirín;* become straight, *maging tuwíd* (*magintuwíd*).

STRAIGHTFORWARD, adj. *ta-pát*.

STRAIN, n. family, race, or breed, *lahì;* quality, *katángian;* trace, *badhá.*—v. to pass through a sieve, *salain, magsalà;* use or force as far as possible, *hapitin, pakápilitin*.

STRAINED, adj. passed through

a strainer, *sinalà;* forced, *pilit, pinilit.*

STRAIT, adj. *makipot.*

STRAND, n. shore, *baybáy-dagat, baybayin;* twisted or ropelike mass, *lubid.*

STRANGE, adj. of or relating to exciting wonder, *kataká-taká;* queer, *kakatwá; kakaibá.*

STRANGER, n. (from a foreign land) *dayuhan;* a person whom one does not know, *taong di-kakilala,* some other person or thing, *ibá.*

STRANGLE, v. *sakalín, manakál, sumakál.*

STRATEGY, n. *laláng.*

STRAW, n. *dayami.*

STRAY, v. *máligáw.*

STREAM, n. (brook) *sapà;* (river) *ilog;* flow, *tulò; agos.*—v. to issue and flow out, *tumulò;* move forward steadily, *umagos.*

STREET, n. *daán; kalye,* Sp.

STRENGTH, n. *lakás.*

STRENGTHEN, v. *palakasín.*

STRESS, n. (Gram.) emphasis of pronunciation on a syllable, *diín.*

STRETCH, v. to reach out, *abutín, iabót, mag-abót, umabót;* expand, *lumapad;* enlarge, *lumaki.*

STREW, v. *isabog, magsabog.*

STRICT, adj. *mahigpít.*

STRIFE, n. *álitan, pagkakaalít.*

STRIKE, v. to hit, smite, *hampasín, humampás, manghampás.* —n. a stopping of work to secure changes in the treatment of labor, *aklas, aklasan; welga,* Sp.

STRIKER, n. one who stops work for better conditions, *mag-aaklás; welgista,* Sp.

STRING, n. small cord, *pisì;*

twine, *panalì;* a musical cord, *bagtíng; kuwerdas,* Sp.

STRIP, v. to deprive of a covering, *talupan;* make naked, *hubó't-hubarán.*

STRIVE, v. to make strenuous efforts, *magsumikap, magsumakit; pagsumikapan, pagsumakitan.*

STROKE, n. *hampás, pukpók;* a line movement, *guhit, kudlít;* sound of clock marking the time, *tugtóg.*—v. to rub gently, *hagpuín, humagpós.*

STROLL, v. *maglakád-lakád; magapsiyál-pasiyal,* Sp.

STRONG, adj. *malakás.*

STRONGHOLD, n. *kutà.*

STRUCTURE, n. *kayarián;* form, *kaanyuán, anyô;* arrangement, *ayos, kaayusan.*

STRUGGLE, n. a violent effort, *pagpupumilit;* contest, *timpalák, páligsahan;* strife, *álitan,* —v. to put forth great effort, *magpumilit, pagpumilitan.*

STUB, n. (of a receipt book or check book) *talón,* Sp.

STUBBORN, adj. *matigás ang ulo.*

STUDENT, n. *mag-aarál, nag-áaral.*

STUDIO, n. *estudyo,* Eng.

STUDIOUS, adj *paláarál; mapag-arál.*

STUMBLE, v. to trip, *mátisod;* fall in walking or running, *márapâ, máparapâ.*

STUMP, n. *tuód.*

STUN, v. to make senseless (as by a blow) *lingmingín,* (become so, *malingmíng*); confuse or daze, *tuligín* (become so, *matulíg*).

STUPENDOUS, adj. *kagilá-gilalás;* wonderful, *kahanga-hangà.*

STUPID, adj. *hangál, uslák.*

STURDY, adj. hardy, *matigás;* robust, *matipunò;* firm and unyielding, *matibay.*

STUTTER, v. *magpautál-utál.*

SUBDUE, v. *supilin, masupil.*

SUBJECT, n. one who owes allegiance to a sovereign, *alagád;* topic, *paksâ;* (in a sentence) *simunò.*

SUBJECTIVE, adj. based on one's own feelings, *pansarili, panarili.*

SUBJUNCTIVE, adj. (Gram.) *pasakalì.*

SUBLIME, adj. great, *dakilà;* exalted, *matayog;* elevated, *malayog.*

SUBMERGE, v. *ilubóg, lumubóg.*

SUBMISSIVE, adj. obedient, *masúnurin;* humble, *pakumbabâ. mapagpakumbabâ.*

SUBMIT, v. to yield to the authority or will of another, *sumailalim, pumailalim;* surrender, *sumukò:* to present for, refer to, the judgment of another, *iharáp.*

SUBORDINATE, adj. (Gram.) dependent, *katulong.*

SUBSCRIBE. v. *sumuskribí,* Sp.; to agree with, *umayon.*

SUBSIDE, v. to sink or fall to the bottom, *tumining;* abate, *humulaw,* (of the rain) *tumilà.*

SUBSIST, v. *manatili;* to continue, *magpatuloy.*

SUBSISTENCE, n. *pang-agawbuhay.*

SUBSTANCE, n. *kalamnán;* real meaning, *buód.*

SUBSTANTIAL, adj. real, *tunay;* solid, strong, *matibay;* valuable, *mahalagá.*

SUBSTITUTE, n. *kapalít, kahalili.*

SUBTERFUGE, n. *laláng, dayà.*

SUBTRACT, v. *magbawas, bawasin.*

SUBTRACTION. n. *pagbabawas;* (Math.) *Palábawasan.*

SUCCEED, v. *magtagumpáy.*

SUCCESS, n. *tagumpáy.*

SUCCESSFUL, adj. *mapanagumpáy.*

SUCCESSION, n. *pagsusunúdsunód.*

SUCCESSIVE, adj. *sunúd-sunód.*

SUCCESSOR, n. *kahalili.*

SUCCOR, v. *saklolohan, sumaklolo.—n. saklolo,* Sp.

SUCCUMB, v. to yield, *sumukò.*

SUCH, adj. *gayón, ganiyán.*

SUCK, v. to draw in (a liquid) with the mouth, *supsupin, sumupsóp;* drink in or absorb, *sipsipin, sumipsíp.*

SUCKLE, v. *sumuso;* to give suck (to), *magpasuso, pasusuhin.*

SUDDEN, adj. *biglâ.*

SUDDENLY, adv. *pabiglâ; dikaginságinsá.*

SUDS, n. bubbles, *bulâ.*

SUE, v. *magsakdál, isakdál.*

SUFFER, v. to feel with pain, *magdusa;* endure, *magtiís.*

SUFFERING, n. *dusa;* the pain borne, *sakit.*

SUFFICE, v. to be enough, *magkásiyá; sumapát.*

SUFFICIENT, adj. *sapát; kainaman.*

SUFFIX, n. (Gram.) *hulapì.*

SUFFOCATE, v. *inisin.*

SUFFOCATION. n. *pagkainís.*

SUFFRAGE, n. vote, *paghalál, paghahalál; supráhiyó,* Sp.

SUGAR, n. *asukal,* Sp.—s. cane, *tubó.*

SUGGEST, v. *magmungkahì, imungkahì.*

SUGGESTIVE, adj. *may-pahiwatig.*

SUICIDE, n. *pagpapakamatáy.*

SUIT, n. courtship, *panliligaw;* a

set of clothes, *terno*, Sp.—v. to fit, *iaŋkóp, ibagay*.

SUITABLE, adj. fitting, *angkóp*; becoming, *bagay*.

SUITCASE, n. *maleta*, Sp.; *maletín*, Sp.

SUITOR, n. a man who seeks to marry a woman, *manliligáw*.

SULK, v. *magtampó*.

SULKY, adj. *nagtátampó; matampuhin*.

SULTRY, adj. *mainit*.

SUM, n. total, *kabuuán*.

SUMMARIZE, v. *buurín*.

SUMMARY, n. *buód, kabuurán*.

SUMMER, n. *tag-araw, tag-init*.

SUMMIT, n. *taluktók*.

SUMMON, v. to call, send for, *ipatawag*; command to appear in court, *paharapín*.

SUMMONS, n. *tawag, patawag*.

SUN, n. *araw*.

SUNBEAM, n. *sinag ng araw*.

SUNDAY, n. *Linggó*.—adj. *panlinggó, pang-Linggó*.

SUNDOWN, n. *takípsilim*.

SUNNY, adj. *maaraw*.

SUNRISE, n. *pagsikat ng araw*.

SUNSET, n. *paglubóg ng araw*.

SUP. v. to take supper, *maghapunan*.

SUPERFICIAL, adj. *paimbabáw*; shallow, *mababaw*.

SUPERFLUOUS, adj. *labis*.

SUPERINTEND, v. *pamanihalaan, panihalaan*; to direct, *patnugutan, mamatnugot*.

SUPERINTENDENT, n. *tagapanihalà*.

SUPERIOR, adj. *nakatátaás*; of better quality, *lalong mabuti*; preferable, *lalong mainam*.

SUPERIORITY, n. *kapanaigan; kalámangan*.

SUPERLATIVE, adj. (Gram.) *pánukdulan; pasukdól*.

SUPERSTITION, n. *pámahiin*.

SUPERSTITIOUS, adj. *mapámahiin*.

SUPERVISE, v. to oversee, *pamahalaan, mamahalà*.

SUPERVISOR, n. *tagapamahalà*.

SUPPER, n. *hapunan*.

SUPPLANT, v. *palitán, halinhán*.

SUPPLEMENT, n. *dagdág*.

SUPPLICATE, v. *mamanhík*.

SUPPLICATION, n. *pamanhík*.

SUPPLY, v. *magtustós, tustusán*; give, *bigyán, magbigáy*.

SUPPORT, v. to uphold, *katigan, kumatig; itaguyod, magtaguyod*; provide for (as to s. a family), *sustentuhín*, Sp.—n. one who upholds, *tagakatig, tagataguyod*; prop, *tukod*.

SUPPOSE, v. *ipagpalagáy*; to imagine, *akalain*.

SUPPOSITION, n. *palagáy; akalà*.

SUPPRESS, v. *sansalain*; to restrain, *pigilin, magpigil*.

SUPREMACY, n. *pangingibabaw, pananaig*.

SUPREME, adj. *kátaás-taasan, kátayúg-tayugan*.

SURE, adj. *tiyák*.—I am s. it's true. *Natitiyák kong tunay ngà*.

SURFACE, n. *ibabaw, pangibabaw*.

SURFEIT, n. *suwà, pagkasawa, pagsasawà*.

SURGE, n. *daluyong, pagdaluyong*.

SURGEON, n. *siruhano*, Sp.; *máninistis*.

SURGERY, n. *siruliya*, Sp.; *paninistis*.

SURLY, adj. *masungít*.

SURMISE, n. *sapantahà*; a guess, *hulà*.

SURMOUNT, v. to overcome, *makapanaig, madaig;* rise above, *makapangibabaw, mapangibabawan.*

SURNAME, n. *apelyido,* Sp.

SURPASS, v. *lumalò, makalalò; makaraig.*

SURPLUS, n. *labis, kalabisán.*

SURPRISE, n. *gulat, manghâ.*— v. to take unawares, *biglaín, gulatin, manggulat;* strike with wonder, *papamanghaín, manghaín;* cause to be surprised, *mágulat, mámanghâ.*

SURPRISING, adj. *kagulat-gulat; kamanghá-manghâ.*

SURRENDER, n. *pagsukò.*—v *sumukò.*

SURREPTITIOUS, adJ. *palihím, patagó.*

SURROUND, v. to inclose on all sides, *palibutan;* besiege, *pikutin, mamikot.*

SURROUNDINGS, n. *palibot.*

SURVEILLANCE, n. *pagmamatyáy.*

SURVEY, n. act of examining carefully, *pagsisiyasat.*—v. to inspect, *siyasatin, tingnán,* measure and determine the features of (as land), *sukatin, magsukát.*

SURVEYOR, n. *mánunukat-lupà.*

SURVIVE, v. *mátirang buháy.*

SURVIVOR, n. *ang nátirang buháy.*

SUSCEPTIBLE, adJ. sensitive, *maramdamın.*

SUSPECT, v. *maghinalà;* (someone) *paghinalaan.*

SUSPEND, v. to hang, *ibitin,* debar, *itiwalag.*

SUSPENSE, n. state of uncertainty, *pag-aalinlangan;* (in a story) *paalinlangan.*

SUSPICION, n. *hinalà.*

SUSPICIOUS, adj. *kahiná-hinalà.*

SUSTAIN, v. *katigan, kumatig;* to maintain or keep up (as an argument) *ipanindigan, manindig.*

SUSTENANCE, n. *sustento,* Sp.

SWALLOW, v. *lunukin, lumunók.*

SWAMP, n. *latian.*

SWARM, n. *kawan.*

SWAY, v. *paugain; ugain.*

SWEAR, v. *manumpâ; sumumpâ; patn.*

SWEAT, n. *pawis.*—v. *pawisan.*

SWEEP, v. *walsán, walisán.*

SWEEPSTAKES, n. *suwipistik,* Eng.

SWEET, adj. *matamís.*—s. potato, *kamote.*

SWEETEN, v. *patamisín, magpatamis; tamisán.*

SWEETHEART, n. *katipán;* a lover, *kasuyò, kasintahan.*

SWELL, v. to enlarge, *lumaki,* (cause to) *palakihín;* bulge out, *bumukol;* be inflated, *bumintóg.*

SWELLING, n. *paglaki;* a bulging out, *bukol; pagbukol;* inflation, *pagbintóg.*

SWIFT, adj. *matulin.*

SWIM, v. *lumangóy.*

SWINDLE, v. *manansô; manubà; manekas.*

SWINDLER, n. *mánanansô; múnunubà; mánenekas.*

SWING, v. to move to and fro regularly, *umuntayon, umindayon.*

SWOON, v. to faint, *himatayin.*

SWORD, n. *tabák.*

SYLLABLE, n. (Gram.) *pantíg.*

SYMBOL, n. *sagisag.*

SYMPATHY, n. *pakikiramay,* compassion, *pagkaawà, pagkahabág.*

SYMPTOM, n. *tandâ, palátanda-an; síntumás,* Sp.

SYNONYM, n. *salitáng kasing-kahuluạán.*

SYNONYMOUS, adj. *kasingka-hulugán.*

SYRUP, n. *harabe,* Sp.; honey, *pulót.*

SYSTEM, n. *sistema,* Sp.; *ayos, paraán.*

T

TAB, n. *ungós; tab,* Eng.

TABERNACLE, n. *dambanà.*

TABLE, n. *mesa,* Sp.; (of bamboo) *hapag;* (low or short-legged) *dulang, latok.*

TABLEAU, n. *larawang-buháy.*

TABLECLOTH, n. *mantél,* Sp.

TABLESPOON, n. *kutsara,* Sp.

TABLET, n. *tablet,* Eng.

TABLEWARE, n. (tablesilver) *kubyertos,* Sp.

TABULATE, v. *pagmangharín.*

TABULATION, n. *manghád.*

TACITURN, adj. *di-masalitâ.*

TACK, n. broad-headed nail, *pakong uluhán;* thumb t., *tamtak,* Eng.

TACKLE, v. to attack (as a problem), *harapín;* fishing t., *bingwít.*

TACT, n. *katalasan.*

TACTFUL, adj. *matalas.*

TACTICS, n. *táktiká,* Sp.; *pamamaraán.*

TADPOLE, n. *ulúuló.*

TAG, n. *tandâ.*

TAIL, n. *buntót.*

TAILOR, n. *mánanahì; sastré,* Sp.

TAILPIECE, n. *pabuntót, pambuntót.*

TAINT, n. *dungis; mansá, mantsá,* Sp.

TAKE, v. to lay hold of, *hawakan;* get, *kunin kumuha.*

TALE, n. *kuwento,* Sp.; *buhay.*

TALEBEARER, n. *satsát, daldál.*

TALENT, n. cleverness, *talino, katalinuhan.*

TALISMAN, n. *antíng-antíng; galing.*

TALK, v. to utter words, *magsalitâ;* express thoughts in words, *magpahayag, manalitâ;* converse, *magsálitaan.*—n. (act of) *pagsasalitâ;* speech, *pananalitâ; pananalumpatì, talumpatì;* conversation, *pagsasálitaan, paguusap.*

TALKATIVE, adj. *masalitâ.*

TALL, adj. *matangkád; mataás.*

TALLOW, n. *sebo,* Sp.; *tabâ.*

TALLY, n. *tara, paya.*

TALON, n. claw, *pangalmót; kukó.*

TAMALE, n. *tamalis,* Mex.

TAMARIND, n. *sampalok.*

TAME, adj. *maamò.*

TAMPER, v. *lumikót, likutín;* to meddle, *makialám, pakialamán.*

TAN, n. (color) *kulay-katad.*—v. to prepare by treating with tannic acid, *magkultí, kultihín,* Sp.

TANGENT, adj. *padaplís, pasapyáw.*

TANGIBLE, adj. *nahíhipò; nádaramá.*

TANGO, n. *tanggo.* Sp.

TANK, n. *tangke,* Sp.

TANNER, n. *mángungultí,* Sp.

TANNING, n. *pangungultí,* Sp.

TANTALIZE, v. *takawin; papaglawayin;* to tease, *tuksuhín.*

TANTALIZING, adj. *nakapagpápalaway;* teasing, *mapanuksó.*

TANTAMOUNT, adj. *katumbás; kasinghalagá.*

TAP, n. faucet, *gripo,* Sp.; rap, *tuktók, katók.*—v. to rap, *tumuktók, kumatók.*

TAPE, n. (for measuring) *panukat;* a narrow strip of paper or cloth, *sintás,* Sp.

TAPER, n. candle, *kandilà,* Sp.

TAPERING, adj. *hubog-kandilà, hugis-kandilà,* Sp.

TAPEWORM, n. *ulyabid.*

TAR, n. *alkitrán,* Sp.

TARDY, adj. late, *hulí.*

TARGET, n. *pátamaán; tudlaan; target,* Eng.

TARIFF, n. *taripa,* Sp.; tax, *buwís.*

TARNISH, v. to dull the brightness of, *papusyawín;* become tarnished, *pumusyáw; mawalán ng kináng.*

TARO, n. (Bot.) *gabi.*

TARPAULIN, n. *trapál.* Sp.

TASK, n. *gáwain, gawâ;* duty, *tungkulin.*

TASSEL, n. *borlas,* Sp.

TASTE, n. flavor, *lasa;* a small quantity tasted, *tikím;* the sense of t., *panlasa;* critical judgment, *panurì.*—v. to perceive or know by the tongue, *malasa;* test the flavor of, *lasahin;* relish, *lasapin.*

TASTELESS, adj. *waláng-lasa.*

TATTERED, adj. *gulá-gulanít; punít-punít.*

TATTOO, n. *tatú,* Eng.

TAUNT, v. *mang-uyám, uyamín; umuyám.*

TAUT, adj. *maigtíng.*

TAUTOLOGY, n. *pagpapaligúyligoy.*

TAX, n. *buwís.*

TAXATION, n. *pagpapabuwís.*

TAXI, n. *taksi,* Eng.

TEA, n. *tsa,* Ch., *saá.*

TEACH, v. *magturò, turuan, iturò.*

TEACHER, n. *tagapagturò; maestro* (a) Sp.; instructor, *gurò.*

TEACHING, n. *pagtuturò.*

TEAM, n. *koponan; tim,* Eng.

TEAMWORK, n. cooperation, *pagtutulungán.*

TEAPOT, n. *tsarera,* Ch.-Sp.

TEAR, n. a lachrymal drop, *luhà.*—To be in tears, *lumuhà.*

TEAR, v. to pull apart, *bakbakín, tanggaíin;* rend, *punitin;* wrench or sever with force or violence, *labnutin.*

TEARFUL, adj. *tigíb-luhà; lumúluhà.*

TEASE, v. *tuksuhín, manuksó.*

TEASPOON, n. *kutsarita,* Sp.

TEASPOONFUL, n. *sangkutsaritą,* Sp.

TEAT, n. *utóng.*

TECHNICAL, adj. *téknikó,* Sp.; having to do with the exact part of any art or science, *maalituntunin.*

TECHNICALITY, n. *pagka-maka-alintuntunịn.*

TECHNICIAN, n. *téknikó,* Sp.; *dalubhasà.*

TECHNIQUE, n. artistry, *kasiningan;* skill, *kadalubhasaan;* methodology, *kapamaraanán, pamamaraán.*

TEDIOUS, adj. wearisome, *nakatiníp, nakákainíp;* tiresome, *nakapápagod, nakákapagod.*

TEETHING, n. *pagngingipín.*

TELEGRAM, n. *telegrama,* Sp. *hatíd-kawad.*

TELEGRAPH, n. *páhatirang-kawad.*

TELEPHONE, n. *teléponó,* Sp.

TELESCOPE, n. *teleskopyo,* Sp.

TELEVISION, n. *telebisyon,* Sp.

TELL, v. *magsabi, sabihin.*

TEMERITY, n. *kapangahasán.*

TEMPER, v. to mix to a proper consistency, *timplahín, magtimplá,* Sp.—n. disposition, *lagáy ng loób;* state of irritation or anger, *init ng ulo;* equanimity, *kahinahunan.*

TEMPERAMENT, See TEMPER, n.

TEMPERAMENTAL, adj. easily irritated, *mayamutín, magagalitín;* sensitive, *maramdamin.*

TEMPERANCE, n. *pagpipigil.*

TEMPERATURE, n. heat, *init;* coldness, *lamíg.*

TEMPESTUOUS, adj. *maguló, maligalig.*

TEMPLE, n. *templo,* Sp.; *sambahan.*

TEMPO, n. *tulin, bilís.*

TEMPORAL, adj. *pamanahón;* transitory, *lumílipas.*

TEMPORARY, adj. *pansamantalá.*

TEMPT, v. to entice (into evil ways), *tuksuhín, udyukán;* allure, *halinahin, manghalina; akitin, mang-akit.*

TEMPTATION, n. *tuksó, panunuksó; udyók.*

TEMPTING, adj. *nakatútuksó; nakaháhalina; kahalí-halina.*

TEN, n. adj. *sampû.*

TENACIOUS, adj. tough, *maganít;* sticky, *malagkít;'* holding fast, *mahígpít kumapit; kapittukô.*

TENANT, n. *ang nangúngupahan.*

TENANTLESS, adj. *walâng-nakatirá.*

TEND, v. *humilig, kumiling.*

TENDENCY, n. aim, *túnguhin, puntahin;* inclination, *hilig.*

TENDER, adj. soft, *malambót;* immature, *murà;* physically painful, (as raw wound) *ma-hapdí, maanták;* sympathetic, *madamayín.*

TENDERLOIN, n. *solomilyo,* Sp.

TENDON, n. *litid.*

TENFOLD, adj. *sampúng ibayo.*

TENNIS, n. *tenis,* Eng

TENOR, n. general meaning or drift, *pinaka-diwà;* highest of adult male voices, *tenór,* Sp.

TENSE, adj. stretched tight, *banát;* rigid, *batíbot, nanínigás;* not lax, *waláng-hinga.* — n. (Gram.) *panahón.*

TENSION, n. strain, *igting;* intensity of feeling, *karubdubán ng damdamin;* mental strain, *kapagalán ng isip.*

TENT, n. *tolda,* Sp.

TENTACLE, n. *galamáy.*

TENTATIVE, adj. provisional, *pansamantalá.*

TENTH, n. adj. *ikasampû, ika-10.*

TEPID, adj. *malahiningá.*

TERM, n. a fixed or limited period of time, *taning; takdáng panahón;* terminology, *talakay.*

TERMS, n. manner of expression, *pagpapahayag;* stipulations, *takdá.*

TERMINAL, adj. *panghanggan;* forming the end, *pandulo, pantapós; pangwakás.*

TERMINATE, v. to bring to an end, *tapusin, wakasán; magtapós, magwakás.*

TERMINATION, n. *katapusán; wakás.*

TERMINOLOGY, n. *talakay.*

TERMITE, n. *anay.*

TERRIBLE, adj. *katakot-takot;* dreadful, *kasindák-sindák;* appalling, *kahilá-hilakbót.*

TERRITORY, n. a large tract of land, *lupaín;* the entire extent of land and water under the control of a ruler or government, *ang nasásakupan.*

TERROR, n. fright, *sindák.*

TERRORIZE, v. *manakot, takutin; manindák, sindakín.*

TERSE, adj. *malamán.*

TEST, n. close examination, *pagsusurì;* experiment, *pagtitikím;* trial, *pagsubok.*—v. to examine, *suriin;* find out by experiment, *tikmán;* try, *subukin.*

TESTAMENT, n. *testamento,* Sp.; *hulíng bilín; pahimakás.*— Old T., *Matandáng Tipán.*— New T., *Bagong Tipán.*

TESTIFY, v. to bear witness, *sumaksí;* give evidence, *magpatunay.*

TESTIMONIAL, n. *katibayan; patibay.*

TESTIMONY, n. *patibay;* affirmation, *patunay;* attestation, *patotoó.*

TETE-A-TETE, (Fr.), n. *pag-uulayaw.*

TEXT, n. *testo,* Sp.; a passage from a book, *sabi.*

TEXTBOOK, n. *aklát na pampáaralan.*

TEXTILE, n. *kayo, habi.*

TEXTURE, n. *pagkakáhabi.*

THAW, v. *tunawin, lusawin.*

THAN, conj. *kaysá,* (personal) *kaysá kay.*

THANK, v. *magpasalamatan.* — Thank you. *Salamat.*

THANKFUL, adj. *nagpápasalamat;* grateful, *kumikilala ng utang na loób.*

THANKS, n. *maraming salamat.* —Thanks to (because of), *salamat sa.*

THANKSGIVING, n. *pagpapasalamat.*

THAT, pron.-adj. (near the person addressed) *iyán;* (far from both person speaking and person addressed) *iyón;* (thing referred to is not within sight) *yaon.*—conj. *na* (or-*ng*).

THE, art. *ang,* (pl. *ang mga, mga*).

THEATER, n. *dúlaan; teatro,* Sp.

THEFT, n. *pagnanakaw.*

THEIR, THEIRS, pron. (prepositive) *kanilá;* (postpositive) *nilá.*

THEM, pron.—to, for, with t., *sa kanilá.*

THEME, n. *paksá; pinag-úusapan.*

THEN, conj. therefore, *samakatwíd.*—adv. at that time, *noón.*

THENCE, adv. from that place, *mulá riyán, mulá roón;* from that time, *mulá noón.*

THEORY, n. *hakà;* hypothesis, *palagáy.*

THERE, adv. (near the person spoken to) *diyán, riyán;* (far from both speaker and addressed) *doón, roón.*

THEREBY, adv. *sa gayón.*

THEREFORE, adv.-conj. *samakatwíd.*

THERMOMETER, n. *termómetró,* Sp.

THESIS, n. *tesis,* Sp.; *akdâ.*

THEY, pron. *sila.*

THICK, adj. *makapál;* dense consistency, *malapot;* close set, *masinsín.*

THICKEN, v. *kapalán;* to make the consistency dense, *laputan.*

THICKENING, n. something added to make the consistency more dense, *pampalapot.*

THIEF, n. *magnanakaw.*

THIEVISH, adj. *mapagnakáw.*

THIGH, n. (Anat.) *hità.*

THIMBLE, n. *dedál,* Sp.

THIN, adj. *manipis;* lacking density, *malabnáw.*

THING, n. *bagay.*

THINK, v. *umisip, isipin; magisíp.*

THIRD, n.-adj. *ikatló, pangatló.*

THIRST, n. *uhaw.*—v. *mauhaw, uhawin.*

THIRSTY, adj. *naúuhaw; uháw.*

THIRTEEN, n.-adj. *labintatló.*

THIRTY, n.-adj. *tatlumpu.*

THIS, pron. *itó* (pl. *ang mga itó*). Of this, *nitó.*

THORN, n. *tiník.*

THOROUGH, adj. *masusì;* complete, *ganáp.*

THOSE, pron.-adj. *ang mga iyán; ang mga iyón.* See THAT.

THOUGH, conj. even if, *kahit na;* and yet, *gayunmán.*

THOUGHT, n. *pag-iisip.*

THOUGHTFUL, adj. given to contemplation, *mapag-isíp;* attentive, *maasikaso,* Sp.; careful, *maingat.*

THOUSAND, adj. *libo.* — Thousands of people, *libo-libong tao.*

THRALDOM, n. *pagkaalipin, kaalipinan.*

THRASH, v. to beat out (grain) from the hull or husk, *gumiik na pahaplít; humaplít, ihaplít;* beat or flog soundly, *haplitín, bugbugín, hambalusin.*

THREAD, n. *sinulid.*

THREADBARE, adj. *gulanít; nisnís.*

THREAT, n. *balà; bantá.*

THREATEN, *magbalà, balaan, pagbalaan;; magbantâ, bantaán, pagbantaán.*

THREE, n.-adj. *tatló.*

THREEFOLD, adj. *tatluhan;* pinagtatló; *tatlóng ibayo.*

THREE-PLY, adj. *tatlóng-sapín.*

THRESH, see THRASH.

THRESHOLD, n. *pintô.*

THRICE, adj. *makátatló, makáitló.*

THRIFT, n. *pagtitipíd, katipirán.*

THRIFTY, adj. *matipíd.*

THRILLING, adj. *makabagbágdamdamin;* causing a shivering or tingling sensation, *nakapangíngilabot.*

THRIVE, v. to prosper, *umunlád;* succeed, *magtagumpáy.*

THROAT, n. (Anat.) *lalamunan.*

THROB, v. *tumibók.*

THRONE, n. *trono,* Sp.

THRONG, n. *karamihang tao.*

THROUGH, prep. from end to end of time, *habang* (as, *habang buhay,* t. *lif3; sa buóng buhay,* t. life) ; by means of, *sa pamamagitan ng.*

THROUGHOUT, prep. *habang, sa buóng.*

THROW, v. *ipukól; iitsá,* Sp.; *ibató.*—To t. away, *itapon.*

THRUST, v. to push, *itulak.*

THUD, n. *lagapák.*

THUMB, n. *hinlalakí.*

THUMP, n. *dagubáng.*

THUNDER, n. *kulóg.*

THUNDERBOLT, n. *kidlát at kulóg.*

THURSDAY, n. *Huwebes,* Sp.

THUS, adv. in this manner, *papaganirí, paganirí;* in that manner, *papaganiyán, paganiyán; papaganoón, paganoón* (For distinctions in the equivalents of "that" see THAT); so, *kayâ;* therefore, *samakatwíd.*

THWART, v. to run counter to, *salungatín;* frustrate, *biguín.*

TICK, v. (of clocks) *tumik-tak.*

TICK, n. blood-sucking insects, (from horses and cattle) *nikník;* (from fowls) *hanip;* (from dogs and cats) fleas, *pulgás,* etc.

TICKET, n. *tiket,* Eng.; *bilyete,* Sp.

TICKLE, v. *kilitiín, mangilitî.*

TICKLISH, adj. easily tickled,

makilítiin; maligawgawin; delicate to handle or achieve, *maselang.*

TIDE, n. *lakí at kati ng tubig.*

TIDINGS, n. news, *balità.*

TIDY, adj. *maimis;* orderly, *maayos.*

TIE, v. *italì, talian;* to make a knot out of loose ends (of string, rope, etc.) *magbuhól, ibuhól.*

TIGER, n. *tigre,* Sp.; *musang.*

TIGHT, adj. not loose, *maigtíng;* (*lapat na lapat*); close-fitting, fastened firmly together, *lapat, masikíp;* taut, *banát.*

TIGHTEN, adj. *igtingán, paigtingín;* to fasten firmly, *ilapat;* make taut, *banatin.*

TILE, n. *tisà,* Sp.; *laryó,* Sp.

TILL, prep.-conj. *hanggáng sa.—* v. to cultivate (the soil), *maglináng, linangín.*

TILT, v. to lean, *tumagilid;* tip, *matiwás, matikwás.*

TIMBER, n. *kalap; kahoy.*

TIME, n. *panahón;* hour, *oras,* Sp.

TIMELY, adj. *nápapanahón.*

TIMID, adj. *mahinang-loób;* fearful, *matakutín;* shy, *mahiyain.*

TIN, n.-adj. *lata.*

TIN FOIL, n. *palarâ.*

TINGE, v. *bahiran;* to be tinged, *mábahiran.*

TINKLE, v. *kumuliling;* (to cause to) *pakulilingín.*

TINSMITH, n. *pandáy-lata.*

TINT, v. *kulayan.—*n. tinge, *bahid, kulay.*

TINWARE, n. *lateriya,* Sp.

TINY, adj. *munsík; katitíng.*

TIP, n. the point of anything tapering, *tulis,* (if sharp) *tilos;* end of a small thing, *dulo;* a fee or present, *pabuyà;* secret advanced information, *tip,* Eng.

TIPSY, adj. *lasíng, langó.*

TIPTOE, v. *tumiyád.* — On t., (adv.-adj.) *patiyád.*

TIRE, v. to become physically weary, *mapagod;* wear out the strength, interest, etc. of someone, *pagurin.*

TIRE, n. (of vehicle) colloq. *goma,* Sp.; *gulóng.*

TIRED, adj. *pagód.*

TIRELESS, adj. *waláng-pagod.*

TIRESOME, adj. *nakapápagod.*

TITLE, n. name of a book, poem, etc. *pamagát;* of dignity, rank, or distinction, *título,* Sp.; legal right to property, *pagka-may-arì;* paper giving such right, *katibayan ng pag-aari.*

TITTER, v. *humilhíl;* (continuously) *maghihilhíl;* (simultaneously) *maghilhilan.*

TOAD, n. *palakâ.*

TOADSTOOL, n. umbrella-shaped poisonous mushroom, *pandóngahas.*

TOAST, v. to brown or heat at the fire, *mag-ihaw, iihaw;* to drink to the health of, *tumagay.*

TOASTMASTER, n. *tagapagpakilala.*

TOBACCO, n. *tabako,* Sp.

TODAY, adv. *ngayón;* at the present time; *sa kasalukuyan.*

TOE, n. *dalirì (ng paá).*

TOGETHER, adv. *magkasama; sama-sama.*

TOIL, v. to work, *gumawâ;* to labor with fatigue, *magpakapagod:* with distress, *magpakasakit, magpakahirap.*

TOILET, n. act of dressing, *pagbibihis;* lavatory with water closet, *pálikuran.*

TOKEN, n. *palátandaan;* memento, *alaala;* symbol, *sagisag;* sign, *tandâ.*

TOLERABLE, adj. *matítiis; mapalálampás; maparáraán.*

TOLERANCE, n. *pagpapalampás; pagpaparaán.*

TOLERATE, v. to put up with, *batahín;* suffer, *tiisín;* allow, *bayaan.*

TOLL, n. *bayad, buwís.*

TOMATO, n. *kamatis.*

TOMB, n. a grave for the dead, *líbingan;* (vault, niche) *nitso,* Sp.

TOMBSTONE, n. *lápidá,* Sp.

TOMORROW, adv. *bukas.*

TON, n. *tunelada,* Sp.

TONE, n. *tono,* Sp.; sound, *tunóg.*

TONGS, n. *sipit.*

TONGUE, n. *dilà.*

TONGUE-TIED, adj. *umíd.*

TONIGHT, adv. *ngayóng gabí; mámayáng gabí.*

TONSIL, n. *tonsil,* Eng.

TOO, adv. also, *din, rin; man; patí;* more than enough, use the prefix *nápaka-* plus the quality meant, as, *nápakahabà,* too long.

TOOL, n. *kasangkapan.*

TOOTH, n. *ngipin.*

TOOTHACHE, n. *sakít ng ngipin.*

TOOTHBRUSH, n. *panghisò; sepilyo ng ngipin.*

TOOTHPICK, n. *panghiningá; palito,* Sp.

TOP, n. the highest part, *tuktók;* summit, *taluktók;* upper part, *ibabaw;* a cone-shaped toy that can be made to spin, *turumpô.* —adj. highest, *pinakamataás.*

TOPAZ, n. *topasyo,* Sp.

TOPIC, n. theme, *paksâ;* subject, *simunò; bagay na pinag-úusapan.*

TOPSY-TURVY, adv. *pabaligtád; patuwád.*

TORCH, n. *sulô; tanglaw.*

TORMENT, n. *dusa, dálitâ.*—v. *papagdusahin, papagdálitain.*

TORNADO, n. *buhawi.*

TORPEDO, n. *turpido,* Eng.

TORPID, adj. dormant, *tulóg;* numb, *ngimáy.*

TORRENT, n. *bahâ, bugsô.*

TORRID, adj. *tuyót, tigáng;* extremely hot, *mainit na mainit.*

TORTUOUS, adj. *twisted, balú-baluktót;* winding, *paikut-ikot.*

TORTURE, n. *pahirap.*—v. *magpahirap, pahirapan.*

TOTAL, n. *kabuuán.*

TOTTER, v. *gumiray-giray, magpagiray-giray.*

TOUCH, v. *humipò, hipuin.*—n. *hipò.*

TOUCHY, adj. *maramdamin; tangkilin.*

TOUGH, adj. *maganít;* firm, *matibay;* hard to influence, *di-máibadling.*

TOUR, n. *paglalakbáy.*

TOURIST, n. *manlalakbáy.*

TOURNAMENT, n. *páligsahan.*

TOW, v. *humila, hilahin.*

TOWARD, prep. *sa dakong; sa gawíng.*

TOWEL, n. *tuwalya,* Sp.

TOWER, n. *tore,* Sp.

TOWN, n. *bayan.*

TOWNSMAN, n. *kababayan; taong-bayan.*

TOWNSPEOPLE, n. *mga taong-bayan.*

TOY, n. *laruán.*

TRACE, v. to follow, as by tracks or vestiges, especially something lost, *bakasín, bumakás;* form lines on transparent paper over original, *sinagín.*—n. mark, *tandâ,* footprint, *bakás.*

TRACHEA, n. (Anat.) *lalaugan.*

TRACK, n. footprint, *bakás;* a beaten path, *landás;* road, *daán.*

TRACTOR, n. *traktor,* Eng.

TRADE, n. occupation, *gáwain; trabaho,* Sp.; means of livelihood, *hanapbuhay;* commerce, *pangangalakal.*

TRADE-MARK, n. *taták.*

TRADITION, n. *sali't saling sabi;* established custom, *kaugalián, pinagkáugalián.*

TRADITIONAL, adj. *kaugalián, pinagkáugalián.*

TRAFFIC, n. *trapik,* Eng.

TRAGEDY, n. *trahedya,* Sp.; *kalunusan,* nc.

TRAGIC, adj. *kalunus-lunos.*

TRAIL, n. footpath, *bagnós;* footprint, *bakás.*—v. to follow, *sumunód, sundán;* grow at some length, *gumapang.*

TRAIN, n. (railway) *tren,* Sp.; series, *kalipunán;* something drawn or dragged behind, *hila; buntót;* (of dress) *kola,* Sp.—v. to drill, *sanayín,* (oneself) *magsanay.*

TRAINING, n. *pagsasanay.*

TRAIT, n. *katángian.*

TRAITOR, n. *taksíl, lilo, sukáb.*

TRAITOROUS, adj. *taksíl, lilo, sukáb.*

TRAMPLE, v. *yumurak, yurakan.*

TRANQUIL, adj. *tiwasáy.*

TRANQUILITY, n. *katiwasayán.*

TRANSCRIBE, v. *isalin; kópyahín,* Sp.

TRANSCRIPTION, n. *salin; kopya,* Sp.

TRANSFER, v. *ilipat, maglipat,* —n. *paglilipat.*

TRANSFIX, v. *tuhugin.*

TRANSFORM, v. *baguhing-anyô.*

TRANSFORMATION, n. *pagbabagong-anyô.*

TRANSFUSION, n. *pagsasalingdugô.*

TRANSGRESS, v. *magkásala;* to break or violate a law, *lumabág, labagín.*

TRANSGRESSION, n. *pagkakasala;* violation, *paglabág.*

TRANSIENT, adj. passing, *dumáraán;* fleeting, *napáparam.*

TRANSITIVE, adj. (Gram.) *palipát.*

TRANSITORY, adj. *lumílipas; napáparam.*

TRANSLATE, v. *isa-* (prefix) plus the language into which to be translated.

TRANSLATION, n. *pagsasalın; salin sa* plus the language into which translated.

TRANSMIT, v. *ipadalá, magpadalá.*

TRANSPARENT, adj. *malinaw.*

TRANSPORT, v. *maglipat.*

TRANSPORTATION, n. *paglilipat;* means of conveyance, *trasportasyón,* Sp.; *sasakyán.*

TRANSPOSE, v. *baligtarín.*

TRANSVERSE, adj. *pahaláng; haláng; nakahalang.*

TRAP, n. *patibóng; umang.*—v. *patibungán; umangan.*

TRAVEL, v. *maglakbáy; lakbayín.*

TRAVELER, n. *manlalakbáy.*

TRAVERSE, v. *bumagtás, bagtasín.*

TRAY, n. *bandeha,* Sp.

TREACHERY, n. *kasukabán, kataksilán, kaliluhan.*

TREAD, v. to step on, *tumuntóng, tuntungán.*

TREADLE, n. *pidál,* Sp.

TREASON, n. see TREACHERY.

TREASURE, n. *yaman, kayamunan.*—v. to value highly, *mahalagahín.*

TREASURER, n. *ingat-yaman, tagaingat-yaman.*

TREASURY, n. *íngatang-yaman.*

TREAT, v. to behave or act toward, *makitungo, pakitunguhan; makisama, pakisamahan;* apply medicine on, *gamutín.*

TREATMENT, n. *pakikitungo,*

pakikisama; application of medicine, *paggamot.*

TREATY, n. *kásunduan.*

TREE, n. *punong-kahoy.*

TRELLIS, n. *balag.*

TREMBLE, v. to shake, *manginíg;* shudder, *mangatál;* shiver with cold (as with malaria), *mangaligkíg.*

TREMENDOUS, adj. exciting fear or terror, *nakapangíngilabot, nakasisindák;* of great size, *nápakalakí;* causing awe or astonishment, *kamanghá-manghá.*

TREMOR, n. *katóg, pangangatóg.*

TREMULOUS, adj. *nangángatóg;* showing fear or timidity, *nangíngimí.*

TRENCH, n. *bambáng.*

TRENCHANT, adj. *matalas, matalím.*

TREND, n. *lakad, hilig.*

TRESPASS, v. to commit any offense, *magkásala;* encroach, *manghimasok, panghimasukan.*

TRIAL, n. act of testing, *pagtitikím, pagsubok;* hardship, *paghihirap;* suffering, *pagdurusa;* judicial examination, *paglilitis.*

TRIANGLE, n. *tatsulók,* cw., nc.

TRIANGULAR, adj. *tatsulukán,* cw., nc.

TRIBE, n. clan, *angkán; lipì.*

TRIBUNAL, n. *húkuman.*

TRIBUNE, n. protector, *tagapagsanggaláng, tagatanggól;* *talibà.*

TRIBUTE, n. tax, *buwís;* acknowledgment, *pagkilala.*

TRICK, n. fraud, *dayà;* deceitful device, *laláng;* a sleight-of-hand feat, *salamangká,* Sp.

TRICKLE, v. to drip, *kumayat, tumulò.*

TRICKY, adj. *madayà, magdarayà; mapaglaláng.*

TRICYCLE, n. *trisiklo,* Sp.

TRIFLE, n. *muntíng bagay.*—v.

to toy with, *maglarô, paglaruán.*

TRIGGER, n. *kálabitan.*

TRILLION, n. *sang-angaw na angaw.*

TRIM, adj. neat, *maimís;* orderly, *maayos.*

TRINITY, n. *Trinidád,* Sp.; *tatluhan.*

TRIO, n. *tatluhan.*

TRIUMPH, n. *tagumpáy.*—v. *magtagumpáy.*

TRIUMPHANT, adj. *mapanagumpáy.*

TROMBONE, n. *trumbón,* Eng.

TROOP, n. *tropa,* Sp.

TROPHY, n. *panalunan.*

TROT, v. *yumagyág.*—n. *yagyág.*

TROUBLE, ·n. *guló, ligalig.*

TROUBLESOME, adj. *maguló, maligalig.*

TROUGH, n. *labangán, sabsaban.*

TROUNCE, v. *bugbugín, mambugbóg;* to flog, *hambalusin.*

TROUSERS, n. *pantalón,* Sp.; *salawál.*

TROWEL, n. *dulós.*

TRUANCY, n. *paglalakwatsa,* Sp.

TRUANT, n. *lakwatsero,* Sp.

TRUCK, n. motor vehicle for heavy loads, *trak,* Eng.

TRUE, adj. *tunay; totoó.*

TRULY, adv. *tunay ngâ; totoó ngâ.*

TRUMPET, n. *trumpeta,* Sp.; *tambulì, pakakak, turutót.*

TRUNK, n. body or stock of a tree, *punò ng kahoy;* body, not including head or extremities, *katawán;* chest, *baúl,* Sp.

TRUSS, n. support for rupture, *saklâ; saló.*

TRUST, n. confidence, *tiwalà, pagtitiwalà;* belief, *paniniwalà;* faith, *pananalig.*—v. to have confidence, *magtiwalà, pagtiwalaan;* believe, *maniwalà, pani-*

walaan; have faith, *manalig, panaligan.*

TRUSTFUL, adj. *mapagtiwalà: mapanalig; mapaniwalaín.*

TRUSTWORTHY, adj. *mapagkakatiwalaan;* dependable, *maáasahan.*

TRUTH, n. *katotóhanan.*

TRY, v. to put to a trial, *magtikím, tikmán;* attempt, *umato, atuhin.*

TRYING, adj. *annoying, nakagagalit;* hard to bear, *di-sukat matiís;* difficult, *mahirap, mabigát;* severe, *mahigpit.*

TRYOUT, n. *pagtitikím.*

TRYST, n. *pagtatagpô.*

TUB, n. *batyâ,* Sp.

TUBE, n. *tubo,* Sp.

TUBER, n. *lamáng-lupà.*

TUBERCULOSIS, n. *tisis,* Sp.; *sakít na tuyô.*

TUBERCULOUS, adj. *tísikó (a),* Sp.; *may-sakít na tuyô.*

TUBEROUS, adj. *bukúl-bukól.*

TUESDAY, n. *Martés,* Sp.

TUFT, n. *uhay; buhók.*

TUG, v. *batakin, hilahin.*—Tug-of-war, *batakán.*

TUITION, n. instruction, teaching, *pagtuturò;* the charge for instruction, *bayad-turò.*

TUMBLE, v. to fall suddenly and hard, *mabuwál, matumbá,* Sp.; roll about, *magpagulung-gulong;* execute gymnastic feats, *magpasirku-sirko,* Sp.

TUMOR, n. *tumór,* Sp.; swelling, *bukol.*

TUMULT, n. *linggál.*

TUMULTUOUS, adj. *malinggál.*

TUNE, n. *himig;* musical tones, *tugtóg;* melody, *awit.*

TUNEFUL, adj. *mahimig.*

TUNNEL, n. *tunél,* Sp.; *nilunggá.*

TURBAN, n. *turbante,* Sp.; *tukaról.*

TURBID, adj. *malabò;* muddy, *maputik.*

TURBINE, n. *turbina,* Sp.

TURBULENT, adj. disorderly, *waláng-kaayusan, maguló;* uncontrollable, *di-masupil;* restles, *di-mápalagáy.*

TURKEY, n. *pabo,* Sp.

TURMOIL, n. *guló; ligalig.*

TURN, v. to make to revolve, *paikutin, magpaikot;* to make to go round, *pihitin, pumihit;* give a round shape through a lathe, *lalikin, maglalik.*

TURNIP, n. (Bot.) *singkamás.*

TURPENTINE, n. *agwarás,* Sp.

TURTLE, n. *pagóng.*

TURTLEDOVE, n. *kalapati.*

TUSK, n. *pangil.*

TUSSLE, n. *bunô;*—v. *magbunô.*

TUXEDO, n. *tuksedo,* Sp.

TWEEZERS, n. *sipit.*

TWELFTH, n.-adj. *ikalabindalawá, ika-12.*

TWELVE, n.-adj. *labindalawá.*

TWENTY, n.-adj. *dalawampû.*

TWICE, adv. *makálawá.*

TWILIGHT, n.-adj. *takípsilim.*

TWIN, adj.-n. *kambál.*

TWINE, n. *pisì, panalì.*

TWINGE, v. *kumirót.*

TWINKLE, v. a wink, *kuráp, kisáp.*—v. *kumuráp, kumisáp.*

TWIRL, v. *paikutin;* to twist, *pilipitin.*

TWO, n.-adj. *dalawá.*

TYPE, n. a specimen or example, *halimbawà;* pattern, *ulirán;* (in printing) *tipo,* Sp.—v. colloq. to write on the typewritter, *magmakinilya,* Sp.

TYPEWRITER, n. *makinilya,* Sp.

TYPHOID, n. (Med.) *tipus,* Lat.

TYPHOON, n. *unós;* storm, *bagyó;* tornado, *buhawi.*

TYPICAL, adj. representative of

a class, *kinatawán;* like others of its kind, *kaurì.*

TYPIST, n. *taypist,* Eng.; *tagapagmakinilya,* Sp.

TYPOGRAPHY, n. art of printing with type, *palálimbagan.*

TYRANNICAL, adj. *mapaniíl;* cruel, *malupít;* despotic, *makaharì.*

TYRANNIZE, v. *maniíl.*

TYRANNY, n. *paniniíl.*

TYRANT, n. *mániniíl.*

U

UDDER, n. *puklô.*

UGLINESS, n. *kapangitan; pagka-pangit.*

UDLY, adj. *pangit.*

UKULELE, n. *ukulele,* Haw.

ULCER, n. *sugat na manaknák.*

ULCERATE, nv. *magnaknák.*

ULTIMATE, *adj. panghulí:* final, *pangwakás.*

ULTIMATUM, n. *hulíng-alay: hulíng-sabi.*

UMBILICUS, n. *pusod.*

UMBRELLA, n. *payong.*

UMPIRE, n. *tagahatol.*

UNABLE, adj. *waláng-kaya, di makákaya.*

UNABRIDGED, adj. *waláng-putol; waláng-nilisanan.*

UNACCUSTOMED, adj. *di-sanáy; di-bihasa.*

UNALLOYED, adj. *waláng-halò.*

UNANIMOUS, adj. *láhatan.*

UNARMED, adj. *waláng-sandata; waláng-armás,* Sp.

UNAVOIDABLE, adj. *di-mailagan; di-maiwasan.*

UNAWARE, adv. *di-handâ.*—To be caught u., *másubok, másubukan.*

UNBEARABLE, adj. *di-matiís; di-mabatá.*

UNBELIEF, n. *kawaláng-paniwalà.*

UNBEND, v. *tuwirín, ituwíd;* to become less severe, *maglubáy.*

UNBIASED, adj. *waláng-kinikilingan.*

UNBIND, v. *kalagín; kalasín.*

UNBOLT, v. to open, *buksán, ibukás.*

UNBORN, adj. *di pa isinísilang.*

UNBOUNDED, adj. *waláng-hanggán.*

UNBRIDLED, adj. *waláng-pigil: waláng-taros.*

UNCALLED-FOR, adj. *di-kailangan;* superfluous, *kalabisán;* out of place, *walâ sa lugár.*

UNCANNY, adj. weird, mysterious, *mahiwagà.*

UNCEASING, adj. *waláng-tigil; waláng-higkát, waláng-likát.*

UNCERTAIN, adj. not sure, *di-tiyák;* doubtful, *alinlangan, nag-áalinlangan.*

UNCHANGEABLE, adj. *di mabábago.*

UNCHARITABLE, adj. *waláng-awà; waláng-habág.*

UNCIVIL, adj. *bastós.*

UNCLE, n. *amaín; tiyó,* Sp.

UNCLEAN, adj. *marumí;* filthy, *nakaáani.*

UNCOMFORTABLE, adj. not at ease, *di-tiwasáy;* causing uneasiness, *nakabábalisa;* without physical ease, *di-maginhawa, waláng-ginhawa.*

UNCOMMON adj, *di-karaniwan;* rare, *bihirà.*

UNCONDITIONAL, adj. absolute, *lubós; waláng pasubalì.*

UNCONFIRMED, adj. *waláng-patunay.*

UNCONSCIOUS, adj. not aware, *waláng-malay;* without feeling, *waláng-pakiramdám.*

UNCONSTITUTIONAL, adj. *labág sa Saligáng-Batás.*

UNCONTROLLED, adj. *walángpigil.*

UNCOUTH, adj. boorish, *bastós;* ungainly, *mabagal:* strange, *kakaibá, kakatwá.*

UNCOVER, v. *buksán.*

UNCTION, n. *unsiyón,* Sp.

UNDAUNTED, adj. *waláng-gulat;* fearless, *waláng-takot.*

UNDENIABLE, adj. *di-matátanggihán;* compelling admission, *cukat-paniwalaan.*

UNDER, prep. *sa ilalim ng.*—adv. *sa ilalim.*

UNDERCLOTHES, n. *damít na pangilalim.*

UNDERCURRENT, n. *agos na pangilalim.*

UNDERDONE, adj. cooked too little, *malasado,* Sp.

UNDERGO, v. to experience, *magdanas, dumanas, pagdanasan;* suffer, *magtiís, pagtiïsán:* endure, *magbatá, batahín.*

UNDERGROUND, adj. *sa ilalim ng lupà;* fig. *pailalím.*

UNDERHANDED, adj, sly, *kublí, pakublí;* secretive, *lihim, palihim.*

UNDERLAY, v. *sapinán, sapnán.*

UNDERLINE, v. *salungguhitan.*

UNDERLINING, n. *salungguhit.*

UNDERLING, n. *tauhan; kampón.*

UNDERMINE, v. *salungguhitan.* To cause to fall by weakening under, *paguhuín;* weaken, *pahinain.*

UNDERNEATH, adv.-prep. *sa ilalim.*

UNDERRATE, v. *muntiín, maltitín.*

UNDERSCORE, v. *salungguhitan.*

UNDERSHIRT, n. *kamiseta,* Sp.

UNDERSIGN, v. to sign below, *lumagdâ; pumirmá,* Sp.—The undersigned, *any nakalagdâ.*

UNDERSTAND, v. to perceive, *máwatasan;* know, *máalaman, alamín;* know the meaning, *maunawaan, unawain; máintindihán, intindihín,* Sp.; be informed of, *mabatíd, matalós.*

UNDERSTANDING, n. the reasoning faculties, *pang-unauà;* state of knowing, *kaalaman;* agreement between two or more minds, *únawaan; intindihan,* Sp.

UNDERSTUDY, n. person trained to take another's place, *panghalili.*

UNDERTAKE, v. *isagawâ, magsagawá.*

UNDERTAKER, n. mortician, *manlilibíng.*

UNDERTAKING, n. the taking upon oneself of a task, *pagsasagawâ;* enterprise, *gáwain.*

UNDESIRABLE, adj. *di-kanaïsnais.*

UNDO, v. to make null and void, *pawaláng-bisà;* destroy, *sirain, gibaín;* loosen, *kalagín, kalasín.*

UNDOING n. *pagkabigô;* loss, *pagkatalo.*

UNDRESS, v. *maghubád; hubarín;* (others) *hubarán.*

UNDOUBTEDLY, adv. *walángpagsala.*

UNDUE, adj. more than proper or suitable, *higít sa nárarapat;* wrong, *malî;* illegal, *labág sa batás.*

UNDULATE, v. *mag-alún-alón.*

UNDYING, adj. never ceasing, *waláng-pagmamaliw;* without end, *waláng-wakás, immortal, waláng-kamátayan.*

UNEARTH, v. *mádukál;* to discover, *mátuklasán.*

UNEASY, adj. aláalá, balisá.

UNEDUCATED, adj. illiterate, mangmáng.

UNEMPLOYED, adj. without occupation, waláng-ginágawâ; out of work, waláng-pinápasukan; not in use, di-ginágamit.

UNEQUAL, adj. di-magkapantáy, di-pareho, Sp.

UNEQUALED, adj. waláng-katulad; di-matularan.

UNESSENTIAL, adj. di-gaanóng kailangan.

UNEVEN, adj. not smooth, magaspáng; bakú-bakó; odd, (not even in numbering), nunes, Sp.

UNEXPECTED, adj. di-akalain; di-ináantáy; sudden, biglâ.

UNFAILING adj. reliable, maáasahan; not liable to fall short, as supply, di-magkúkulang; not growing less or weaker, di-manghíhinà.

UNFAIR, adj. tricky, madayà, maydayà; dishonest, di-marangál; not just, di-tapát.

UNFAITHFUL, adj. taksíl.

UNFASTEN, v. kalagín.

UNFATHOMABLE, adj. di-matarók.

UNFAVORABLE, adj. adverse, salungát; discouraging, nakapanghíhinà ng loób.

UNFEIGNED, adj. tunay; without pretense, waláng-pakunwarì.

UNFINISHED, adj. di tapós.

UNFIT, adj. not suitable, di-bagay; improper, di-dapat; di-akmâ.

UNFOLD, v. to spread open, ibuká, ibukadkád, iladlád; to open, as a flower, bumukád.

UNFORTUNATE, adj. sawî; sawing-palad; regrettable, kahiná-hinayang.

UNFOUNDED, adj. waláng-pinagbábabatayan.

UNFURL, v. iladlád.

UNGRACIOUS, adj. uncivil, waláng-pakundangan; rude, waláng-galang, bastós; offensive, mabagsík.

UNGRATEFUL, adj. waláng utang na loób.

UNHAPPY, adj. malungkót; nalulumbáy.

UNHEALTHY, adj. unwell, maykaramdaman; injurious, nakasásamá.

UNIFORM, n. uniporme. Sp. — adj. magkakatulad (in form, sa anyó; in shape, sa hugis; in character, sa katángian).

UNIFY, v. to form into one, pagisahín.

UNIMPEACHABLE, adj. di-mapag-áalinlanganan.

UNION, n. pagkakáisá.

UNIQUE, adj. bukód-tangì.

UNIT, n. yunit, Eng.; pagka-isá.

UNITE, v. to join together, pagsamahin; combine so as to make one, pag-isahín.

UNITY, n. pagkakáisá; (in Literature) kaisahán.

UNIVERSAL, adj. pansansinukuban; panlahát; pandaigdíg.

UNIVERSE, n. sansinukob, santinakpán, loosely, the world, daigdíg, sandaigdigan; sangkalupaán.

UNIVERSITY, n. unibersidad, Sp.; pámantasan, cw.

UNJUST, adj. di-matuwíd; not according to legal justice, waláng-katárungan.

UNKEMPT, adj. guló, gusót; not combed, di-sinukláy; slovenly, nanlílimahid.

UNKIND, adj. malupít.

UNKNOWN, adj. not apprehended, di-alám; not recognized, di-kilala.

UNLAWFUL, adj. labág sa batás.

UNLESS, conj. máliban kung.

UNLIKE, adj. ki-katulad, di-kawangis.

UNLIKELY, adj. waláng kasiguruhán, Sp.

UNLIMITED, adj. waláng-hanggán.

UNLOAD, v. mag-ibís maglapág, ilapág.

UNLOCK, v. buksán.

UNLOOSE, v. alpasán.

UNLUCKY, adj. waláng-kapalaran; sinásamá.

UNMISTAKABLE, adj. di-mapagkakamalán.

UNNATURAL, adj. di-katutubò.

UNNECESSARY, adj. di-kailangan.

UNOCCUPIED, adj. not busy, waláng-ginágawá; not inhabited, waláng-tumítirá; untaken (as, seat), waláng-umúupô.

UNPARALLELED, adj. waláng-kahambíng.

UNPARDONABLE, adj. di-mapatátawad.

UNPLEASANT, adj. nakayáyamot.

UNPRECEDENTED, adj. waláng-ulirán; novel, bago.

UNPREJUDICED, adj. waláng-kiníkilingan.

UNPREPARED, adj. di-handâ.

UNPROFITABLE, adj. di-mapakíkinabangan; waláng-pakinabang.

UNRULY, adj. di-masupil.

UNSATISFACTORY, adj. di-nakasísiyáng-loób.

UNSATISFIED, adj. di nasísiyahán.

UNSEEN, adj. di-kita, di nákikita.

UNSTABLE, adj. mabuway.

UNSTRUNG, adj. habsô, talihabsô.

UNTIDY, adj. dirty, marumí; slovenly, nanlílimahid.

UNTIL, prep.-conj. hanggáng sa.

UNTOLD, adj. di-maulatan.

UNTRUE, adj. di-totoó.

UNUSUAL, adj. di-karaniwan, di-pangkaraniwan.

UNUTTERABLE, adj. di-masabi; beyond description, di-máilarawan.

UNWARRANTABLE, adj. waláng-matuwid.

UNWARY, adj. kulang sa alagà.

UNWILLING, adj. ayaw.

UNWISE, adj. di-dapat.

UNWORTHY, adj. di-karapatdapat.

UNWRITTEN, adj. di-násusulat; di-nakasulat.

UP, adv. sa itaás.—prep. sa itaás ng.

UPHOLD, v. magtaguyod, itaguyod; to maintain, manindig, ipanindigan.

UPLIFT, n. progress, pag-unlád.

UPON, prep. on, sa; on top or surface of, sa ibabaw ng.

UPPERMOST, adj. káitaasan.

UPRIGHT, adj. nakatayô, patayô; patindig.

UPRISING, n. pagbabangon.

UPROAR, n. pagkakaingáy, pagkakaguló.

UPROOT, v. bunutin.

UPSET, v. guluhin.

UPSIDE, adv.-adj. upside down, patiwarík; baligtád, tuwád.

UPSTAIRS, adj. sa itaás.

UPWARD, adv. pataás, paitaás.

URGE, v. ipasagawâ.

URGENT, adj. mádalian; important, mahalagá.

URINATE, v. umihì.

URINE, n. ihì.

URN, n. urna, Sp.

US, pron.—to, for, with us, (all)

sa *atin,* (excluding person addressed), sa *amin.*

USABLE, adj. *magágamit, nagágamit.*

USAGE, n. *paggamit, kagamitán.*

USE, v. *gumamit, gamitin.*—n. as USAGE.

USEFUL, adj. *mapakikinabangan.*

USELESS, adj. *waláng-kagamitán; waláng-saysáy.*

USUAL, adj. *karaniwan; kaugalián.*

USURER, n. *magpapátubò.*

USURIOUS, adj. *mapagpatubò.*

USURP, v. *mangagaw ng tungkulin ng ibá.*

USURY, n. *pagpapatubò.*

UTERUS, n. (Anat.) *bahaybatà; bahaytao.*

UTILIZE, v. see USE.

UTMOST, adj. greatest, *kalubúslubusan;* farthest, *kálayu-layuan;* extreme, *kasukdulán.*

UTTER, v. to pronounce, *bigkasín;* speak, *magsalitâ, magwikà.* —adj. absolute, *lubós.*

UTTERLY, adv. fully, *buong-buô;* absolutely, *lubós na lubós.*

V

VACANCY, n. *pagka-bakante,* Sp.; emptiness, *pagka-waláng-lamán.*

VACANT, adj. *bakante,* Sp.; empty, *waláng-lamán.*

VACATE, v. to give up the possession of, *iwan;* colloq., go away, *umalís.*

VACATION, n. *bakasyón,* Sp.; *pahingá.*

VACCINATE, v. *magbakuna, bakunahan,* Sp.

VACCINE, n. *bakuna,* Sp.

VACILLATE, v. *mag-urung-sulong; mag-alangán.*

VACUUM, n. *alangaang,* nc.

VAGABOND, n.-adj. *hampaslupà.*

VAGARY, n. *isip na ligáw;* irresponsible dreaming, *pangangarap;* whim, *kapritso,* Sp.; *kibót ng isip.*

VAGRANT, adj. *ligáw, náliligáw.* —n. a tramp, *hampaslupà.*

VAGUE, adj. not clear, *di-malinaw;* hazy, *malabò;* not sure, *ditiyák.*

VAIN, adj. valueless, *walárghalagá, waláng-kabuluhán, waláng-saysáy.*—In v., to no purpose, *waláng-kapararakan.*

VAINGLORIOUS, adj. *mapagparangalan; palalò;* boastful, *hambóg.*

VAINGLORY, n. excessive vanity or pride, *kapalaluán;* boastfulness, *kahambugán;* vain pomp or show, *pagka-mapagparangalan.*

VALEDICTORIAN, n. (of a graduating class) *unang dangál.*

VALEDICTORY, n. *talumpating pamamaalam.*

VALIANT, adj. brave, *matapang;* heroic, *magiting.*

VALID, a d j. *may-bisà;* well-grounded, *may-kabuluhán.*

VALIDATE, v. to ratify, *pagtibayin;* give legal force to, *bigyáng-bisà.*

VALLEY, n. *labák; lambák; libís.*

VALOR, n. fearlessness, *pagkawaláng-takot;* bravery, *katapangan.*

VALUABLE, adj. *mahalagá.*

VALUATION, n. *paghahalagá.*

VALUE, n. *halagá;* precise import, *kabuluhán;* exact meaning, *kahulugán.*—v. to put a price on, *halagahán,* esteem highly, *pahalagahán, mahalagahín;* hold dear, *mahalín, itangì.*

VALUED, adj. dearly prized, *mahál, minámahál.*

VALVE, n. *bárbulá,* Sp.

VAN,—in the v., *nasa-unahán, nangúnguna.*

VANGUARD, n. *talibà.*

VANISH, v. to disappear, *mawalâ;* pass out of existence, *maparam.*

VANITY, n. conceit, *kapalaluán;* triviality, *pagka-waláng-kapararakan.*

VANQUISH, v. to conquer, *manlupig, lupigin;* defeat, *talunin;* get the better of, *daigín.*

VAPOR, n. *singáw; halipawpáw,* O.T.; mist, *ulap.*

VAPOROUS, adj. *masingáw.*

VARIABLE, adj. *pabagu-bago.*

VARIED, adj. *ibá-ibá.*

VARIETY, n. *sarisari.*

VARIOUS, adj. *ibá't ibá.*

VARNISH, n. *barnís,* Sp. — v. *magbarnís, barnisán,* Sp.

VARY, v. to alter, *pagbagu-baguhin;* make unlike one another, *pag-ibá-ibahín;* undergo a change, *mabago.*

VASE, n. *haro, saro,* Sp.

VASSAL, n. *kampón.*

VAST, adj. *malawak;* huge, *malakí.*

VAT, n. *kawa.*

VATICAN, n. *Batikano,* Sp.

VAUDEVILLE, n. *bódabíl,* Fr.

VEER, v. *pumihit, pumalig.*

VEGETABLE, n. *gulay.*

VEHEMENCE, n. *karubdubán; kaalaban.*

VEHEMENT, adj. *marubdób; maalab.*

VEHICLE, n. *sasakyán.*

VEIL, n. *belo,* Sp.; *talukbóng;* mantilla, *lambóng.*—v. to cover with a v., *talukbungán.*

VEIN, n. *ugát.*

VELOCITY, n. speed, *bilís;* swiftness, *tulin.*

VENERABLE, adj. worthy of reverence, *kapitá-pitagan;* worthy to be taken as sacred, *kapintupintuhò.*

VENERATE, v. to regard as sacred, *pintuhuin, mamintuhò;* revere, *pamitaganan.*

VENERATION, n. worship, *pamimintuhò;* respect and reverence, *pamimitagan.*

VENGEANCE, n. *higantí; paghihigantí.*

VENIAL, adj. pardonable, *mapatátawad.*

VENISON, n. *karning-usá.*

VENOM, n. *kamandág;* poison, *lason.*

VENOMOUS, adj. *makamandág;* poisonous, *may-lason.*

VENT, n. hole, opening, *butas;* outlet, *pálabasan.*—To give' v. to one's feelings, *ihingá ang mga damdamin.*

VENTILATE, v. *pahanginan, gawíng maaliwalas.*

VENTILATED, adj. *maaliwalas.*

VENTRAL, adj. *pantiyán.*

VENTURE, v. to risk or chance, *magbakasakalì;* dare, *mangahás.*

VENTURESOME, VENTUROUS, adj. daring, *pangahás;* having the quality of taking risks or chances, *mapagbakasakalì.*

VERACITY, n. accordance with truth, *pagka-ayon sa katotóhanan.*

VERB, n. (Gram.) *pandiwà.*

VERBAL, n. (Gram.)—v. noun,

pandiwang makangalan; v. adjective, *pandiwang makaurì, pandiwarì.*

VERBOSE, adj. *maligoy.*

VERBOSITY, n. *kaliguyan.*

VERDANT, adj. *lunti, luntián.*

VERDICT, n. *hatol; pasiyá.*

VERDURE, n. *kaluntián; pagkaluntî.*

VERGE, n. brink, *gilid, gulod;* extreme edge, *tangwá.*

VERIFY, v. to prove the correctness of, *patunayan, magpatunay;* examine so as to prove, *siyasatin kung totoó.*

VERNACULAR, n. *sariling wikà.*

VERSE, n. *tulâ.*

VERSIFY, v. *tumulâ; tulaín.*

VERTICAL, adj. upright, *patayô, patindíg.*

VERTIGO, n. (Med.) *lulà, hilo.*

VERY, adj.-adv. Use *nápaka-* (prefix) plus the quality modified, as, *nápakabutì,* very good; *nápakagandá,* very beautiful.

VESPER, adj. *panghapon, panggabí.*

VESSEL, n. container, *sisidlán, lolagyán;* ship, *sasakyáng-dagat, bapór,* Sp.

VEST, n. *tsaleko,* Sp.

VESTIGE, n. mark, *tandâ;* trace, *bakás.*

VESTMENT, n. *kabihisan.*

VESTRY, n. *sákristiya,* Sp.

VETERAN, n. *beterano,* Sp.; possessing experience, *may-karanasan;* long trained, *sanáy.*

VETERINARIAN, n. *beterinaryo,* Sp.

VETO, n. *beto,* Sp.

VEX, v. *mangyamót, yamutín.*

VEXATION, n. *kayámutan.*

VEXATIOUS, adj. *nakayayamót.*

VIANDS, n. *pangulam.*

VIBRANT, adj. resonant, *mataginting.*

VIBRATE, v. to quiver, as *voice, kumatál-katál;* resound. *tumaginting.*

VIBRATION, n. *pagkatál-katál;* resonance, *taginting.*

VICAR, n. *bikaryo,* Sp.

VICE, n. *bisyo,* Sp.—adj. next in rank, *pangalawá.*—V.-president, *pangalawáng pangulo.*

VICINITY, n. nearness, *kalapitan.*

VICTOR, n. *ang nagwagí, ang nagtagumpáy.*

VICTORIOUS, adj. *mapagwagí, mapanagumpáy.*

VICTORY, n. *pagwawagí; tagumpáy.*

VICTUALS, n. *pagkain.*

VIEW, n. the act of seeing, *pagtingín;* picture of a scene, *tánawin;* spectacle, *pánoorín;* opinion, *palagáy.*—v. to see, *tingnán,* gaze at, *tanawín.*

VIGIL, n. *paglalamay, pagpupuyát.*

VIGILANCE, n. watchfulness, *maingat na pagbabantáy;* caution, *pangangalagà.*

VIGILANT, adj. alert, *gising,* wary, *maingat, maalagà.*

VIGOR, n. *lakás.*

VIGOROUS, adj. *malakás;* energetic, *masiglá.*

VILE, adj. *hamak;* mean, ignoble, *imbí.*

VILLAGE, n. *nayon; baryo,* Sp.

VILLAIN, n. *belyako,* Sp.; *taong tampalasan; kontrabida,* Sp.

VILLAINOUS, adj. *tampalasan.*

VILLAINY, n. *katampalasanan.*

VINDICATE, v. *mananggaláng.*

VINDICTIVE, adj. *mapanghigantí.*

VINE, n. *baging.*

VINEGAR, n. *sukà.*

VIOLATE, v. to transgress, *lu-*

mabág, labagín; treat roughly or severely, dahasín, mandahás; use ill, rape, gahisín, manggahís.

VIOLATION, n. transgression. paglabág; ill-treatment, rape, panggagahís; severe treatment. pandadahás.

VIOLENCE, n. karahasán.

VIOLENT, adj. marahás.

VIOLET, n. lila, Sp.; biyoleta, Sp.

VIOLIN, n. biyolín, Sp.

VIRGIN, n.-adj. birhen, Sp.; dalaga.

VIRILE, adj. may-pagka-lalaki.

VIRTUE, n. effectiveness, bisà; worth. halagá; merit, kagálingan, kabutihan; rectitude, pagka-matuwíd; chastity kalinísang-puri.

VIRULENT, adj. makamandág; may-lason.

VISAGE, n. pagmumukhâ.

VISAYAN, n.-adj. Bisayà.

VISIBLE, adj. in sight, kita; obvious, litáw; apparent, halatâ.

VISION, n. larawang-diwà; bisyón, Sp.; guníguní.

VISIT, v. dumalaw, dalawin; bumisita, bisitahin, Sp.

VISITOR, n. dalaw; bisita, Sp.

VISUALIZE, v. ilarawan sa diwù.

VITAL, adj. pambuhay; essential, kailangan.

VITALITY, n. lakás.

VITAMIN, n. baytamín, Eng.

VIVACIOUS, adj. masiglá.

VIVID, adj. masidhî; animated, buháy.

VOCABULARY, n. talásalitaan; bukabularyo, Sp.

VOCAL, adj. pertaining to the

voice, pantinig, or speech, pansalitâ; having voice, may-tiniq; voiced, tininigan.

VOCATION, n. hilig, kináhihiligan.

VOCATIONAL, adj. panghilig-yaman.

VOCATIVE, adj. (Gram.) patawág.

VOCIFEROUS, adj. maingay; malinggál.

VOICE, n. tinig; (Gram.) tingig.

VOID, adj. empty, waláng-lamán; useless, waláng-kagamitán; waláng-saysáy.

VOLATILE, adj. maígahin; madaling maigá.

VOLCANO, n. bulkán, Sp.

VOLITION, n. kaloobán, buluntád, Sp.; determination, decision, pasiyá.

VOLTAGE, n. bultahe, Sp.

VOLUBLE, adj. masalitá.

VOLUME, n. a book, aklát, libró, Sp.; tomo, Sp.; size, lakí.

VOLUNTARY, adj. kusà.

VOLUNTEER, n. buluntaryo, Sp.

VOMIT, v. sumuka, magsuká.

VORACIOUS, adj. masibà.

VOTE, n. boto, Sp.; halál.—v. bumoto, botohan, Sp.; ihalál.

VOTER, n. botante, Sp.; manghahalal.

VOUCH, v. to confirm, patunayan, magpatunay; bear witness, saksihán, sumaksí; guarantee, akuin, umakò.

VOUCHER, n. one who bears witness, saksí; guarantor, ang umáakò; paper or receipt for payment, botser, Eng.

VOUCHSAFE, v. igawad, ipagkaloób.

VOW, n. pangakò.—v. mangakò.

VOWEL, n. (Gram.) *patinig.*

VOYAGE, n. *paglalayág; paglalakbáy-dagat.*

VULGAR, adj. *pangkaraniwan;* low, *mababà;* mean, *hamak.*

VULNERABLE, adj. *matátalbán.*

VULTURE, n. *buwitre,* Sp.

W

WAG, v. *magpauli-ulì.*

WAGE, n. pl. (wages) *sahod, kita.*—v. To w. war, *mandigmâ.*

WAGER, n. *pustá,* Sp.—v. *pumustá.*

WAGON, n. *bagón,* Sp.

WAIST, n. (Anat.) *baywáng.*

WAIT, v. *maghintáy, hintayín.*

WAITER, n. *tagapaglingkód; weyter,* Eng.

WAKE, v. *gumising, mágising.*

WAKEKFUL, adj. *gising;* unable to sleep, *di-mákatulóg.*

WAKEN, v. *gisingin.*

WALK, v. *lumakad, maglakád;* to take a stroll, *magpasiyál,* Sp.

WALK-OUT, n. *welga,* Sp.; *aklasan.*

WALL, n. fence of stone, brick, etc., *padér,* Sp.; room partition, *dingdíng.*

WALLET, n. folding pocketbook, *pitakà,* Sp.

WALLOW, v. to roll about in mud, *lumublób;* live in vice or filth, *gumumon.*

WALTZ, n. *balse,* Sp.

WAN, adj. sickly, *masasaktín.*

WAND, n. *batutà,* Sp.

WANE, v. (applied to the moon) *magtunáw.*

WANT, n. *pangangailangan.* — v. *mangailangan.*

WANTING, adj. lacking, *kulang:* missing. *nawáwalâ.*

WANTON, adj. malicious, *masamang-budhî;* loose in morals, *mahalay.*

WAR, n. *digmâ;* (actual and being fought) *digmaan.*

WARBLE, v. to trill, *humuni;* carol, *umawit.*

WARD, n. district, *purók;* person under guard or protection, *alagà;* section of a hospital, *salà,* Sp.—v. to w. off, *magsanggalâng, magtanggól.*

WARDEN, n. *alkayde,* Sp.

WARDROBE, n. closet for clothes, *aparadór,* Sp.

WAREHOUSE, n. *bodega,* Sp.; *pintungan.*

WARFARE, n. *digmaan, pagdirigmaan.*

WARM, adj. *mainit, mabanás.*

WARMTH, n. *init.*

WARN, v. to put on guard, *papag-ingatin;* make aware of possible danger, *pagsabihan, pangunahan;* advise against something, *paalalahanan.*

WARNING, n. *paálaala.*

WARP, v. to become twisted, *mamaluktót.*

WARRIOR, n. *mandirigmâ.*

WARSHIP, n. *bapór na pandigmâ.*

WART, n. *butíg.*

WARY, adj. *maingat.*

WASH, v. *maghugas, hugasan; maglabá, labhán.*

WASHSTAND, n. *hugasán; lababo,* Sp.

WASP, n. *laywán.*

WASTE, v. to destroy, *gibaín, siraín;* spend or use recklessly or unprofitably, *mag-aksayá, aksayahín; sayangin.*

WASTEFUL, adj. *mapag-aksayá.*

WATCH, n. small timepiece, *relós,* Sp.; guard, *bantáy.*—v. to keep guard, *magbantáy, bantayán.*

WATCHFUL, adj. *maingat, maalagà.*

WATCHMAKER, n. *relohero,* Sp.

WATCHMAN, n. *bantáy; tanod.*

WATCHWORD, n. *hudyát.*

WATER, n. *tubig.*—v. to sprinkle with w., *diligín, magdilíg.*

WATER-CLOSET, n. *inodoro;* Sp.

WATERMELON, n. *pakwán.*

WATERFALL, n. *talón.*

WATERPROOF, adj. *di-mabasâ, di-matatalbán ng tubig; may-sagabi.*

WAVE, n. *alon.*

WAVER, v. *mag-ulik-ulik.*

WAX, n. *pagkít.*

WAY, n. passage, *daán;* manner, *ugalì;* method, means, *paraán.*

WAYLAY, v. *abatán.*

WAYSIDE, n. *tabíng-daán.*

WAYWARD, adj. *suwaíl.*

WE, pron. (all) *tayo;* (excluding the person addressed) *kamì.*

WEAK, adj. *mahinà.*

WEAKEN, v. to r e d u c e in strength, *pahinain;* become less strong, *manghinà.*

WEAKNESS, n. *kahinaan.*

WEALTH, n. *yaman, kayamanan.*

WEAN, v. *iwalay; awatin; ibitíw.*

WEAPON, n. *sandata; armás,* Sp.

WEAR, v. *magsuót, isuót.*

WEARISOME, adj. *nakapápagod.*

WEARY, adj. *pagód, napápagod.*

WEATHER, n. *panahón.*

WEAVE, v. (reeds or the like) *lumala, maglala, lalahin;* (threads into cloth) *humabi, maghabi, habihin.*

WEB, n. cobweb, *bahay-álalawà, bahay-gagambá.*

WED, v. to marry, *mag-asawa, pakasál,* Sp.

WEDDING, n. *boda,* Sp.; *kasál,* Sp.; *pag-iisáng-dibdíb.*

WEDGE, n. *kunyás,* Sp.; *sinsél,* Sp.

WEDNESDAY, n. *Miyérkulés,* Sp.

WEED, n. *damó.*—v. to remove undesirable grass or plants, *gumamas, gamasin.*

WEEDY, n. *madamó.*

WEEK, n. *linggó.*

WEEKLY, adv. once a week, *lingguhan;* every week, *linggú-linggó.*

WEEP, v. to cry, *umiyák;* shed tears, *lumuhà.*

WEIGH, v. *magtimbáng, timbungín.*

WEIGHT, n. heaviness, *bigát;* unit of heaviness, *timbáng.*

WEIGHTY, adj. heavy, *mabigát;* having much weight, *matimbáng.*

WEIRD, adj. *nakapangíngilabot.*

WELCOME, n. *masayáng pagtanggáp.* — adj. *kalugúd-lugód, nakalúlugód.*—v. to receive with hospitality, *tanggapíng mahinusay.*

WELD, v. *maghinang, ihinang, hinangin.*

WELDING, n. *hinang.*

WELFARE, n. *kagálingan.*

WELL, n. waterhole, *b a l ó n;* spring, *balong, batis.*

WELL, adj.-adv. *magalíng.*

WELL-TO-DO, adj. *mariwasâ.*

WELT, n. red swollen mark on the skin made by a blow, *latay.*

WEST, n.-adj. *kanluran.*

WESTERLY, adj.-adv. *pakanlurán.*

WESTERNER, n. *tagakanluran.*

WESTWARD, adj.-adv. *pakanlurán.*

WET, adj. *basâ.*—W. nurse *sisiwa.*

WHALE, n. *dambuhalà; isdángbalyena,* Sp.

WHARF, n. *dáungan.*

WHAT, pron-adj. *anó.*

WHATEVER, pron.-adj. *anumán, anó man.*

WHATSOEVER, pron.-adj. *anumán, anó man.*

WHEAT, n. *trigo,* Sp.

WHEEL, n. *gulóng.*—v. *umikot.*

WHEN, adv. *kailán.*

WHENCE, adv. *sa anóng dahilán.*

WHENEVER, adv. *kailanmán at, kailanmá't.*

WHERE, adv. *saán.*

WHEREAS, conj. *yáyamang.*

WHEREFORE, adv. (relative use) *sa anong dahilán;* (interrogative use) *bakit.*

WHEREIN, adv. (interrogative use) *saán.*

WHEREVER, adv. *saanmán.*

WHET, v. to sharpen (as a knife), *ihasà, maghasà.*

WHETHER, conj. *kung.*

WHETSTONE, n. *hasaán.*

WHEY, n. *patís ng gatas.*

WHICH, pron-adj. *alín.*

WHICHEVER, pron. *alinmán.*

WHILE, conj. *habang, samantala.*

WHINE, v. *dumaíng.*

WHIP, n. *látikó,* Sp.

WHIR, v. *umugong, humiging.*— n. *ugong, higing.*

WHIRL, v. *umikot, uminog.*

WHIRLPOOL, n. *puyó, ng tubig.*

WHIRLWIND, n. *ipuipo.*

WHISKER, n. *bigote,* Sp.

WHISKY, n. *wiski,* Eng.

WHISPER, n. *bulóng.*—v. *bumulóng;* (to) *bulungán.*

WHISTLE, v. *sumipol;* (at) *si-*

pulan.—n. (act of) *sipol;* an instrument for whistling, *pito,* Sp.; *silbato,* Sp.

WHITE, adj.-n. *putî, maputî.*—W ant, *anay.*

WHITEN, v. *paputiín;* become white, *pumuti, mamutî.*

WHITHER, adv. *pasaán.*

WHO, pron. *sino.*

WHOEVER, pron. *sínumán.*

WHOLE, n.-adj. *buô; lahát.*

WHOLE-HEARTED, adj. *buóngpusò.*

WHOLESALE, n. *pakyawan, pakyáw.*

WHOM, pron. to w., *kanino.*

WHOSE, pron. *kanino, nino.*

WHY, adv. *bakit.*

WICK, n. *mitsá,* Sp.

WICKED, adj. evil, *masamâ;* immoral, *mahalay;* sinful, *makasalanan.*

WIDE, adj. *maluwáng.*

WIDEN, v. *paluwangín;* to broaden, *palaparin.*

WIDESPREAD, adj. *kalát, laganap.*

WIDOW, WIDOWER, n. *balo; bao.*

WIDTH, n. *luwáng;* breadth, *lapad.*

WIFE, n. *asawa (asawang babae).*

WIG, n. *peluka,* Sp.

WILD, adj. *mailáp;* uncultivated, *ligáw;* savage, *labuyò.* — W. boar, *baboy-ramó.*—w. cat, *alamíd.*

WILL, n. *kaloobán;* command, *utos.*

WILT, v. *malantá.*

WILY, adj. *mahibò; magdarayà.*

WIN, v. *manalo.*

WIND, n. current of air, *hangin.*

WIND, v. to twist round and round something, *magpulon, pulunin.*

WINDOW, n. *bintanà*, Sp.; *dúru-ngawán.*

WINDSHIELD, n. *panalóng-hangin.*

WINDY, adj. *mahangin.*

WINE, n. *alak.*

WING, n. *pakpák.*

WINK, v. *kumindát, kumuráp, kumisáp.*

WINSOME, adj. *kahalí-halina.*

WINTER, n.-adj. *taglamíg; tagginaw.*

WIPE, v. *magpunas, punasan.*

WIRE, n. *kawad.*

WISDOM, n. *kaalaman;* knowledge, *karunungan.*

WISE, adj. *maalam;* knowing, *marunong.*

WISH, v. *naisin, nasain.*

WISHFUL, adj. *mapagnais, mapagnasa.*

WISTFUL, adj. *paláisíp.*

WIT, n. *katalasan.*

WITCH, WIZARD, n. *mangkukulam, manggagaway.*

WITH, prep. *sa,* (However, there are numerous cases in which "with" is not translated, the meaning being included in a word or in the context.)

WITHDRAWAL, v. to retire, *umurong; umalis;* take back (as money deposited in a bank) *kumuha.*

WITHER, v. *malantá.*

WITHERED, adj. *lantà.*

WITHIN, adv. *sa loób.*—prep. *sa loób ng.*

WITHOUT, adv. *sa labás.*—prep., not prep. but adv. in Tagalog; lacking, *walá.*

WITHSTAND, v. *matiís;* to resist, *mapaglabanan.*

WITLESS, adj. *tangá, hangál.*

WITNESS, n. *saksí.*—v. *sumaksí.*

WOE, n. *pighatî.*

WOEBEGONE, adj. *lungkót na lungkót.*

WOEFUL, adj. *namímighatî.*

WOMAN, n. *babae.*

WOMANHOOD, n. *pagka-babae.*

WOMANISH, adj. *parang babae.*

WOMANKIND, n. *kababaihan.*

WOMB, n. uterus, *bahaybatà; bahaytao.*

WONDER, n. *pagtataká.*—v. *magtaká, pagtakhán.*

WONDERFUL, adj. *kataká-taká; kahanga-hangà.*

WOO, v. *manligaw, mangibig.*

WOOD, n. *kahoy.*

WOODLAND, n. *kakahuyan.*

WOOL, n. *lana,* Sp.

WORD, n. *salitâ.*

WORK, n. *gáwain;* trabaho, Sp.—v. *gumawà; magtrabaho,* Sp.

WORKMAN, n. *manggagawà; trabahador,* Sp.

WORKSHOP, n. *gáwaan.*

WORLD, n. *daigdíg;* mundó, Sp.

WORM, n. *bulati.*

WORN-OUT, adj. *sirâ, gibá;* tired out, *pagód.*

WORSE, adj. (comparative) *lalong masamâ.*

WORSHIP, v. *sumambá, sambahín; mamintuhò, pintuhuin.*

WORST, adj. (superlative) *kásamá-samaan; nápakasamâ.*

WORTH, n. value, *halagá;* merit *kagálingan.*

WOUND, n. *sugat.*

WOUNDED, adj. *nasugatan; may sugat.*

WRANGLE, v. *magtaltalan.*

WRAP, v. *balutin.*—n. cloak, *balabal.*

WRAPPER, n. *pambalot.*

WRATH, n. *galit.*

WRENCH, v. *pilipitin.*

WREST, v. *agawin.*

WRESTLE, v. *magbunô.*

WRINKLE, n. *kulubót.*

WRIST, n. *galanggalangán; pupulsuhan,* Sp.

WRITE, v. *sumulat, sulatin.*
WRITER, n. *mánunulat.*
WRITHE, v. *mamilipit.*

WRONG, adj. *malî; lisyâ;* incorrect, *di-wastô.*

X

X-RAY, n. *eks-ray,* Eng.
XYLOGRAPH, n. *ukit sa kahoy.*
XYLOID, adj. *parang kahoy.*

XYLOPHONE, n. *sílopón,* Eng.
XYSTER, n. *pangayod.*

Y

YACHT, n: *batél,* Sp.; *yate,* Sp.
YAM, n. (Bot.) *tugî; lamî.*
YAP, n. *tahól, kahól; yapyáp.*
YORD, n. *yarda,* Sp.
YARN, n. *estambre,* Sp.
YAWN, n. *hikáb.*—v. *humikáb, maghikáb.*
YEAR, n. *taón.*
YEARLY, adj. *santáunan.*—adv. once a year, *minsan isáng taón;* every year, *taún-taón.*
YEARN, n. *magnais; maghangád.*
YELL, n. *hiyáw, sigáw.*—v. *humiyáw, sumigáw;* (at someone) *hiyawán, sigawán.*
YELLOW, n. *diláw, mariláw, amarilyo,* Sp.; (fig.) coward, *duwág.*
YELLOWISH, adj. *madiláw-diláw.*
YES, adv. *oo.*
YESTERDAY, adv. *kahapon.*

YET, adv. *pa.*
YIELD, v. to produce, as fruit, *bumunga, magbunga;* assent, *pumayag;* surrender, *sumukò.*
YOKE, n. *pamatok.*
YOLK, n. *pulá ng itlóg, burok.*
YONDER, adj. *iyón, yaón.*—adv. *doón.*
YOU, pron. (sing., prepositive) *ikáw,* (postpositive) *ka;* (pl. and honorific) *kayó.*
YOUNG, adj. *batà.*
YOUNGSTER, n. *batà.*
YOUR, pron. (sing., prepositive) *iyó,* (postpositive) *mo;* (pl., prepositive) *inyó,* (postpositive) *ninyó.*
YOURS, pron. (sing.) *iyó;* ,(pl.) *inyó.*
YOUTH, n. *kabataan.*
YULE, YULETIDE, n. *paskó, kapaskuhán.*

Z

ZEAL, n. *siglá, sigyá; sikap.*
ZEALOUS, adj. *masiglá, masigyá; masikap.*
SENITH, n. the greatest height, *káitaasan;* summit, *taluktók.*
ZERO, n. *sero,* Sp.; nothing, *walá.*
ZEST, n. spicy flavor, *linamnám;* keen enjoyment, *lasáp.*

ZIGZAG, n. *sigsag,* Eng. — adj. *pakilú-kiló.*
ZINC, n. *siín, sim,* Sp.
ZITHER, n. *sítará,* Sp.; *kudyapî.*
ZONE, n. *sona,* Sp.
ZOO, n. *paláhayupan.*
ZOOLOGY, n. *soolohiya,* Sp.
ZOOM, v. *sumibad.*

APPENDIX A

USEFUL TERMINOLOGIES

1. WEIGHTS, MEASURES, AND STANDARDS

A. Length. *Habà.*

Kilometer, *kilómetró,* Sp.
Meter, *metro,* Sp.
Decimeter, *dcsímetró,* Sp.
Centimeter, *sentímetró,* Sp.
Miilimeter, *milímetró,* Sp.
Mile, *milya,* Sp.
Yard, *yarda,* Sp.
Foot, *talampakan*
Inch, *dalì*

B. Surface. *Pangibabaw.* (*Lawak, lakí, lapad*)

Square kilometer, *kilómetróng parisukát.*
Hectare, *ektarya,* Sp.
Are, *arya,* Sp.
Centare, *sentarya,* Sp.
Square centimeter, *sentímetróng parisukát.*
Liter, *litro,* Sp.
Cubic meter, *metro kúbikó,* Sp.
Cubic centimeter, *sentímetró kúbikó,* Sp.

C. Weight. *Bigát.*

Ton, *tunelada,* Sp.
Quintal, *kintál,* Sp.
Kilogram, *kilo,* Sp.
Gram, *gramo,* Sp.
Centigram, *sentígramó,* Sp.
Milligram, *milígramó,* Sp.
Pound, *libra,* Sp.
Ounce, *onsa,* Sp.
Dram, *drakma,* Sp.
Grain, *grano,* Sp.; *butil.*

D. Time Measure. *Tagál ng Panahón.*

Second, *segundo,* Sp.; *saglít, sandalí.*
Minute, *minuto,* Sp.
Hour, *oras,* Sp.
Day, *araw.*
Week, *linggó.*
Month, *buwán.*
Year, *taón.*
Century, *dantaón.*

2. MONETARY UNITS

P 0.01, one centavo, *isáng pera; isáng séntimós.*

0.05, five centavos, a nickel, *walóng-kuwarta* (in Batangas, *isáng bagól*) ; *singko.*

0.10, ten centavos, *labing-anim na kuarta; diyés.*

0.15 fifteen centavos, *saikapat-apat; kinse.*

0.20, twenty centavos, *isáng piseta; beinte* (in Batangas, *isang bilyón*).

0.25, twenty-five centavos, *kahatì.*

0.30, thirty centavos, *kahati't-waló.*

0.35, thirty-five centavos, *kahati't-labing-anim.*

0.50, fifty centavos, *isáng salapî.*

0.60, sixty centavos, *tatlóng piseta.*

0.75, seventy-five centavos, *anim na saikapat.*

0.80, eighty centavos, *apat na piseta.*

1.00, one peso, *piso.*

1.10, one peso and ten centavos, *piso't labing-anim na kuwarta.*

1.20, one peso and twenty centavos, *anim na piseta.*

1.25, one peso and twenty-five centavos, *sampúng saikapat.*

1.50, one peso and fifty centavos, *tatlóng salapî.*

2.00 two pesos, *dalawáng piso.*

2.50, two pesos and fifty centavos, *limáng salapî.*

3.00, three pesos, *tatlóng piso.*

3.50, three pesos and fifty centavos, *pitóng salapî.*

10.00, ten pesos, *sampúng piso.*

100.00, one hundred pesos, *sandaáng piso.*

3. NUMERATION

1—*isá.*
2—*dalawá, dalwá.*
3—*tatló.*
4—*apat.*
5—*limá.*
6—*aním.*
7—*pitó.*
8—*waló.*
9—*siyám.*
10—*sampû.*
11—*labing-isá.*
12—*labindalawá, labindalwá.*
13—*labintatló.*
14—*labing-apat.*
15—*labinlimá.*
16—*labing-anim.*
17—*labimpitó.*
18—*labíngwaló*
19—*labinsiyám.*

20—*dalawampú.*
21—*dalawampú't isá.*
30—*tatlumpû.*
40—*ápatnapû.*
50—*limampû.*
100—*sandaán.*
101—*sandaá't isá.*
110 —*sandaá't sampû.*
200—*dalawandaán.*
1,000—*sanlibo.*
10,000—*sanlaksâ; sampúng libo.*
100,000—*sangyutà; sandaáng libo.*
1,000,000—*sang angaw.*
1,000,000,000—*sanlibong angaw.*
1,000,000,000,000—*sang-angaw na angaw.*

4 NUMERICAL DISTRIBUTION

One for each, *tigisa.*
Two for each, *tigalawá.*
Three for each, *tigatló.*
Four for each, *tigapat.*
Five for each, *tiglilimá.*
Six for each, *tiganim.*
Seven for each, *tigpipitó.*
Eight for each, *tigwawaló.*
Nine for each, *tigsisiyám.*
Ten for each, *tigsasampû.*
Eleven for each, *tiglalabing-isá.*
Twenty for each, *tigdadalawampû.*
A hundred for each, *tigisang daán.*
Two hundred for each, *tigalawang daán.*
A thousand for each, *tigisang libo; manlibo.*

5. MONETARY DISTRIBUTION

One centavo each, *mamera.*
Two centavos each, *tigalawáng pera.*
Five centavos each, *tigwawalóng-kuwarta* (in **Batangas**, *mambagól*) ; *tigsisingko.*
Ten centavos each, *tiglalabing-anim na kuwarta; tigdidiyés.*
Twenty centavos each, *mamiseta;* (in **Batangas**, *mambilyón*) ; *tigbebeinte.*
Twenty-five centavos each, *mangahatì.*
Fifty centavos each, *manalapî; tig-sisingkuwenta.*
One peso each, *mamiso.*

6. NUMERICAL ORDER

First, *una.*
Second, *ikalawá; pangalawá. (Ika-2).*

Third, *ikatló; pangatló.* *(Ika-3)*.
Fourth, *ikapat; pang-apat.* *(Ika-4)*.
Fifth, *ikalimá; panlimá.* *(Ika-5)*.
Sixth, *ikanim, ikaanim.* *(Ika-6)*.
Seventh, *ikapitó.* *(Ika-7)*.
Eighth, *ikawaló.* *(Ika-8)*.
Ninth, *ikasiyám.* *(Ika-9)*.
Tenth, *ikasampû.* *(Ika-10)*.

7. DIRECTIONS

North, *hilagà.*
Northeast, *hilagang-silangan.*
Northwest, *hilagang-kanluran.*
South, *timog.*
Southeast, *timog-silangan.*
Southwest, *timog-kanluran.*
East, *silangan.*
West, *kanluran.*
Northward, *pahilagâ.*
Southward, *patimóg.*
Eastward, *pasilangán.*
Westward, *pakanlurán.*

8. DAYS AND MONTHS

A. Days of the week. *Mga araw ng linggó.*

Monday, *Lunes,* Sp.
Tuesday, *Martés,* Sp.
Wednesday, *Miyérkulés,* Sp.
Thursday, *Huwebes,* Sp.
Friday, *Biyernes,* Sp.
Saturday, *Sábadó,* Sp.
Sunday, *Linggó.*

B. Months of the year. *Mga buwán ng taón.*

January, *Enero,* Sp.
February, *Pebrero,* Sp.
March, *Marso,* Sp.
April, *Abril,* Sp.
May, *Mayo,* Sp.
June, *Hunyo,* Sp.
July, *Hulyo,* Sp.
August, *Agosto,* Sp.
September, *Setyembre,* Sp.
October, *Oktubre,* Sp.
November, *Nobyembre,* Sp.
December, *Disyembre,* Sp.

APPENDIX B

COMMON AFFIXES

Simple Rules for Affixiation

The student should bear in mind that a great wealth of vocabulary can be within easy reach if he or she understands the meaning of the affixes and masters the rules for affixiation.

1. *Prefixing.*—The general rule for prefixing is simply place a prefix before a root-word.—*taga*bundók, *ma*tao, *mala*kanin, *palá*birô.

  a. If a prefix ends in a consonant and the root-word to be attached begins with a vowel, requiring a slight pause in pronunciation between, a hyphen should be used.—*pag*-asa, *mag*-aral, *mang*-abala, *tag*-ulán. Exceptions are in prefixes ending in *-ng* in which the pronunciation of *-ng* is combined with the initial vowel of the root: *pangaral, mangibig, pangulo,* etc.

  b. Root-words that begin with a capital letter require a hyphen when a prefix is attached to them.—*maka*-Pilipino, *tagá*-Batangan, *pang*-Paskó.

  c. Prefixes ending in *-ng* are governed by the following rules:

   (1) The *-ng* ending is retained before root-words whose initial letters are the vowels *a, e, i, o, u,* and the consonants, *k, g, h, m, n, ng, w,* and *y.*—*pang*-aso, *mang*ipit, *pang*gamót, *mang*harang, *pang*marami, *pang*nannám, *pang*ngalan, *pang*wakás, *mang*yari. NOTE: The consonant *k* of the root-word disappears: *pang*+*kuhit, pang*uhit; *mang*+kalat, *mang*alat.

   (2) The *-ng* ending becomes *-n* before root-words that begin with *d, l, r, s,* and *t.*—*Man*durukot, *magkan*luluhód, *pan*rigalo, *san*sinukob, *san*tinakpán. — Sometimes the initial *s* or *t* *disappears: pan*sulat (*pan*ulat) ; *man*tahî (*mana*hî).

2. *Infixing.*—There are really only two infixes,—*um-*, and *-in-*. Both are usually inserted after the first consonant of the root-word. —*tum*awa, *sin*aing. NOTE: In certain verbs the infix *ni* is used after the prefix *i-*, *ini*habol.

3. *Suffixing.* — There are two sets of suffixes.—*an, -in* and *-han, -hin.*

a. *-AN* and *-IN* are suffixed to root-words that end in consonants and the glottal vowel.—Balut*an*, hula*an*, bilang*in*, bati*in*.

b. -HAN and -HIN are suffixed to root-words that end in the liquid vowel.—Sama*han*, ubu*hín*.

c. The following are irregular forms of suffixiation:

(1) The use of *-nan* or *-nin* instead of *-han* or *-hin* after certain words that end in a liquid vowel: tawa*nan* (instead of tawa*han*) ; ku*nin*, from kuha*nin* (instead of kuha*hin*).

(2) The omission of a vowel or a syllable of the root-word upon taking a suffix. — *alsán* (from alis*án*), *dakpín* (from daki*pín*), *dalhán* (from dala*hán*) *hipan* (from hihi*pan*), *alalahanin* (from alaala*hin*), *halinhán* (from halili*han*), *kilanlín* (from kilala*hin* or kilala*nin*).

COMMON AFFIXIAL MEANING

I. FOR NOUNS

1. —AN, —HAN.

a. Place where many or much of what is mentioned by the root-word is found. *Aklatan*, library; *palayan*, rice-field.

b. Place where the action mentioned in the root-word is done. *Gúpitan*, barber-shop; *táhian*, tailoring shop.

c. Season for certain acts. *Pasukán*, school season; *anihán*, harvest season.

d. Utility, apparatus, or instrument. *Sulatán*, desk; *orasán*, clock.

e. Source of aid in time of need. *Dúlugan*, person to whom one goes when in need; *híraman*, person or place where one borrows.

f. Exchange, reciprocity, or simultaneousness of actions. *Abuluyán*, mutual aid; *tangkilikán*, mutual support; *digmaan*, warfare.

2. —IN, —HIN.

a. As prefix and infix: an action accomplished or something that passed through the process mentioned in the root. *Inakáy*, birdlings; *inihaw*, roasted piece; *binatà*, bachelor, unmarried man; *tinapay*, bread; *tinapá*, smoked fish or meat.

b. As suffix: more as an adjective than as a noun, but there are some used as nouns meaning: common occurrence, common usage for a thing or action mentioned by the root. *Inahín*, hen; *inumín*, drinking water; *panauhin*, guest; *simulain*, principle; *súliranín*, problem; *tuntunin*, rule, regulation.

3. KA..AN, KA..HAN.

a. Gives the abstractness of the idea of the root. *Kamátayan*, death; *kabutihan*, goodness; *kasamaán*, evilness.

b. Collectiveness. *Katagalugan*, Tagalog region; *kabisayaan*, Visayan region; *kailukuhan*, Ilocos region; *kapuluán*, archipelago.

c. Currency, frequency or intensity of an act or occurrence. *Kasagsaán*, peak of abundance; *kasasalán*, high intensity; *katanghalian*, high noon; *kabilugan*, full roundness.

d. Centricity of a place or extremity of a distance. *Kabayanan*, downtown; *kalunuran*, far west; *kalautan*, far at sea; *kaduluhan*, extremity.

e. Maturity, fulness, limitation, surplus. *Kabuwanán*, month of maturity; *kaarawán*, day of fulfillment, anniversary; *kapupunán*, completion; *kasapatán*, sufficiency.

f. Obligation, authority, or place where such obligation or authority is done or applied. *Katungkulan*, duty; *karapatán*, right; *kapangyarihan*, authority; *kágawarán*, department; *káwanihán*, bureau.

g. Exchange, reciprocity, and also alternation or contest in sound or noise. *Kásunduan*, accord; *káibigán*, mutual consent; *káingayán*, collective tumult; *kágalitán*, mutual quarrel.

4. MAG—.

a. When added to a simple noun: relation, companionship, and referring to only two. *Mag-iná*, mother and child; *mag-*

asawa, husband and wife; *magpanginoón,* master and servant.

b. When prefixed to a root whose first syllable is reduplicated: occupation. *Magbibigás,* rice dealer; *magsasaka,* farmer; *magnanakaw,* thief; *magsasabóng,* cockpit habitué.

c. Many Filipino surnames use this prefix. *Magbitang, Magpayo, Magpantáy, Magsalin, Magsaysáy.*

5. MANG—, MAM—, MAN—. (Similar in usage to 4. *b.*)

6. PA—. (This prefix is also for verbs and adverbs.)

   a. Utility. *Pangalan,* name; *pamagát,* title; *palayaw,* nickname; *patibóng,* snare; *patabâ,* fertilizer; *paliwanag,* explanation; *paunawà,* notice; *patunóg,* whistle, noisemaker.

   b. Something ordered, asked to be done, or paid for. *Pabili,* what is asked to be bought; *padalá,* something sent to someone else; *pahatíd,* message; *pamana,* inheritance given; *patahî,* something ordered to be sewn; *pautang,* credit or loan granted.

   c. Advertisement or application of a thought, rule, decision, or policy. *Pahayag,* proclamation; *palakad,* policy; *palagáy,* thought, opinion; *panahón,* time, season; *panata,* vow; *paraán,* method, device; *parusa,* punishment, sentence.

   d. When prefixed to compound words: figurative meaning. *Pakitang-gilas,* act of showing-off; *pakitang-loób,* generosity shown, *palipád-hangin,* bluff.

7. PA..AN, PA..HAN.

   a. Place or building where something is done. *Páaralán,* school; *págawaan,* factory; *pálamigan,* refrigerator, refreshment parlor; *pálaruan,* gymnasium, athletic field; *párusahán,* penal district, *páminggalan,* cupboard.

   b. Full exchange or simultaneous action. *Páalaman,* farewells; *pátawarán,* mutual forgiving; *pásunuran,* mutual obedience; *pámilihan,* market (place where people buy at the same time), *pánakbuhan,* act of running away simultaneously.

   c. Place where some specialized knowledge is applied. *Págamutan,* infirmary, hospital; *pálimbagan,* printing shop; *págandahan,* beauty shop; *pákulutan,* hair-dressing shop.

  d. Name of the result of an act. *Páhayagán,* newspaper; *pámahalaán,* government; *pángasiwaán,* administration; *panagimpán,* dream; *panalunan,* winnings.

8. **PAG—.** (This is the most common prefix for nouns. It forms a verbal noun, i. e. it is derived from verbs.)

  a. If from an UM or MA verb, it is attached to the root and means: "act of." *Pag-alís,* departure; *pagkuha,* act of getting; *pagdating,* arrival; *pagtulong,* act of aiding; *pagbasa,* act of reading.

  b. If from a MAG verb, the first syllable of the root is reduplicated. *Pagtuturò,* act of teaching; *pag-iisip,* act of thinking.

9. **PAG..AN, PAG..HAN.** (With the first syllable of the root reduplicated.)

  a. Exchange, reciprocity, mutuality. *Pag-iíbigan,* mutual loving; *pag-uútangan,* mutual borrowing (of money or favor); *pagdirigmaan,* battling.

  b. Vying, surpassing, or contest. (*Pa* or *ma,* reduplicated, is added to the prefix.) *Pagpapágandahan,* vying in beauty; *pagmamáliksihan,* vying in quickness.

  c. Simultaneousness or abundance. *Pag-aánihan,* harvesting all together; *pagbubúlaklakan,* profuse blooming.

  d. Imitation, simulation. (With reduplication, not only of the first syllable of the root, but also of the whole root.) *Pag-iiná-inahan,* acting like a mother, playing mother; *pagbabaháy-bahayan,* playing house.

10. **PAGKA—.**

  a. Abstractness, naturalness, beingness. (Uses a hyphen after it.) *Pagka-bathalà,* godhood; *pagka-tao,* humanness; *pagka-harì;* kingship; *pagka-babae,* womanhood.

  b. Action happening to self involuntarily. *Pagkaabala,* delay; *pagkaawà,* pity; *pagkalantá,* withering.

  c. Manner, cause or condition of an occurrence. (Reduplicates the KA.) *Pagkakáawit,* manner of having sung; *pagkakápatáy,* manner of having killed (been killed).

  d. Condition of having. (Originates from the verb MAGKA—

and reduplicate KA.) *Pagkakabulaklák*, condition of having flowers; *pagkakadamít*, condition of having clothes; *pagkakaroón*, condition of having.

e. If used with *pag* (PAGKAPAG): reason for.—If with further reduplication of *ka* (PAGKAKAPAG): manner of. *Pagkápag-asawa*, reason for having married. *Pagkakápagasawa,* manner of having married.

11. PANG—, PAM—, PAN—. (This is properly a prefix for adjectives, although the same form is used as nouns.)

a. Instrument, apparatus, utility. *Panggabí*, adj. for evening; *pambansá*, adj. national; n. something that concerns the nation; *pangulay*, adj. coloring; n. dye.

b. Referring to the application of a thing. *Pandiníg*, organ of hearing; *pantukoy*, article; *pang-urì*, adjective; *pandiwà*, verb; *panghalíp*, pronoun.

e. Act of. (From the verbs MANG—, MAM— or MAN—, with the first syllable of the root reduplicated.) *Panggagamót*, act of curing; *panghihingî*, act of asking; *pamimitagan*, act of respect, reverence.

12. PALA..AN, PALA..HAN.

a. Place or instrument commonly used as basis, or used in putting, caring, or applying something. *Palábabahán*, window-sill; *palárindingan*, wall-support; *paláisdaan*, fish-pond.

b. Method, custom, or problem. *Palátandaan*, distinguishing mark; *palásumpaan*, form for oath; *pálabunután*, method of electing by pulling sticks of different lengths; *palábugtungan*, riddles.

c. Art or collection of rules for analysis or study. *Palátitikan*, orthography; *palábaybayan*, rules in spelling; *palágitlingan*, hyphenation; *palábantasan*, punctuation.

13. SANG—, SAM—, SAN—.

a. Oneness. *Sandalî*, a second; *sanlinggó*, a week.

b. With -*an*. Oneness, wholeness, completeness. *Sambayanán*, whole town; *sambahayán*, whole household; *sanlibután*, whole universe; *sandaigdigan*, whole world.

c. With *ka*— and —*an*. Whole expanse, allness. *Sangkalangi-*

tán, all heaven; *sangkalupaán*, all earth; *sangkatauhan*, all humanity.

14. **TAG—.**

a. Season, period, epidemic. *Tag-ulán*, rainy season; *tagginâw*, cold season; *taggutom*, famine; *tagkólera*, cholera epidemic.

b. With *-an* or *-han*. Season, period of action or occurrence. *Tagtániman*, planting season; *taghálalan*, election time.

15. **TAGA—.**

a. Native of, resident of. *Taga-Batangan*, native of Batangas; *taga-Sebú*, native of Cebu.

b. Person having the duty of. *Like tagapag.—Tagalutò*, cook; *tagalinis*, cleaner; *tagaalagà*, carer; *tagalimbág*, printer.

16. **TALA..AN, TALA..HAN.** List of. *Taláaklatan*, catalog of books; *taláarawan*, calendar; *talátinigan*, dictionary; *taláawitan*, songbook; *talábansahan*, list of nations.

II. FOR ADJECTIVES

1. **MA—.** Having, possessing. (Often: having much). *Magandá*, beautiful; *matao*, crowded; *mabundók*, mountainous; *mabulaklák*, flowery; *matabá*, fat.

2. **MAKA—.**

a. Inclined, supporting. *Makatao*, humanitarian; *makabayan*, patriot; *makabago*, modern. *Maka-Rizal*, pro-Rizal; *maka-Quezon*, pro-Quezon.

b. Able to cause or do, possible to happen. (Prefixed to compound words). *Makabasag-bungô*, skull-breaking; *makadurog-pusò*, heart-rending.

3. **MALA—.** Seeming, apparently, almost like. *Malalangit*, heavenlike; *malasarili*, almost autonomous; *malakanin*, ricelike; *malasutlâ*, silklike.

4. **MAPAG—.** Always, customarily, having the habit of. *Mapaglibót*, wandering; *mapagsalitâ*, talkative; *mapagbirô*, always joking; *mapagtamád*, customarily lazy; *mapagbanál*, always saintly.

5. MAPANG—, MAPAM—, MAPAN—. (Like MAPAG—, except that MAPANG—is more objective.) *Mapang-abala*, bothersome; *mapamihag*, captivating; *mapanirà*, destructive.

6. PALA—. (Like MAPAG—.) *Palábirô, mapagbirô*, always joking; *palásabí, mapagsabí*, always telling.

7. PANG—, PAM—, PAN—, Instrument, use, or intention.

    a. Instrument: *Pang-halò*, for mixing; *pambilang*, for counting; *pansulat*, for writing.

    b. Use: *panggatong*, for fuel; *pamundók*, for mountain use; *pang-alís*, for taking out something.

    c. Intention: *pang-akin*, for myself; *panlahát*, for all; *pambayan*, municipal.

8. —AN, —HAN.

    a. Oversize or excess in number. *Bibigán*, big-mouthed; *butuhán*, bony; *sungayán*, horny.

    b. Full of, having. *Pulahán*, very reddish; *putikán*, very muddy; *duguán*, very bloody.

9. —IN, —HIN. (Sometimes infix, often suffix.) (Compare with —IN, —HIN for nouns.)

    a. Cut, style, class, or kind. (Infix.) *Binalimbing*, made into the shape of a balimbing fruit; *sinampalok*, tamarindlike; *sinampaga*, kind of rice.

    b. Proneness to a disease or characteristic. *Lantahin*, easily withered; *sípunin*, easily affected by colds; *gálingin*, having a lucky streak; *súgatin*, always having wounds, easily wounded.

    c. Quality or characteristic. *Báligtarin*, can be turned inside-out; *pítasin*, can be easily picked.

    d. Quantity or amount. (With reduplication of first of root.) *Pipisuhin*, of one-peso denomination; *sasampuín*, of ten-peso denomination.

    e. Source, origin (directional). (Similar to *taga*— in nouns.) *Silangunin*, from (of) the east; *kanluranin*, from (of) the west.

10. MA..IN, MA..HIN. (Like MAPAG—, and PALA.) *Masintahin*, loving, tender; *maramdamin*, sensitive; *masúnurin*, habitually obedient; *mahiyain*, habitually shy.

11. **PA..IN, PA..HIN.** What is to be done or given, or needed to be done or given. *Pálamuníng baboy;* pig that must be fed; *pátabaíng manók,* chicken to be fattened; *págalingíng sakit,* sickness to be cured.

III. FOR VERBS

1. **UM.** As prefix before roots that begin with a vowel, and infix inserted after the first consonant of roots that begin with a consonant. UM verbs commonly express inner motion.

   a. Impersonal acts; acts of nature; self-change through time or care of man. *Lumindól,* the earth to quake; *bumagyó,* to storm; *umulán,* to rain; *kumidlát,* the lightning to flash; *humangin,* the wind to blow. *Tumubò,* to grow; *sumilang,* to shine; *sumiból,* to spring up. *Pumutî,* to become white; *dumami,* to multiply; *tumabâ,* to become fat; *pumayát,* to become thin. *Tumapang,* to become brave; *bumuti,* to improve.

   b. Acts of parts of the body, will, the intellect, the soul, or the emotion. *Tumangô,* to nod; *umilíng,* to shake the head; *tumingín,* to look; *tumawa,* to laugh; *lumuhód,* to kneel; *kumain,* to eat; *uminóm,* to drink. *Umisip,* to think; *dumamdám,* to feel; *umabuloy,* to succor; *umibig,* to love; *umasa,* to hope.

   c. Acts of taking a part from the whole. *Humiwà,* to cut a slice; *pumitás,* to pick; *humirám,* to borrow; *tumawad,* to ask for a discount; *humatì,* to take half.

   d. Acts of going towards or away from a place. *Pumakanan,* to turn to the right; *pumakaliwâ,* to turn to the left; *pumagitnà,* to go to the center; *sumalangit,* to go to heaven; *tumabí,* to come near; *umalís,* to go away.

2. **MAG—.** In general: to do, perform, or accomplish acts of thinking, feeling, and willing, and involving external motion. *Maysayáw,* to dance; *maglutò,* to cook; *mag-aral,* to study; *magbigáy,* to give; *magsanay,* to practice; *magmahál,* to hold dear, esteem highly; *magsundalo,* to perform the function of a soldier; *maghangád,* to aspire.

   a. **MAG..AN, MAG..HAN.** Indicates reciprocity, mutuality, and simultaneousness of action. *Magpálitan,* to exchange;

magdamayán, to succor each other; *magsáyawan,* to dance simultaneously.

b. MAGKA—. To have, to come to possess. *Magkabahay,* to have a house; *magkaasawa,* to have a husband (wife); *magkatinapay,* to have bread; *magkapanahón,* to have time.

c. MAGMA—. (The additional MA— is the start of an adjective.) To act as if possessing the quality expressed. *Magmabutí,* to appear as good; *magmagandá,* to make oneself look beautiful.

d. MAGPA—. (This is MAG— plus a PA noun.) To order something done. *Magpabilí,* to order (something) bought; *magpasabi,* to send a message; *magpatindá,* to have (something) offered for sale.

e. MAGPAKA—. To exert effort to become. *Magpakabuti,* to try hard to be good; *magpakalagót,* to insist on doing something or continuing in some act or condition.

f. MAGPATI—. To do something voluntarily, due to despondency or force of circumstances. *Magpatiwakál,* to commit suicide; *magpatihulog,* to let oneself fall; *magpatibuhat,* to start from a certain place.

g. MAGSA—. To imitate, simulate the characteristic or qualities of another person, a situation, or an animal. *Magsaparì,* to act like or imitate a priest; *magsamayroón,* to act like one who has; *magsapagóng,* to pretend to like the contrary of what one wants to happen.

h. MAGSI—. (Plural or collective form of MAG verbs.) *Magsialís,* to depart in company or at the same time; *magsisama,* to join the company, go with, in a group.

3. MA—. In general: to be able to do or perform an act, or something to happen without the volition of the doer or the person affected. *Makuha,* to be able to get; *mákuha,* to happen to get.

a. The other affixial derivatives of MA— which carry more or less the same significance to their roots are:—

Ma..an   *Máalaman,* to be able to learn of.
Mai—.   *Máilabás,* to be able to take out.
Maipa—.   *Máipabasa,* to be able to have someone read.

Maipag—.	*Máipagbilí*, to be able to sell.
Maka.—	*Makaalís*, to be able to go away.
Makapag—.	*Makapagbihis*, to be able to change the dress.
Makapang—.	*Makapandayà*, to be able to cheat.
Mapa—.	*Mapadulás*, to be able to make (a thing) slippery.

b. But MAKI— and MAKIPAG— verbs generally mean to join, ask a favor, or perform an act together with others. *Makiusap*, to ask a favor; *makisama*, to join others; *makiawit*, to join in the singing; *makiraan*, to ask permission to pass; *makipag-awit*, to sing with the others; *makipag-away*, to quarrel with others.

4. MANG—, and its plural and collective form MANGAG— (and derivatives) generally mean, like MAG— verbs, —to perform acts of external motion. In MANG— the receivers of the action are more indefinite or greater in number. *Mangharang*, to hold up; *mambatak*, to pull (or influence) other people; *manulat*, to write (producing literature for public consumption). *Mangag-aral*, to study (collectively); *mangagsipanalo*, to win together or collectively; *mangagsipuntá*, to go together or in groups or simultaneously; *mangagsipagpakuha*, to ask or order something to be taken (collective asking or ordering).

5. —AN, —HAN. To perform the act, build or make the thing, effect the quality, expressed by the root, on a person, animal, or thing. *Tawagan*, to call; *bambangán*, to put a ditch; *lambután*, to soften; *pintasán*, to find faults.

6. I—. (Prefix for passive verbs, as —*an* and —*in* are suffixes for passive verbs.)

a. In general: to use a thing according to the act called for. (In this sense, a function of IPAG— and IPANG— is similar.) *Isulat* (*ang pluma*), to use (the pen) for writing; *itangláw* (*ang plaslait*), to use the flashlight to illuminate with; *ipunas* (*ang basahan*), to use the rug to wipe with. *Ipagtangláw, ipantangláw; ipagsulat, ipanulat, ipagpunas, ipamunas*.

b. The same form of *I*— and *Ipag*— (*not Ipang*—) may be used to mean to do for someone else. *Isulat mo akó*.

You write for me. *Ipagsulát mo akó. Itangláw mo si Juan.* You light (a candle) for Juan. *Ipagtangláw mo siyá sa prusisyón.* Light a candle for him in the procession. *Ipunas, ipagpunas,* to do the wiping for (someone).

c. To perform the act expressed by the root on or for the subject of the verb. *Isabit and sumbrero,* to hang the hat. *Ilagà ang manók,* to boil the chicken. *Ipukól ang bató,* to throw the stone. *Itulak ang bangká,* to push the boat. *Iligtás ang maysakít,* to save the patient. *Ilihim ang katotóhanan,* to hide the truth. *Ihayág ang lihim,* to expose the secret. *Isanglâ ang singsing,* to pawn the ring. *Ibili ng sapatos ang batà,* to buy shoes for the child.

7. IKA—. To be the reason for a condition or an act. *Ikabuti,* to be the reason for the well-being; *ikasamâ,* to be the cause for (a thing) being or become bad or worse; *ikaalís,* to be the reason for departure; *ikátiwalág,* to be the reason for having been dismissed (from a job).

8. —IN, —HIN.

a. To perform the act expressed by the root on the subject of the verb. *Aklatín ang mga papel,* to bind the papers into book form. *Lagariin ang kahoy,* to saw the wood. *Suklayín ang buhók,* to comb the hair. *Ibigin ang kapwà mo tao,* love your fellow men. *Ayusin ang silíd,* to put the room in order.

b. To happen to the subject. Either there is no doer of action **or** the agent is an act of nature or something beyond the control of the subject. To suffer from a disease, to be lucky, or unlucky, etc., are the denotations included in this meaning of—IN verbs. *Lagnatín,* to suffer from fever; *galingín,* to become lucky; *samaín,* to become unlucky; *palarin,* to become fortunate.

9. IPA—. To order, request, that something be done by someone else. *Ipagawâ,* to have (something) made or repaired; *ipabili,* to have (something) bought; *ipakuha,* to order someone else. to get (something).

a. The action that is done for someone else is expressed by IPAG—. (See 6b).

b. The definite impression of request is given by IPAKI— and IPAKIPA—. *Ipakiabót mo ngâ ang aklát sa akin.* Please hand me the book. *Ipakisama ngâ ninyó ang aking sulat.* Please include my letter. *Ipakipabilin mo ngâ ang kapatíd ko.* Please have someone send for my broιher (sister).

10. ISA—. To accomplish, put into effect; or translate into another language. *Isagawâ,* to accomplish; *isaulì,* to return; *isaayos,* to put in order; *isa-Tagalog,* to translate into Tagalog; *isa-Inglís,* to translate into English.

11. KA..AN, KA..HAN. This is of the —AN family and gives the same general meaning. More particularly, however, KA..AN expresses an act of the feelings, the will, or the mind, on the subject of the verb. *Kalimutan ang nakaraan,* to forget the past. *Kagalitan ang alilà,* to scold the servant.

12. PA..AN, PA..HAN. To have (something) done on or for the subject of the verb. *Palagyán ng uhalis ang barò,* to have buttonholes put in the dress. (*Pauhalisan ang barò.*) *Paalisán ang dumí ang kahón,* to have the dirt taken out of the box. *Palagyán ng asin ang karné,* to have salt put on the meat. (*Paasinán ang karné,* to have the meat salted.)

13. PA..IN, PA..HIN.

    a. To cause something to happen or to be done to the subject of the verb. *Palinisin ang sahíg,* to make the floor clean. *Patulinin ang takbó,* to accelerate the speed. *Pakintabín ang sapatos,* to make the shoes shiny.

    b. To cause or permit the subject of the verb to perform the act expressed by the root. *Paiyakín ang sanggól,* to cause the baby to cry. *Pasayawín ang panauhin,* to make the guests dance. *Paraanin ang kalabáw,* to let the carabao pass. *Patakbuhín ang kabayo,* to get the horse to run.

14. PAG..AN, PAG..HAN.

    a. To express an act affecting the emotion or the will of the subject-receiver. *Pagdamutan ang kaibigan,* to refuse to give (something) to a friend. *Pagtananan ang amá,* to escape from the father. *Paglingkurán ang vámahalaán,* to serve the government. *Pagdasalán ang Mahál na Bir-hen*, to pray to the Holy Virgin.

b. To indicate the place where or person to whom the action expressed by verb is done or performed. *Ang bahay na pagdárausan ng pagtitipon*, the room where the get-together will be held. *Ang taong pagbibigyán ng sulat*, the man to whom the letter will be given.

15. PAPAG..AN, PAPAG..HAN.   To allow someone to perform an act in or on a place or on a person. (Similar to PA..AN.) *Papagsayawán ang salas*, to allow (some people) to use the living-room for dancing. *Papaglaruán ang harapán ng ba-hay*, to allow (some people) to use the front of the house for playing. *Pakainan ang mesang bago*, to allow the new table to be used for eating.

16 PAPAG..AN, PAPAG..HAN.   To allow or order the subject to perform the act expressed by the root. *Papagsayawín*, to allow or get (someone) to dance. *Papag-aralin*, to allow or order (someone) to study.

17. PAKA..AN, PAKA..HAN.   Indicates extraordinary perform-ance of an act. (Also PAKAPAG..AN.) *Pakábutihan*, to exert much effort to produce good results. *Pakátaasán*, to make too high. *Pakáiklián*, to make too short. *Pakáhabaán*, to make too long.

18. PAKI..AN, PAKI..HAN; PAKI..IN, PAKI..HIN.   Both *paki- an* and *paki- in* express a request about something to be done, but the essential difference between the suffixes —*an* and —*in* is maintained. The suffix —*an* indicates an action to be done on something, while the suffix —*in* ex-presses the thing to be done about something. *Pakigawán mo ngâ ng paraáng makuha natin ang aklát.* Please find a way by which we may get the book. *Pakigawín mo ngâ ang silyang itó.* Please make this chair.

APPENDIX C

Orthography of Geographical Names

Abra, *Abra*
Abulug River, *Ilog Abulog*
Abyssinia, *Abisinya*
Acapulco, *Akapulko*
Afghanistan, *Apganistan*
Africa, *Apriká*
Agno River, *Ilog Agno*
Agus River, *Ilog Agos*
Agusan, *Agusan*
Aklan, *Aklán*
Akron, *Akron*
Alabama, *Alabama*
Alaska, *Alaska*
Albania, *Albanya*
Albany, *Albani*
Albay, *Albáy*
Aleutian Islands, *Kapuluang Alyutyan*
Algeria, *Alherya*
Alhambra, *Alhambra*
Alps Mts., *kabundukan Alpes*
Amazon, *Amasón.*
Amboina, *Amboyna*
Amburayan River, *Ilog Amburayan*
Amoy, *Amoy*
Anatolia, *Anatolya*
Andes Mts., *Kabundukang Andes*
Angat, *Angát*
Angeles, *Anghelés*
Ankara, *Angkara*
Annam, *Anám*
Antipolo, *Antipulo*
Antique, *Antike* (*Hantík*)
Aparri, *Apari*
Apayao, *Apayáw*
Apo, Mt., *Bundók Apò.*
Arabia, *Arabya*
Aravat, *Arayat*
Argao, *Argáw*
Argentina, *Arhentina*
Aringay, *Aringay*
Arizona, *Arisona*
Armenia, *Armenya*

Aroroy, *Aruroy*
Asia, *Asya*
Athens, *Atenas*
Atimonan, *Atimunan*
Atlas Mts., *Kabundukang Atlás*
Australia, *Australya*
Azerbaijan, *Aserbayán*
Babuyan Is., *Pulóng Babuyan*
Babylon, *Babilonya*
Bacolod, *Bakulod*
Bagobo, *Bagubo*
Bagonbayan, *Bagumbayan*
Baguio, *Bagyo*
Bais, *Bais*
Balabac, *Balabak*
Balanga, *Balangà*
Balayan, *Balayang*
Baler, *Balér*
Balete, *Balitì*
Bali, *Bali*
Baliangao, *Balyangáw*
Baliuag, *Baliwag*
Balkan, *Balkan*
Baltic Sea, *Dagat Báltikó.*
Baltimore, *Báltimore*
Baluchistan, *Balusistán*
Banahao Mt., *Bundók Banahaw*
Banaue, *Banawe*
Banda Is:, *Pulóng Bandá*
Bangkok, *Bangkók*
Bangued, *Banggéd*
Bangui, *Banggi*
Bantay, *Bantáy*
Bantayan, *Bantayan*
Barcelona, *Barselona*
Barili, *Barili*
Basco, *Basko*
Basey, *Baséy*
Basilan, *Basilan*
Bataan, *Bataán*
Batac, *Baták*
Batan I., *Pulô ng Batán*
Batanes, *Batanes*
Batangas, *Batangan*

Batavia, *Batabya*
Batayan, *Batayan*
Battas, *Batas*
Bauan (La Union), *Bawan*
Bauan (Batangas), *Bawáng*
Baybay, *Baybáy*
Bayombong, *Bayumbóng*
Belfast, *Belpás*
Belgium, *Bélhiká*
Belgrade, *Belgrado*
Belize, *Belís*
Bengal, *Benggál.*
Benguet, *Benggét*
Bergen, *Bergen*
Berlin, *Berlín*
Bethlehm, *Belén*
Bicol, *Bikol*
Bilbao, *Bilbáw*
Biliran, *Biliran*
Binondo, *Binundók*
Birmingham, *Birminghám*
Biscay, Bay of, *Loók ng Biskáy*
Black Sea, *Dagat Itím*
Boac, *Buwák*
Bogo, *Bugó*
Bohemia, *Buhemya*
Bohol, *Buhól*
Bokhara, *Bukkara*
Bolbok, *Bulbók*
Bolivia, *Bulibya*
Bombay, *Bumbáy*
Bondoc, *Bundók*
Bontoc, *Buntók*
Bordeaux, *Burdú*
Borneo, *Borneó*
Boro-Budur, *Búrubudúr*
Borongan, *Burungan*
Bosporus, *Bósporús*
Boston, *Boston*
Botocan, *Butukán*
Brazil, *Brasíl*
Bremen, *Bremen*
Breslau, *Breslo*
Brisbane, *Brisbein*
British Empire, *Imperyo Británikó*

British Isles, *Mga Pulóng Británikó*
Brittany, *Britanya*
Brunei, *Brunáy*
Brussels, *Bruselas*
Bucharest, *Bukarés*
Budapest, *Budapés*
Bued River, *Ilog Buwéd*
Buenos Aires, *Buenos Aires*
Buffalo, *Búfaló*
Bukidnon, *Bukidnón*
Bulacan, *Bulakán*
Bulalacao, *Bulalakaw*
Bulgaria, *Bulgarya*
Bulusan, *Bulusan*
Burias, *Buryas*
Burma, *Burma*
Butuan, *Butuan*
Cabagan, *Kabagan*
Cabanatuan, *Kabanatuan*
Cadiz, *Kadis*
Cagayan, *Kagayán*
Cairo, *Kayro*
Calais, *Kalais*
Calamba, *Kalambá*
Calamian Is., *Mga Puló ng Kalamyán.*
Calapan, *Kalapán*
Calasiao, *Kalasyáw*
Calbayog, *Kalbayog*
Calcutta, *Kalkuta*
California, *Kaliporniya*
Calivo, *Kalibo*
Callao, *Kalyáw*
Calumpit, *Kalumpít*
Camarines Norte, *Hilagang Kamarines*
Camarines Sur, *Timog Kamarines*
Cambodia, *Kambodya*
Camiguin I., *Pulóng Kamiging*
Camiling, *Kamilíng*
Canada, *Kanadá*
Candaba, *Kandaba*
Candon, *Kandón*
Canlaon, *Kanlaón*
Canton, *Kantón*

Cape Bojeador, *Tangos Bohiyadór*
Cape Bolinao, *Tangos Bulináw*
Cape Engaño, *Lungos Ingganyo*
Capiz, *Kapís*
Caraballo Mts., *Kabundukang Karabalyo*
Caracas, *Karakas*
Caramoan Peninsula, *Tangwáy ng Karamuan*
Carcar, *Karkar*
Carigara, *Karigara*
Carolina, North, *Hilagang Karolina*
Carolina, South, *Timog Karolina*
Catanduanes, *Katanduwanes*
Catarman, *Katarmán*
Catbalogan, *Katbalugan*
Catubig River, *Ilog Katubig*
Caucasus, *Káwkasó*
Cauit, *Kawit*
Cavite, *Kabite*
Cebu, *Sebú*
Celebes, *Salibís*
Central America, *Gitnáng Amériká*
Central Europe, *Gitnáng Europa*
Central Luzon, *Gitnáng Lusón*
Central Mindanao, *Gitnáng Mindanáw.*
Central Panay, *Gitnáng Panáy*
Cervantes, *Serbantes*
Ceylon, *Seylón*
Chattanooga, *Satanuga*
Chicago, *Tsikago*
Chico River, *Ilog Tsiko*
Chile, *Tsile*
China, *Tsina*
China Sea, *Dagat Tsina*
Chosen, *Tsosen*
Claveria, *Klaberya*
Cleveland, *Kliblan*
Cochin-China, *Kutsin-Tsina*
Cologne, *Kolón*
Columbia, *Kolombiya*
Colombo. *Kulumbo*

Colorado, *Kulorado*
Columbia, *Kulumbiya*
Columbus, *Kulumbus*
Congo, *Konggo*
Constantinople, *Kustantinopla*
Cordillera, *Kurdilyera*
Corregidor. *Kurehidor*
Cotabato, *Kutabató*
Cuba, *Kuba*
Culion, *Kulyón*
Currimao, *Kurimáw*
Cuyo, *Kuyo*
Czechoslovakia, *Sekoslobakya*
Dagupan. *Dagupan*
Dairen, *Dayrén*
Dakota, North, *Hilagang Dakota*
Dakota, South, *Timog Dakota*
Damaskus, *Damasko*
Damortis, *Damortis*
Dansalan. *Dansalan*
Danube River, *Ilog Danubyo*
Danzig, *Dansig*
Dapitan, *Dapitan*
Dardanelles, *Dardanelas*
Data, Mt., *Bundók Datá*
Davao, *Dabaw*
Dead Sea, *Dagat na Patáy*
Delhi, *Delhi*
Denmark, *Dinamarka*
Denver, *Denber*
Detroit, *Detroit*
Dinagat, *Dinagat*
Dipolog, *Dipulóg*
Diuata Mts., *Kabundukan ng Diwatà*
Dnieper River, *Ilog Niyeper*
Dominican Republic, *Repúblikáng Dominikano*
Donnai River, *Ilog Dunáy*
Dublin, *Dublin*
Duluth, *Dulút*
Dumaguete, *Dumagete*
Dumaran, *Dumarán*
Dutch East Indies, *Silangang Indiyong Ulandés*

Echague, *Etsagwe*
Ecuador, *Ekwadór*
Edinburgh, *Edinbur*
Egypt, *Ehipto*
England, *Inglatera*
Eritrea, *Eritrea*
Ermita, *Ermita*
Estancia, *Istánsiya*
Estonia, *Estonya*
Ethiopia, *Etyopya*
Etna, Mt., *Bundók Etna*
Euphrates River, *Ilog Yuprates*
Europe, *Europa*
Everest, Mt., *Bundók Eberés*
Fabrica, *Pábriká*
Fiji Is., *Kapuluang Pidyi*
Finland, *Pinlandiya*
Florence, *Florensiya*
Florida, *Plorida*
Formosa, *Pormosa*
France, *Pránsiya*
Fujiyama, *Pudyiyama*
Fusan, *Pusán*
Galveston, *Gálbestón*
Gandara, *Gandará*
Gapan, *Gapáng*
Germany, *Alemanya*
Gibraltar, *Hibraltár*
Great Britain, *Dakilang Britanya*
Greece, *Gresya*
Greenland, *Lupanluti, Grinland*
Guagua, *Guwaguwa, Wawâ.*
Guam, *Guwám*
Guatemala, *Guwatemala*
Guayaquil, *Guwayakíl*
Gubat, *Gubat*
Guimaras, *Gimarás*
Habana, *Habana*
Hagonoy, *Hagunoy*
Hainan, *Haynán*
Haiphong, *Haypóng*
Haiti, *Hayti*
Halcon, Mt., *Bundók Halkón*
Hankow, *Hangkáw*

Hanoi, *Hanóy*
Hawaiian Is., *Kapuluán ng Hawáy*
Heidelberg, *Hidelberg*
Helsingfors, *Helsingpors*
Helsinki, *Helsingki*
Himalaya, *Himalaya*
Hokkaido, *Hokaydo*
Holland, *Olanda*
Hondagua, *Ondagwa*
Hong Kong, *Hongkong*
Honolulu, *Honolulu*
Honshu, *Honsiyu*
Hood, Mt., *Bundók Hud*
Hudson Bay, *Loók Hudson*
Hungary, *Unggarya*
Hwang Ho, *Huwangho*
Iba, *Ibà*
Ibanag, *Ibanág*
Iberia, *Iberya*
Iceland, *Lupangyelo, Aisländ*
Idaho, *Idahó*
Ifugao, *Ipugáw*
Igorot, *Igurót*
Ilagan, *Ilagan*
Iligan, *Iligan*
Illinois, *Ilinoy*
Ilocos Norte, *Hilagang Iluko*
Ilocos Sur, *Timog Iluko*
Iloilo, *Iluilo*
Ilongot, *Ilunggót*
Imus, *Imus*
Inca, *Ingka*
Indang, *Indáng*
India, *Indiya*
Indian Empire, *Imperyong Indiyo*
Indian Ocean, *Karagatang Indiyo*
Indiana, *Indiyana*
Indo-China, *Indutsina*
Infanta, *Impanta*
Iowa, *Ayowá*
Iran, *Irán*
Iraq, *Irák*
Ireland, *Irlanda*
Iriga, Mt., *Bundók Iriga*
Irosin, *Irosín*

Irrawaddy River, *Ilog Irawadi*
Isabela, *Isabela*
Isarog, Mt., *Bundók Isaróg*
Isinay, *Isináy*
Istanbul, *Istambúl*
Italy, *Italya*
Iwahig, *Iwahig*
Jamaica, *Hamayka*
Janiuay, *Haniway*
Japan, *Hapón*
Japanese, *Haponés*
Jaro, *Haro*
Java, *Diyaba, Haba*
Jerusalem, *Herusalém*
Jolo, *Holó*
Jordan River, *Ilog ng Hordán*
Kabugao, *Kabugaw*
Kalinga, *Kalingga*
Kamchatka, *Kamsatka*
Kansas City, *Lunsód ng Kansas*
Karachi, *Karatsi*
Kashmir, *Kasmír*
Kentucky, *Kentaki*
Kiangan, *Kiyangan*
Kiel Canal, *Kanál ng Kiyél*
Kiev, *Kiyeb*
Kimberley, *Kimberlí*
Klondike, *Klondaik*
Kobe, *Kobe*
Korea, *Koreá*
Krakatao, *Krakatáw*
Kuala Lumpur, *Kuwala Lumpúr*
Kuenlun Mts., *Kabundukan ng Kuwenlún*
Kyoto, *Kiyoto*
Kyushu, *Kiyusyu*
Labrador, *Labradór*
La Carlota, *Lakarlota*
Laguna de Bay, *Dagatang Laguna*
Lake Baikal, *Dagatang Baykál*
Lake Bato, *Dagatang Bató*
Lake Buhi, *Dagatang Buhi*
Lake Danao, *Dagatang Danáw*
Lake Erie, *Dagatang Iri*
Lake Lanao, *Dagatang Lanáw*
Lake Mainit, *Dagatang Mainit*

Lake Michigan, *Dagatang Mísigán*
Lake Naujan, *Dagatang Nawhán*
Lake Ontario, *Dagatang Untaryo*
Lake Superior, *Dagatang Supiryor*
Lake Taal, *Dagatang Taál*
Lake Titicaca, *Dagatang Titikaka*
Lamon Bay, *Loók ng Lamón*
Lanao, *Lanáw*
Laoag, *Lawág*
Laoang, *Lawáng*
La Paz, *Lapás*
Larena, *Larena*
Latvia, *Latbiya*
Legaspi, *Legaspi*
Lemery, *Lemeri*
Leningrad, *Léningrád*
Leyte, *Leyte*
Liaotung, *Liyawtúng*
Lima, *Lima*
Limay, *Limáy*
Lingayen, *Linggayén*
Lipa, *Lipá*
Lisbon, *Lisbon*
Lithuania, *Litwanya*
London, *Londres*
Los Baños, *Losbanyos*
Louisiana, *Luwisyana*
Lubang Island, *Pulóng Lubáng*
Lubuagan, *Lubwagan*
Lucban, *Lukbán*
Lucena, *Lusena*
Luzon, *Lusóng*
Lyon, *Liyón*
Maasin, *Maasim*
Macabebe, *Makabebe*
Macao, *Makáw*
Macassar, *Makasar*
McKinley, Mt., *Bundók Makinley*
Mactan, *Maktán*
Madagascar, *Madagaskár*
Madeira, *Madeyra*
Madras, *Madrás*
Madrid, *Madríd*
Magalan, *Magalang*
Magat River, *Ilog Magát*
Mahagnao, *Mahagnáw*

Mahatao, *Mahatáw*
Malabang, *Malabáng*
Malabon, *Malabón*
Malacañan, *Malakanyáng*
Malacca, *Malaka*
Malate, *Maalat*
Malaybalay, *Maláybaláy*
Malinta, *Malintâ*
Malitbog, *Malitbóg*
Malolos, *Malulos*
Mamanuas, *Mamanwás*
Mambajao, *Mambahaw*
Manchester, *Mansestér*
Manchuria, *Mansurya*
Mandalay, *Mandaléy*
Mangaldaŋ, *Mangaldán*
Mangyan, *Mangyán*
Manila, *Maynilà*
Mankayan, *Mangkayán*
Maqueda Bay, *Loók ng Makeda*
Maquiling, Mt., *Bundók Makiling*
Maribojoc, *Maribuhók*
Marinduque, *Marinduke*
Mariquina, *Marikina*
Mariveles Mt., *Bundók Maribeles*
Marseille, *Marseyla*
Martinique, *Martinika*
Masbate, *Masbate*
Massachusetts, *Masatsusets*
Mauban, *Mauban*
Mayon, Mt., *Bundók Mayón*
Mediterranean Sea, *Dagat Mediteráneó*
Melbourne, *Melborn*
Mesopotamia, *Mesopotamya*
Messina, *Mesina*
Mexico, *Méksikó, Méhikó*
Meycauayan, *Meykawayan*
Miagao, *Miyagáw*
Michigan, *Mísigán*
Milan, *Milán*
Milwaukee, *Milwoki*
Mindanao, *Mindanáw*
Mindoro, *Mindoro*
Minneapolis, *Minyápolís*

Minnesota, *Minesota*
Misamis, *Misamis*
Mississippi, *Misisipi*
Missouri, *Misuri*
Moluccas, *Mulukas*
Mongolia, *Munggolya*
Montevideo, *Montebídeó*
Montreal, *Montreál*
Moravia, *Morabya*
Morocco, *Moroko*
Moroland, *Kamorohan*
Morong, *Morong*
Moscow, *Moskú*
Mountain Province, *Lalawigang Bulubundukin*
Mukden, *Mukdén*
Muñoz, *Munyós*
Naga, *Naga*
Nagasaki, *Nagasaki*
Naguilian Road, *Daáng Nagilyan*
Naic, *Naik*
Nanking, *Nangking*
Naples, *Nápolés*
Navotas, *Nabotas*
Negros Occidental, *Kanlurang Negros*
Negros Oriental, *Silangang Negros*
Netherlands, *Olanda*
Nevada, *Nebada*
New York, *Niyuyork*
Niagara, *Niyágara*
Nikko, *Niko*
Nile, *Nilo*
Normandy, *Normandiya*
North America, *Hilagang Amériká*
North Sea, *Dagat Hilagà*
Norway, *Norwega*
Novaliches, *Nubalitses*
Nueva Ecija, *Bagong Esiha*
Nueva Vizcaya, *Bagong Biskaya*
Obando, *Ubandó*
Odessa, *Odesa*
Ohio, *Ohayo*
Oklahoma, *Oklahoma*
Olongapo, *Ulunggapó*

Omaha, *Omahá*
Orani, *Oraxi*
Oregon, *Oregón*
Ormoc, *Urmók*
Oroquieta, *Orokyeta*
Osaka, *Osaka*
Ottawa, *Utawa*
Pacific Islands, *Kapuluáng Pasipikó*
Paco, *Pakò*
Paete, *Paitè*
Pago Pago, *Panggo-panggo*
Pagsanjan, *Pagsanghán*
Palawan, *Palawan*
Palembang, *Palembang*
Palestine, *Palestina*
Pampanga, *Kapampangan*
Panama, *Panamá*
Panaon, *Panaón*
Panay, *Panáy*
Pandacan, *Pandakan*
Pandan, *Pandán*
Pangasinan, *Panggasinán*
Panguil Bay, *Loók ng Pangil*
Pansipit River, *Ilog Pansipit*
Parañaque, *Palanyag, Paranyake*
Paris, *París*
Pasig, *Pasig*
Patagonia, *Patagonya*
Pateros, *Patero*
Peiping, *Peyping*
Peñaranda, *Penyaranda*
Pennsylvania, *Pensilbanya*
Persia, *Persya*
Peru, *Perú*
Philippines, *Pilipinas*
Pittsburgh, *Pitsburg*
Polillo, *Pulilyo*
Pototan, *Putotan*
Prague, *Praga*
Puerto Princesa, *Portoprinsesa*
Puerto Rico, *Portoriko*
Pulangi River, *Ilog Pulanggí*
Pulog, Mt., *Bundók Pulog*
Pulupandan, *Pulupandán*
Pyrenees, *Pirineó*

Quebec, *Kuebék*
Quito, *Kito*
Rangoon, *Rangyun*
Richmond, *Ritsmond*
Riga, *Riga*
Rio de Janeiro, *Riyo-de-Haneyro*
Rizal, *Risál*
Romblon, *Romblón*
Rome, *Roma*
Rotterdam, *Róterdám*
Rumania, *Rumanya*
Russia, *Rusya*
Saar, *Saar*
Sahara, *Sahara*
Saigon, *Saygón*
Salinas, *Salinas*
Samar, *Samar*
Samarkand, *Samarkánd*
Samoa, *Samoa*
Sampaloc, *Sampalok*
Savannah, *Sabana*
Seattle, *Seatel*
Seoul, *Seyól*
Shanghai, *Shangháy*
Siam, *Siyám*
Siargao, *Siyargáw*
Siberia, *Siberya*
Sibul, *Sibúl*
Sibuyan, *Sibuyán*
Sicily, *Sisilya*
Sierra Madre, *Siyéramadre*
Silang, *Siláng*
Silay, *Siláy*
Sinait, *Sinait*
Singalong, *Singgalong*
Singapore, *Singgapúr*
Siquijor, *Sikihór*
Solano, *Sulano*
Sorsogon, *Sorsogón*
South America, *Timog Amériká*
Spain, *Espanya*
Sual, *Suwál*
Subic Bay, *Loók ng Subik*
Sudan, *Sudán*
Suez Canal, *Kanál ng Suwés*
Sulu, *Sulú*
Sumatra, *Sumatra*

Surabaya, *Surabaya*
Surigao, *Surigáw*
Sydney, *Sidney*
Syria, *Sırya*
Taal, *Taál*
Tablas, *Tablas*
Tacloban, *Takloban*
Tacoma, *Takoma*
Tanauan, *Tanawan*
Tagudin, *Tagudín*
Taiwan, *Taywán*
Talavera, *Talabera*
Tarlac, *Tarlak*
Tasmania, *Tasmanya*
Tawitawi, *Tawitawi*
Tayabas, *Tayabas*
Tennessee, *Ténesí*
Ternate, *Ternate*
Texas, *Teksas*

Tibet, *Tibet*
Ticao, *Tikáw*
Tokyo, *Tokyo*
Toledo, *Toledo*
Tondo, *Tundó*
Tuguegarao, *Tugegaráw*
Urdaneta, *Urdaneta*
Uruguay, *Urugwáy*
Valencia, *Balensiya*
Valparaiso, *Balparaiso*
Vancouver, *Baṅgkuber*
Venezuela, *Beneswela*
Venice, *Benesya*
Vesuvius, *Besubyo*
Vienna, *Biyena*
Vigan, *Bigan*
Visayan Islands, *Kapuluang Bisa-yà*.
Zambales, *Sambales*
Zamboanga, *Sambuwangga*